Chad Holland

# SCARS OF BLUE

## A STORY OF POLICING, CORRUPTION, MENTAL HEALTH, AND SURVIVAL

Print ISBN: 978-1-09836-168-6

eBook ISBN: 978-1-09836-169-3

# CONTENTS

Foreword.................................................................................................... 1

Dedication............................................................................................... 5

Chapter 1: The Beginning of the End................................................... 9

Chapter 2: From Whence I Came....................................................... 13

Chapter 3: My First Real Job, My First Born, and My Big Break.......... 26

Chapter 4: Somerdale............................................................................ 45

Chapter 5: My First Lessons in Politics................................................ 51

Chapter 6: An Old Friend to the Rescue.............................................. 56

Chapter 7: Camden................................................................................ 62

Chapter 8: He's Was Alive, and Now He's Dead.................................. 68

Chapter 9: The Angry Fried Chicken Lady.......................................... 75

Chapter 10: The Good Guys Are the Bad Guys................................... 91

Chapter 11: And So, It Begins............................................................. 102

Chapter 12: Setup to Fail.................................................................... 110

Chapter 13: Time for Me to Go.......................................................... 114

Chapter 14: Tale of the Tape.............................................................. 118

Chapter 15: From My Past Emerges My Future................................. 124

Chapter 16: Back Where It All Began................................................. 129

Chapter 17: How I Stopped Being Such a Dick!................................ 132

Chapter 18: A Time to Kill.................................................................. 140

Chapter 19: My First Breakdown....................................................... 182

Chapter 20: Everyone Wants Me to Leave......................................... 202

Chapter 21: Popping Pills................................................................... 213

Chapter 22: Back From the Dead....................................................... 223

Chapter 23: One Last Life to Save...................................................... 233

Chapter 24: The Home Stretch.......................................................... 245

Chapter 25: A Wrongful Death........................................................... 253

Chapter 26: There's Only One Truth.................................................. 257

Chapter 27: PTSD-Depression & Suicide........................................... 266

Special Thanks..................................................................................... 273

# FOREWORD

Law enforcement is at a pivotal point. Never before have we experienced this level of hatred toward police, nor suffered from the complete abandonment of the political establishment. Our duty, and what his right or wrong, is overshadowed by what makes splashy headlines and is subject to placating those who just wish to spread evil and destruction.

Much too often law enforcement leadership fails the rank and file. "Leaders" in law enforcement are failing to support their officers, choosing instead to side with the politicians and protect their own careers. This lack of leadership not only crushes moral, but creates a culture where law enforcement turns against one another, and "eats their own." We are conditioned to *kill or be killed*. Promotions are no longer based upon the best candidate, but rather upon hook-ups, connections, favors, or who you know. This results in even the most loyal and dedicated officers becoming disenchanted with the job, isolated, distant, and ultimately bitter.

Scars of Blue- *A story of Policing, Corruption, Mental Health, and Survival* is a look at what happens when a good officer suffers the consequences for trying to do the right thing. This writing perfectly articulates how cops not only suffer from the trauma they face on the street, such as with Chad's deadly encounter with a suicidal individual. But, how cops oftentimes suffer just as much trauma while dealing with the administration on the inside, as they face a leadership and a bureaucracy that is more interested in asserting its authority and crushing its adversaries. This book provides a clear insight into the root cause of what is becoming a mass exodus within our profession. Whereas, officers are not fleeing from police work. They are running from the byzantine administrations that control many of these agencies. Chad is a prime example of how good cops get caught up in the nefarious motives of those who just seek power. All the while, the officer on the street must still battle crime and withstand horrible events.

This book provides you with the insight into how frivolous retaliation from the same leaders who are supposed to support us, eats away at your mental health. Which contributes just as much to the suicide epidemic currently going on in law enforcement, and as much as anything our officers will face on the street. Compounding the problem, is the attitude these agencies have toward officers asking for help. Which is all too often looked upon as a sign of weakness. Chad's articulation about being predisposed to mental health issues, his dealing with the worker's comp bureaucrats after suffering an injury, being forced to take medication, along with the need to break the stigma are all important points for you to read, learn, and understand. Agencies need to understand that waiting to treat officers once they develop PTSD is often, too late. There has never been a more important time in our history where pre-PTSD screenings, discussions of burnout and depression, and the use of medication to cope with these things is openly needed for discussion in law enforcement.

Scars of Blue forces the reader to ask themselves some cold-hard questions. Questions, such as: When (and if) I break, who will be there for me? Who will suffer from *your* personal mental devastation? What can you do to protect yourself from suffering from mental health issues? What are you doing to not only protect yourself, but to help others you live or work around to deal with their issues? And lastly. Are you part of the problem contributing to the stigma, or are you going to be part of the solution? Chad's raw and vivid account of his suffering in describing how he pushes away the very same people he loves and is fighting for, and the isolation he suffers from which almost causes his death, is something which needs to be read and burned into your soul. I know his suffering firsthand. I know how "the job" abandons you, and the emptiness you feel. Which can only be filled by the people you truly love.

If this profession is to have a future, then it will need more Chad Hollands, not less. Officers who have spoken up and paid the price. However, the goal is for officers to be able to speak freely, and not suffer for doing so. We need more officers who put the greater cause in front of their self-interest. There are many officers who have suffered from, and are currently suffering from poor leadership, exposure to tragic events, and who are in pain. We must, as a profession, speak up and "be our brother's/sister's keeper." Be the voice for your agency. Take a leadership role. Even if you don't wear bars, stars, or stripes. Learn from the experiences of people like Chad, and help facilitate change by insisting mental health wellness become a top priority within your agency. Together, we can change the culture of law enforcement by following the examples of heroes like Chad. We can eliminate the toxic environment that officers too often face within the four walls of their station house. Remember your oath:

"On my honor, I will never betray my badge, my integrity, my character, or the public trust. I will always have the courage to hold myself and others accountable for our actions. I will always uphold the Constitution, the community, and the agency I serve, so help me God."

Be the change!

-Sergeant Nick Ruggiero (Ret.)

Author of Amazon's bestselling law enforcement book- Police Mental Barricade-*A survivor's guide to poor law enforcement leadership*

Host of the Roll Call Room Podcast- With over 100K listeners

Owner of the Roll Call Room Café, located in Dumfries, VA

www.rollcallroom.com

www.mentalhealthbarricade.com

# DEDICATION

This book is dedicated to my family, my Blue family, and everyone who has ever loved and cared for me. I wouldn't be here without any of you.

This book will hopefully serve as a reference for anyone who has ever struggled, or is struggling with Mental Health issues. Remember-*you are not alone.*

For those of you still on the job, *Hold the Line.*

This is my story. The events in this book are told as I alone recall them. All events in this book are factual.

All names and identities have been changed, except for those who gave permission.

*Never be embarrassed by your struggle. Never apologize for the things you've worked hard for. Every part of your journey has beauty in it, so never let anyone drag you down for climbing to a better place.*

Vex King

# CHAPTER 1

# THE BEGINNING OF THE END

"Jesus Christ, drop the fucking knife! Just drop the knife. Drop the knife. Drop the fucking knife!"

Since I first set foot in the apartment, I have spent almost thirty minutes talking with Mark. The minutes felt like hours because of the tension in the room. And the fact that I wasn't making any progress in convincing him to abandon his suicidal plans made it even more challenging. The only thing I wanted to do was convince him that his life was worth living. But the talking was over now. He no longer wanted to listen. Now, he's walking toward me with the knife clasped in his hand—that huge knife! Fourteen inches of shiny hardened stainless steel. He is holding it in his left hand with his arm is bent at the elbow, the knife is just even with his shoulder. He looks like one of those Hollywood killers as he is holding the knife— monsters like Jason Voorhees from *Friday the 13th* or Michael Myers from the *Halloween* films.

Mark is slowly moving toward me, as he's very labored in his approach. He's moving just like one of those horror film killers as they stalk their hapless victims…walking ever so slowly…dragging his feet…and holding the knife-menacingly. But, I'm not a helpless victim who is desperately trying to run away. I am an armed and trained police officer standing my ground. All my senses are on fire, and I am completely focused in the moment.

I am backing up—my gun is raised with my sights on him, and my finger is on the trigger. I am alternating between shouting at the top of my lungs at him and speaking softly.

"Don't do it! Just drop it. We were doing fine Mark. Let's just keep talking." I beg him.

I don't want to have to kill him. I don't want this to end grimly.

*I want to help him. I'm here to help him! Why can't he just understand that? Why can't he understand I am here to help him and not hurt him?*

I want to be the one who helps him make it out of this apartment alive—not the one who puts him in his grave. However, Mark won't stop coming toward us with the knife. I look into his eyes. His eyes have that blank thousand-yard stare, and I feel as though he is looking right through me. I am screaming at him so loudly that I can be heard clear across the apartment complex. But, he isn't even listening to me anymore. It's as if I'm not even in the room with him, and as if he *won't* hear me. Mark's mind is made up. He either wants to die, or he wants to kill us, or both. I just can't be sure which it is. Mark's steps are staggered and almost drunk like, as he is dragging one foot right after the other across the carpet. It reminds me of how the Frankenstein monster first ambled in the movie, right after being given life by the crazed Doctor Frankenstein. Except this isn't a movie, this is real life. This isn't a nightmare, but a horror playing out right before my eyes.

I have a sudden notion of being a little kid again. It was the strangest sensation in a moment like this, and it came out of nowhere. When you are so young and so small that any adult you're standing in the presence of seems to be towering over you, as if you're looking up at a giant. That is exactly how Mark appears to me at this moment, like he is a giant! He looks so damn huge in this tiny apartment. It's as if he is taking up the whole room—and is larger than life. I am still backing up, using shuffle steps so I don't trip.

The apartment is a darkened and dank shithole, and not the kind of place where someone should want their life to end. It's definitely not how anyone would picture spending their last moments on Earth. As we usually have some vision of ourselves surrounded by family as we lay in a hospital bed, or dying within our home, as we say our goodbyes. At least that is the version of death we're all taught to embrace. This won't be a peaceful or quiet demise. It will be a loud and violent death. This is a result I am praying and hoping to still avoid.

The place completely reeks of cigarettes and stale beer. Every piece of trash imaginable is tossed about on the floor. Empty pizza boxes, empty beer cans, and fast food wrappers are everywhere. As I continue to back up, I sense I'm running out of room to retreat. I can feel the wall coming up behind me, as I am cornered in the apartment. My senses are off the charts, so much so that I can even smell sweat. However, it's not my own sweat that I smell, even though it's now pouring down my back and my chest underneath my body armor. It's the smell of *his* sweat, and he is standing about six feet away from me. My body is tense and tight. I feel afraid, I feel fear, and yet I also feel in control. My mind has thousands of thoughts racing through it in just milliseconds. Some of these thoughts I am conscious of; others are just my training, my reactions, and my instincts. I can almost *hear* the thoughts going through my head one by one.

It's so damn hot and suffocating in the apartment, and the air is thick and heavy making it hard for me to breathe. Actually, the air feels more than thick—the air feels *alive*! There's an electricity in it, like when you walk across the rug with socks on your feet then touch something, or someone, and get a shock. I have a funny taste in my mouth. It tastes like I am chewing on a piece of metal. My heart is pounding. My eyes are darting from the knife to Marks's face, then back to the knife. I tighten my grip on my weapon because my palms are so sweaty, and the adrenaline is making my hands start to tremble. I am afraid the gun will slip right from my hand. I practice combat breathing. Breath in for a four count, hold for four, exhale for four, hold for four–repeat. I'm still moving backwards, but I'm running out of room—quickly!

I take another step backwards and suddenly–I slip! My foot slips on something slick on the rug. My back leg and foot slide so quickly that I almost come crashing down to the floor, and I gasp for air as my heart skips a beat. If I fall down he can be on top of me in a fraction of a second, and he will start stabbing away at me with that huge knife. I have a quick vision in my mind of this happening. I can see Mark on top of me, his eyes staring into mine as he stabs into my chest and through my vest, literally tearing me apart. This vision terrifies me. For the first time during this ordeal I feel true horror in my gut. This is when the moment begins to feel the most real, and yet, it also feels the most dreamlike at the same time. I know that probably doesn't make any sense. Nothing in this moment is making any sense. I feel like I'm watching something unfold which I am not actually a part of, almost from a third-person point-of-view. Yet, here I am–front and center. Mark has stopped. He sees the Sergeant off to his left. He is now rocking backwards and putting all of his weight onto his back foot.

"Mark, no!" I shout. "Mark–don't do it." I plead.

He springs forward toward me. Just as he leaps forward a thought enters my mind clear as day–*I don't want to die!*

# CHAPTER 2

# FROM WHENCE I CAME

For anyone who knew me as a kid, my becoming a police officer is the last occupation anyone would have suspected to be what lie ahead in my future. As a boy, I was a skinny, scrawny, hyperactive, ADD-inflicted smartass with a big head of blonde curly hair. I had a loud mouth and a lot of attitude, but not much to back it up. Why was I like this? It took me a long time to figure that one out. Eventually, I realized it was because I have always felt as though I never fit in anywhere, so I would lash out. I still feel very much like that today, like I often don't fit in. I may be smiling and socializing when I am someplace, but inside I feel like I am the odd man out. I assume it was because I was never a part of any particular group, nor was I very close with any one person in particular, except one girl–Tina. She was my version of a "best friend" through high school. Sadly, she passed away after being ravaged by cancer.

I didn't have much family outside my mother and brothers. What little family we did have didn't really speak with each other anymore once my parents divorced. Nonetheless, I have had ample opportunity to make and maintain close friendships, but I have failed to do so. I imagine it's because I never created those feelings of obligation, or a sense of duty one develops with friendships. I was never bitten by the "best friend bug," so to speak. I am the oldest child in my family of four brothers. Older than my next brother by almost six years. Quite an age gap. So, while growing up I wasn't able to have any of my brothers' act as my "best friend" with whom I could confide in, because they were too young. To make matters worse, I had a father who really didn't want anything to do with parenting, let alone being part of a family. This helped to create my sense of being alone and on my own very early on. Detached may be a better way to describe it. Either way, I sometimes feel as though I am better off just staying at home, rather than going out and trying to socialize. This may sound like a pity party, but trust me, these are not good feelings, and they are feelings I wish I didn't have to live with.

As a kid, you don't know how to rationalize these emotions or how to navigate them. So my reaction, or my defense to pretty much every slight or criticism was to be a little sonofabitch. When we moved to Brooklawn, I had a hard time making any friends for the first couple of years. The town was very insular, and everyone seemed to be related to everyone else. I really only made one real friend early on, Michelle, with whom I miraculously still keep in contact with until this day. So, I guess I'm not completely awful at friendship after all.

Upon my arrival in Brooklawn, I was quickly labeled by the neighborhood kids as "the dirt bag Philly kid." Being branded, along with being a complete outsider with no ties to the community whatsoever, made my integration that much more difficult. I spent more time fist fighting those first couple of years (and getting my ass kicked) then I did playing with the any of the neighborhood kids. It certainly didn't help matters any with my being small in stature and completely insecure, while having a big mouth and cocky attitude. I didn't exactly endear myself to many people. That list included kids, teachers, and other parents. To top it off, I wasn't a good student. It wasn't an intelligence issue. It was because I was so hyperactive and so out of control that I could barely sit still in my chair, let alone settle down enough to focus and learn. Today, I would have been diagnosed as

ADD or ADHD, along with ODD (oppositional defiance disorder). Back then, I was just a smart mouth pain in the ass!

Another problem I had was I hated being told what to do. Especially, by the teacher when I was in front of the entire class. It embarrassed me to be corrected in front of the same kids who were just looking for a reason to hate me. "Sit down," "Stand over here," "Go stand in the corner," "Go to the principal's office," "Stop talking," "Stop fidgeting," etc. I drove my teachers crazy! Then I would make everything worse with my attitude and my big mouth, my defense mechanisms. More than one person from those early years has told me they found it ironic that I became a cop—the portrait of authority—since I always displayed resentment toward authority.

I particularly resent authority when it's in the hands of someone I deem doesn't deserve it. Someone who only got into the positon because of who they know are the worst in my eyes, and I despise them. These feelings of resentment had manifested during those early childhood years, and they would continue to grow. My apathy of power would also cost me professionally later on down the line. To be frank, I still have these feelings from time to time, as I now work in the corporate world. I have a habit of comparing the corporate desk jockeys, keyboard warriors, and telephone tough guys I now deal with to the heroes I worked with on the street. Needless to say, the comparison often falls short for obvious reasons, and I tend to lack respect for those I am around in the business world. My negative outlook toward those in charge has caused me to have blown through a series of jobs since I retired from law enforcement. This is not something I am proud of.

My first year in the New Jersey school system was horrible. Not only was I fighting and getting picked on all the time (today it would be called bullying), but the curriculum in my new school was so far advanced compared with that of the school I attended in Philadelphia, that I wound up having to repeat the grade. Of course, this just added to my feelings of ineptitude. Not only was I an outsider who already felt hated and constantly picked on, but I felt like I was stupid when comparing myself with the other students. Let me clarify one thing. It was not in any way, the fault of my teachers' that I was lagging behind. I was simply the product of a school district that was running about two years behind the curriculum of my current school. By January of my first school year in New Jersey, it had already been determined that I would have to repeat the grade. So I sat in a classroom every day knowing that I didn't have to do a damn thing, because nothing I did mattered. This idle time was not a good thing for a hyperactive and frustrated kid. Needless to say, I spent a lot of time in detention or in the principal's office. I acted out purposely in class out of sheer boredom, and just to get tossed out. Once the other students found out I was going to have to repeat the grade, I became "the retarded kid from Philly."

At home things weren't much better. My father worked at an oil refinery. He was verbally, mentally, and physically abusive toward my mother, and toward me, especially.

He eventually left my mother and their four sons for a woman he worked with at the refinery when I was fourteen years-old. Sadly, I remember having feelings of relief when my dad finally left. He constantly belittled me, while almost taking joy in getting me upset. He took zero interest in me as a son. We never played sports together, or did anything father–son related. We hardly spent any time together at all. Although, he was not violent, or overly physically abusive per se, he wasn't shy about smacking me around when the opportunity presented itself. Often, he would poke me, or flick my cheek with his finger. Not hard enough to leave a mark, but enough to hurt me. It was more the mental abuse with his constant put-downs and disparagement that wore me down. The only time I can say he was actually physically violent was about a year or so after he had left.

One weekend, my mother and my brothers were away at her new boyfriend's campground. I was at home alone when my dad showed up and walked right in the front door of the house, as if he still lived there. He was obviously drunk, and we got into it right away.

It started out as yelling and screaming at first. Then, at one point, he cracked me pretty good across the face with the back of his hand. A "back hand" as he would call it. His go-to move when he did lay heavy hands on me. Enraged, I picked up one of those miniature baseball bats you would get at a baseball souvenir stand. My brother had been playing with it the day before in the living room, and he had left it on the couch. I picked up the mini-bat and swung it at him, right at his head, but I missed. Now furious, he stepped forward and nailed me good with a closed fist to the face. He then took the bat from my hand and hit me with it about five or six times in my head and shoulders. I was able to somewhat block about two of the blows with my forearm as I fell to the floor, but two or three of the other blows got through. I was hit in the face and the head.

In order to get my father to stop hitting me, I thought it best to act like I was unconscious. He stopped swinging the bat at me, and after a second or so of standing over me and mumbling something I couldn't understand (mostly because of the ringing in my ears), he dropped the bat next to me and onto the floor. He then stumbled out the front door. For a quick second, I thought of picking up the bat, running up behind him, and giving him a blow to the back of his head. However, the second I tried to stand up I almost fell onto the floor face first. I was concussed and so dizzy. I laid on the floor for a few minutes trying to gather my wits. I didn't know what a concussion was at the time, but I know now that's what was going on in my head.

After a while, I was able to crawl over to the couch and lean on it, and then stand up. I went directly into the bathroom to assess the damage. While lying on the floor, I noticed that I had begun to bleed. I had an intrusive thought while I was in the bathroom looking at my smashed face. I suddenly became very afraid that my mother was going to come walking in any second, along with my brothers. I didn't want them to see me beaten and bleeding all over the place. Even though they weren't due to come home for a couple of more days. It was an irrational thought, but it scared me into action, nonetheless. I quickly cleaned myself up and put some ice on my face and my forearm. Still feeling dizzy and foggy, I took some aspirin and I went to bed. I still have the scar through my eyebrow from where one of the blows hit my head and split it open.

It may interest you to know that I have never told anyone about this incident until now, writing about it in this book. This night has been buried inside me for a long time. As horrible as this experience sounds, it feels good for me to finally get it out in the open. Primarily, and as not to embarrass my father, I had kept this episode to myself. I once asked my father about his memories of this night. He had absolutely no recollection of this event ever having taken place. I know there are plenty of people out there who have had it worse. People, who have been mentally and physically abused repeatedly for years. This occurrence doesn't remotely compare to their horror. I am simply sharing this story with the hope that someone who reads this book realizes that no matter what life throws at you, you can make it through–and you're not alone.

For the rest of the weekend I worked on reducing the swelling. The cut above my eye through my eyebrow was deep, but not large. And I didn't get any stitches. Opting instead to bandage it and hope for the best. I was also working on an alibi to tell my mother when she and my brothers came home. I couldn't tell her the truth—she would have lost her mind! When my mother saw me two days later, all black and blue and swollen, I told her I had gotten jumped by a bunch of guys while walking in Gloucester City. She asked some of the normal questions you would expect.

"Why were you walking alone at night?"

"Did you recognize any of them?"

"Why would they pick you?"

"Did you call the police?"

And the like. I answered them all with lies, and that was that. There was no call to the police. I never told her the truth. I didn't want my mother to ever feel bad for not being there. She was away with my brothers, and she was trying to enjoy herself. Plus, God only knows what my father would have done to her if she and my brothers were at home that night. Who knows how far things would have gone. I just look at it as having taken one for the team.

\* \* \*

After my father left our family it seemed as if I had to grow up overnight, and I did. Gone was the hyperactive, cocky kid. He was replaced by a much more mature and calmer young man. I had huge responsibilities now. I had to take care of my three younger brothers, and even though I love my mother very much, she wasn't up to the task. My mother, at forty years-old, had been a housewife for twenty years. My dad had handled the money, the bills, everything. As a result, my mom had no clue how to run a home. She was completely overwhelmed. I started thinking about how to make money and how to help pay our bills. I learned how to make repairs (somewhat) to the house on the cheap, since my father left us with nothing. He literally took every dime we had. We found out during the divorce proceedings that he had been planning his exit for quite some time. So, with him handling all the money, and my mom never asking any questions, he was able to put away a nice nest egg for him and his new love to build their new life together.

Each night, I would help my brothers with their homework, and I would cook them dinner (when we had food). At night, I helped them get their baths, and then I would put them into bed. I was more like a father, and not their big brother, anymore. Ironically, and although it was a struggle, I often credit my father's leaving as the best thing to ever happen to me. Prior to his departure, I think I was heading down a path of self-destruction. My father's constant disparagement and lack of interest in me had me feeling like the only way I could get his attention was to act out. This led to him frequently punishing me, which led to continuous reminders of how much of a disappointment I was to him. This constant negativity was sending me down a deep hole mentally and emotionally. It's a terrible thing when the one you want approval from the most is the same person who is causing you to suffer the greatest. My lack of self-esteem and my lack of self-worth was growing every day I was around him.

My father leaving us forced me to make a choice. My choices seemed to boil down to two paths: I could become a useless piece of shit, and wind up in trouble all the time, while becoming a total loser. In the process, I would be letting my mom and my brothers down. Or, I could step up and take care of my family, help out at home, and do the best I could. I chose the latter. So, even though the past few paragraphs may have sounded as though I hated my father, or that I am blaming him for all that was wrong in my world, I assure you that is not the case. I don't hate my father, but I do feel sorry for him. He missed seeing his four young boys grow into great men. That is something he can never get back.

We eventually lost the house to foreclosure just after I graduated high school, and we bounced around from rental home to rental home for the next couple of years. We had a pattern of moving out of whatever home we were living in right before we could be evicted. Landlords looked at us as if we were "white trash," and I suppose they were right. At least to a certain extent. We were flat broke. There were nights I would skip dinner so my brothers would have enough to eat. I would purposely stop over a friend's house right around dinner time, praying that their mom or dad would invite me to stay for dinner, just so I could eat. Sometimes they would. Other times, they would politely say it was time for me to go. I would leave their home with tears in my eyes knowing I wasn't going to eat that night, but too embarrassed to tell them the truth. Many times our electricity was turned off, and we would be at home with no lights, no television, nothing! It was a hell of a way to live.

My goal coming out of high school was to go into the Navy. As I said, I wasn't much of a student, so I wanted to go into the Navy because I knew I wasn't going to college. I hated to be ridiculed (again, from my childhood insecurities), so I didn't share the idea of my going into the military with anyone out of fear of being told I wouldn't make it, or that it was a dumb idea. I didn't even tell my mother, or my brothers. One day, after school during my senior year, I went to a recruiter and told them I wanted to sign up. Truth be told, I didn't understand the whole process. I simply went to a recruiter's office and told them what I wanted to do, and that was that. I wasn't eighteen years-old yet, so I was going to need my mom to sign the paperwork, or I just had to wait until December after my eighteenth birthday to do it myself. I opted to wait, and I signed up right after my birthday on my own, because I didn't want my mom to know.

My plan was to get into the military and hopefully get to do fun stuff along the way. However, the real driving force in my wanting to join the military was so I wouldn't be a burden on my mother anymore. I wanted to help out the family by living on the military's dime, and send my paychecks back home. I had been giving my mom my paychecks since I started working at the local five-and-dime store when I was fifteen years-old, stocking shelves. However, my plans for a future in the military went to shit when I crashed on my motorcycle the week of my high school graduation. I severely broke my lower right leg—both bones, the tibia and fibula. The doctors put a rod put in my lower leg to stabilize it. I was so angry with myself that I had done something so stupid. I had ruined my dream, my way out, but my anger and disappointment was nothing compared to that of my Navy recruiter, who had come to my high school graduation.

He arrived in his dress uniform, only to find me sitting in a wheelchair on the football field during the ceremony. I hadn't had a chance to call him, there were no cell phones then. I went straight from the hospital directly to my graduation ceremony. The only reason I was released early from the hospital was because of my graduation. Otherwise, I still would have been there. When my recruiter saw me his jaw dropped, and he turned beat red with anger. Then, he began to let me have it! He was screaming and yelling at me how he had to "pull a lot of strings" to get me in so quickly, and that "I had failed him, failed myself, failed my family, failed my country, and failed the United States Navy." Pretty heavy stuff to put on an eighteen year-old kid on his graduation day. The Naval officer shouted at me that since I had to have surgery, and because of how jacked up my leg was, that I could forget about getting into the Navy for at least the next two years. Then he stormed off–and I was crushed. I felt like the biggest piece of shit ever. I had let my family down. I had let myself down.

I spent the summer after high school in a cast from my toes to my hip. I was deeply depressed, and I felt lost about what to do next with my life. I continued to work at my part-time job for the rest of the year while I was healing and trying to figure out my next move. That was until I got bored and quit. After that, I bounced from job to job. I did a couple of semesters at a community college, but without any clue as to what to do with my life. I had zero direction. I didn't dare try to enter the Navy, or any other military service. My recruiter had shamed me into giving up that idea. During my senior year of high school my mom had met a new boyfriend. He was a *much younger* Korean-American man, who ironically happened to be in the Navy. After we got evicted from our latest rental house, and after only two years or so of dating this man, my mom informed me that the family was moving up to Groton, Connecticut to live on the U.S. Naval Base with him.

"Mom, I don't want to live in Connecticut." I pleaded.

"Well, Chad." My mom began. "I kind of figured you wouldn't want to go. And I know you and Nick [my mom's boyfriend] don't really get along. So, I figured maybe you can find a friend to live with here in New Jersey, or maybe, stay with your father."

"What! Mom, are you telling me you're taking my brothers and leaving me here?"

That was exactly what she was saying. My mom and I had been caught up in a rapidly deteriorating relationship. We argued, and Nick would always jump in. Then he and I argued. It was becoming a freaking mess. This was her way of kicking me out, without her actually kicking me out. It wasn't so much that it seemed like my mom was kicking me to the curb that hurt me, it was that she was separating me from my brothers. I had taken care of them their whole lives. I was their protector. Now, I was going to be a four-hour drive away.

It hurts to write about and think about this part of my life, even today. Once my mother did move away, taking my brothers with her, not only did it forever change my relationship with her, but my brothers and I inevitably grew apart because of it. It permanently altered our relationships with each other. Sadly, since they grew up away from me during their teenage years our bonds suffered, and have never fully recovered. Even to this day, I am only truly close with one of my three brothers. After trying multiple times to pull my family back together, time and effort has failed to bring us close again.

Once my mom and my brothers moved away I tried living on my own for a while. At twenty years-old I had no skills, and I worked at whatever job I could find during that time. I rented a room from a friend, and stayed at their parent's house. Without anyone to answer to, or anyone depending on me, I went out drinking until all hours of the night with my friends, and slept with whatever girls I could pick up. It got to a point where I was repeating this exercise day in and day out over the next several months. Needless to say, I quickly wore out my welcome wherever I stayed, and rightfully so. It was around this time that my father and I started to have some contact.

He didn't fight my mom when she told him she was moving away with my brothers. I believe it actually relieved him from the awkwardness and from his obligation of having to come over and pick them up whenever it was his weekend. Mind you, he never wanted them (or me) to come over to his house and stay for overnight visits once he moved out. He was happy to come over at about noon every other Sunday (or whenever he showed up) and take my brothers out to McDonald's for lunch, or maybe to a movie. I always refused to go with him. He would then drop them back off a few hours later, thus fulfilling his obligation. The whole thing was uncomfortable, because without fail he and my mother would always wind up in an argument about money. Especially, when the bank was foreclosing on our family home.

My father had stopped paying the $600 a month mortgage on the family home once he moved out. His logic was since he didn't live there anymore the mortgage wasn't his problem, even though his ex-wife and four kids were still living there. So, whenever he came to the house they would argue, and I would wind up involved somehow. My father and mother would yell, my brothers would cry, and I would scream at him to leave. It was just a preposterous situation that repeated.

One day, I got a message from one my friends whose home I had recently been living at. He said my father had stopped by looking for me. I had no idea how he found out where I had been staying. It bothered me that he showed up there, so I called him.

"Chad, can I see you tonight? I want to talk to you about something." He sounded desperate.

Skeptically, I met with him in the parking lot of a local Kmart, because I didn't know exactly what was going on, and I didn't trust him.

"Chad, Jamie and I are splitting up. I'm going to get an apartment, and I wanted to see if you wanted to live with me."

Jamie was the woman my father had left our family for. The woman he had worked with at the refinery. Apparently, *the grass was no longer greener on the other side.* My first thought was *no fucking way!* Still, there was a problem I was about to have—it's called homelessness. I had just lost my job because I had been acting like an idiot, and I was about to lose my place to live because of lack of funds. Reluctantly—very reluctantly—I agreed to live with my father until I could get on my feet.

Awkward would not even begin to describe how it felt to live with him again. I was 20 years-old, and I didn't remotely have a clue as to what I was going to do with the rest of my life—a life my father hadn't really been a part of since he left about six years earlier. He and I were basically strangers at this point. We had nothing in common, we never really did. The fact that we hadn't really been on speaking terms for the past several years just magnified those differences. Plus, there was a ton of anger and resentment I still harbored toward him. It didn't take long for me to realize that living with my father would not be a long-term solution. Nevertheless, at the moment I had no choice. But I was about to finally get a break.

# CHAPTER 3

---

# MY FIRST REAL JOB, MY FIRST BORN, AND MY BIG BREAK

The father of a friend I attended grade school and high school with was the local postmaster for the U.S. Postal Service office of Gloucester City, New Jersey.

John was such a warm and wonderfully gregarious Italian-American man. When he had an opening in the post office for what they called a Casual Letter Carrier position (basically a part-time letter carrier with no benefits) I applied, and he gave me the position. They promised only a twenty-hour work week, but it paid something like $9 an hour—which was well above minimum wage at that time. John always made sure I got my twenty hours and then some. Usually, he would get me as close to forty hours per week as possible. I was finally making some decent money (at least by my standards at the time), and I enjoyed being outside all day walking, talking, and meeting new people while I delivered the mail. For the first time, I felt as though I was working at a place where I could actually have a future.

The Postal Service was known to be a lifelong job which paid decent money and offered good benefits. After a year, I got promoted to a position where I was guaranteed forty hours per week. I also received a $3 per hour raise. I was now making $12 dollars an hour—big bucks for me! It was by far the most money I had ever made in my short lifetime. In the meantime, I waited to take the Postal Exam in an attempt to get a permanent position. It was 1993. I was twenty-one years-old, and my life was about to change again.

I'm not going to bore you with all the details, but during this time I met my first wife and the mother of the older of my two sons. I met her initially when I was nineteen, and we dated off and on. We got pregnant when I was twenty-one, and we got married and had our son just before my twenty-second birthday. It was during the time I was with Cindy that I became a cop, at age twenty-three. We were separated before my twenty-fourth birthday, and divorced by the time I was twenty-five. In the interim, I learned how a relationship can go to hell in a hurry. In fairness to us both, we were married only because we had a child. We had nothing in common. Our backgrounds were similar only in that we both came from homes of divorced parents. Otherwise, we had nothing—no love, no trust, nothing.

This relationship is one of the biggest regrets of my life, as well as one of my most painful memories. The *only* good to come of this relationship was the birth of our awesome son, Chad. Still, the pain of having raised our son in a divorced household will never go away. I swore I would never do that to my kids after having been through it myself. I will always feel as though I let him down. However, the relationship with his mother got away from me so quickly, and it became so volatile so fast, that there was no way to salvage it. What more can I say. It was a mistake. The relationship was emotionally relentless, mentally draining, physically violent, and it took a huge toll on the both of us.

After the birth of our son, Cindy suffered from severe postpartum depression from which I think she never truly recovered. She refused to seek help, and the arguments between us grew in frequency and eventually, in violence. I never laid a hand on her. That I can promise you. On the other hand, I never knew if I was going to have something thrown at my head when I walked in the door each night, because I never knew *who* I was coming home to. She became obsessed with the idea that there were other women. The last thing I wanted to deal with during this time was another woman. I was focused on trying to salvage what we had and trying to raise our son together. Still, there was no way to salvage a marriage made of necessity and not of love. This is something that I will forever be ashamed of.

I had been working for the Postal Service for a couple of years when something started to happen to me—I began to get very bored. When I get bored I don't stop being bored until I have made some type of change. Sometimes the change is good, often times it turns out to be too impulsive, and is a mistake I come to regret. While working for the Postal Service, not only did I start to become bored with the job, but I had been forced to move to another office. I moved from Gloucester City where I loved working, to the Deptford office, which I came to hate. I had to make the move in order to land a permanent position with the Postal Service, but I was miserable. I questioned myself everyday about whether I could continue to do this job for the rest of my life. However, I had a wife and son to care for. I couldn't just quit and move on without a plan, like I used to so often do. However, something had to give. I felt like my job was soulless and soul killing.

Then one day, in September 1995, while I was picking up the mail in one of our satellite offices in Woodbury Heights, my big bulky battleship gray first-generation Motorola cell phone rang.

"Hello?"

"Is this Chad?"

"Yes, it is."

"Chad, its Frank McMillan."

I had known Frank McMillan since shortly after we had moved to Brooklawn from Philadelphia. In my father's never-ending attempt to remain out of our house and away from the family as much as possible, he had joined the Brooklawn Volunteer Fire Department for the sole purpose of being able to play on their men's softball team. Frank and my father had played together on the team, and I used to go to some of the games. Frank knew me from my days as a skinny little kid running around the softball field like a little madman–covered in dirt. He was also familiar with the problems my family had from when he had to show up at our house in his capacity as a police officer, after my mom had called the police on my dad a few times when things got out of hand. Frank was now the Chief of Police in Brooklawn, and Brooklawn was looking to hire a new officer. My name came up on their Civil Service list from the test I had taken about four years prior.

During my senior year of high school, in 1991, we were permitted to leave for the day to take the Civil Service Exam. The exam lasted only about three or four hours, but you were excused for the entire day if you took it. So, a few of my buddies and I paid the $10 bucks to take the exam in order to get out of school for the day. I hadn't studied for it, and when I took it I had no real interest in becoming a cop. Especially, after my results came back. I had scored an 85.4, and was ranked something like tenth on Brooklawn's list. Which for a small department, wasn't a high enough ranking to seriously be considered for a position any time soon. Brooklawn was a police department of only five or six full-time officers at the time (today there are still only eight full-time officers and a couple of part-timers). So, I never really gave any serious thought to becoming a police officer. It just wasn't on my radar.

"Chad, your name came up on the list from the test you took back in '91. We have three people we're looking at, but I think you would be the best fit, if you're interested?" Frank said.

"Damn right I am interested." I replied, a bit too enthusiastically.

This was my chance to get out of this soul-sucking postal job.

"What do I have to do, Chief?"

Over the coming months I went through the background check and the interviews. I still have a copy of my original application, with my answers hand printed in my terrible handwriting. I am embarrassed to look at it now. It was totally unprofessional. But at the time, I didn't know any better. Speaking of being unprofessional, I almost blew my getting the job during my final interview because of my eager propensity towards pure honesty.

During my final interview, one of the council persons on the panel had asked if there was any law I would be reluctant to enforce. Without hesitation, I blurted out,

"Yes, speeding. I wouldn't write a speeding ticket to anyone."

Out of the corner of my eye I could see the Chief's jaw drop, along with the jaws of a couple of the other officers in the room.

"Excuse me!" the council person began. "Did you just say that as a police officer you wouldn't write anyone a speeding ticket?"

"Yes sir, that's what I said." After a brief pause I asked, "May I explain why."

"Yes, please do." He replied, somewhat perplexed. "I really want to hear this."

I sensed I was dangerously close to blowing it. I knew this story was either going to make or break me. So, I began to tell them why I felt the way I did.

"When I was sixteen years-old, I had managed to save up enough money on the side to buy my first car—a 1979 Chevy Camaro Z28. It cost me twelve hundred bucks, and it was a piece of junk. I spent the next year fixing it up the best I could, while I waited to turn seventeen and get my license. Once I got my license, I was in complete shock at the price of car insurance for a new driver. The cost for a first-year driver in a 'sports car' was eighteen hundred dollars for liability insurance only. More than I paid for the car! My mother wouldn't let me put the car in her name, which would have saved me a ton of money, but she didn't want her car insurance to go up, since she was paying like five hundred bucks a year."

I continued, "I worked my butt off to pay for the car, for gas money, for the insurance payment, and I would give what little money remained to my mom to help feed our family. I would go to school all day, go to football practice after school during the season, then straight from practice to my part-time job. One night, a buddy and I were driving home from work in Deptford Township. It was late, and I had to be up early for school the next day, so I was speeding. I got pulled over for driving sixty-five in a fifty mile-per-hour zone."

"After I got pulled over, the officer decided that he was going to search my car because he felt we were 'acting suspicious.' He never did tell us what was suspicious about us in the first place. My friend and I were still wearing our work clothes, and I had already told the officer we were coming from our jobs, but that didn't seem to matter. After tearing my car apart, he wrote the speeding ticket for driving sixty-five in a fifty. A four-point ticket. On the advice of friend, I went to court in order to try to get it reduced to something with no points. The officer would not budge. When asked by the prosecutor if he had any objections to reducing the ticket down to something with no points and just a hefty fine he said,"

'I'm sick of these punk kids being able to think they can rip around my town and then come to court and get off scot free. No, I won't agree to reduce the ticket, and I will take it to trial if need be.'

"The prosecutor said there was nothing he could do. That if I went to trial and lost—basically a foregone conclusion—I would have to pay the fine *and* the court costs, which was something I could not afford to do. At this time, the electricity was turned off in our house. So, I was hoping that I could actually save some of the money by getting the ticket reduced, and get the electric turned back on. I also had an insurance payment coming up that I had been saving for. I literally begged the officer and the prosecutor with tears in my eyes to reduce the ticket, while always taking full responsibility for my actions. Still, nothing I said was going to change his mind. I went to the window and paid the four-point speeding ticket, then waited for the insurance company to inform me what my new rate would be. I got a letter in the mail from the insurance company about a month later."

[Dear Mr. Holland, due to your recent conviction for speeding sixty-five miles per hour in a fifty mile-per-hour zone, a four-point speeding offense in the State of New Jersey, your annual premium of eighteen hundred dollars will now be adjusted to twenty seven hundred dollars, and a surcharge of one hundred dollars will be assessed to you for the next three years.]

"I was forced to sell the car. I wound up buying a motorcycle, since that was the only thing I could afford. While riding the motorcycle I crashed. I broke my leg so badly that I couldn't enter into the Navy, like I had planned to do. So, that one speeding ticket helped to change the entire trajectory of my life!"

I could see the council persons' faces beginning to soften. So I continued.

"I had to sell my car due to one mistake. I lost my job because I was unable to get to my job on time after school, because I no longer had a car. And before I was able to save enough to buy a motorcycle. My family suffered because I could no longer give my mom the little bit of money I had been making, which had made all the difference in the world to us. I lost my spot in the Navy, because I bought the only thing I could afford, a motorcycle, which almost killed me. The toll that one speeding ticket took on me and my family was immeasurable."

I finished by explaining to the council that I was willing to stop someone for speeding, but I would simply use one of the other laws on the books to cite them, if it was required. Since I saw firsthand how financially damaging a speeding ticket could be, I felt this was a fair way of sticking to my principles, while still enforcing the law. After I finished my story, the council persons sat there in silence for what seemed like forever. I thought I had blown the opportunity. They looked at each other, made some gestures toward each other, and whispered back and forth. After a few moments, the chairperson on the panel then made his statement.

"Mr. Holland, I am only going to speak for myself for the moment. I am of the belief that if you have convictions that are so strong, that you were willing to risk not getting this position by stating them, and although you are not yet an officer, you have the foresight to see what repercussions your actions may have upon a person whom you are enforcing the law, then you are, in my opinion, not only far ahead of the game, but the perfect person to enforce the laws in Brooklawn. It is because you have an understanding that although you have an obligation and a duty to the townspeople you serve, you must also take into account the human factor of your actions, and that you realize already there is a balance which must be maintained. That, in my opinion, is what makes the perfect officer."

Another council person immediately spoke up and said,

"I second that."

Then another, and then another. It was unanimous. They thanked me for my candor and honesty and said they would let me know their final decision.

[Note: Right about now you may be calling me a hypocrite, or worse. Right or wrong, I don't put all violations of law in the same "mistake" bucket. Meaning, if you drink and drive that's not a mistake, that's intentional. If you have drugs in the car that's not a mistake, that's a problem. If you forget to put on your seat belt that's usually a mistake, since most people don't intentionally neglect to wear their seatbelt. If you forget to renew your vehicle registration, or you forget to get your car inspected it's most likely an error. Even though speeding can be intentional, it can also be a mistake at times. Right or wrong, that is how I rationalize it, and that's the distinction I made to the council.]

"You fucking blew it!" One of the officers I had known since we were kids said to me once we had left the room. "You can't tell them you're not going to enforce the law because you don't agree with it!"

"That's not what I said." I shot back. "I said I would stop people for speeding, I just wouldn't write them the ticket for that particular offense. So, I'm still enforcing the law, I'm still stopping them from speeding—I'm just not crushing them financially."

"You're a fucking idiot! They may agree with you now, but when the Solicitor [the town's legal counsel] gets done with them there is no way they'll hire you." He continued,

"Let me ask you—what are you going to do if they don't have anything else wrong when you stop them for speeding? If their car is registered, if it's insured, and they're wearing their seat belt, then what?"

"Well, I can always just give them a warning, right?" I replied, somewhat modestly.

"Dude, I'm sorry but they are not hiring you. You fucking blew it."

I feared he was correct, and I felt defeated. Then I got a call from Chief the next day.

"Jesus Christ, Chad, you scared the shit out of me!" The Chief began. "I thought there was no way they were hiring you after you said you wouldn't write speeding tickets. Congratulations, they want you."

I was on cloud nine. For what felt like the first time in my life, I stuck by what I believed in and it worked out in my favor.

"Chief, thank you!" I said, while trying not to get choked up. "But let me ask you something if I may. How do *you* feel about me not writing speeding tickets?"

"If they're okay with it, I'm okay with it." He replied. "You just better be writing *something*."

During my seventeen year-long career I would stop many people for speeding, but I held to my convictions and I *never* wrote someone a speeding ticket. I know there are officers out there who think this was the wrong thing to do. All I can say is, to each their own!

I started at the Camden County Police Academy, which was located at the time on the campus of Camden County Community College in Blackwood, New Jersey, in January of 1996. After sixteen weeks of training, I graduated on May 17, 1996 with Class 24. There were forty-two cadets who entered the class and all forty-two graduated on time. A 100% success rate! Which is extremely rare. Our class was made up of cadets from several different departments. Camden City, Gloucester Township, Gloucester City, Cumberland County Sheriffs, Department of Health and Human Services police, and even Cherry Hill High School campus police, to name a few.

While I was going through the police academy my life at home was becoming pure hell! I was up at 4:30 am every day, out of the house by 5:00 am, and not back home until 6 or 7 pm each night. I had to prep my meals, iron my clothes, shine my gear, and complete my homework before going to bed every night. That part was fine. I actually enjoyed learning how to perform those tasks, and the discipline that goes along with it. However, when I would walk into the apartment after a long day at the police academy, I didn't know if I was coming home to a hug and a kiss from my wife, or to something being thrown at me. The relationship—and her moods— were truly that volatile. I would walk in the front door and she would literally shove our son into my arms before I even had a chance to put down my gear.

"Here, I'm done! You take care of your son. It's your fucking turn! I have to do it alone all day while you're at the stupid police academy." She often would say.

I had made it a point to spend my first hour at home each night playing with our son. Partly, to just give her a break. But mostly, so I would have some bonding time with him. Still, after that hour I really needed to eat, get a shower, do my homework, and take care of all the things I have already mentioned. By the time I was done with my tasks I would get to bed around 11:30 pm, and sometimes after midnight. It was usually while I was completing these responsibilities that the fighting would start.

"I'm so sick of this shit! You're gone all day. Then you come home at night and you can't even take care of your son. You even took a pay cut! For what? To be a fucking cop. You're such a piece of shit!"

This is just a small sample of the verbal thrashing I would receive. I would just take it in silence. Mind you, this is 1996. I went to the police academy when it was only sixteen weeks long, not the twenty-six (or more) weeks it is now. It felt like four years, not four months. I did take a pay cut from working at the Postal Service. I was making $36,000 per year at the Postal Service. I plunged to $24,480 for my first year as an officer. A huge cut. Still, I did so while looking ahead at what was to come in the near future. After just three years of being a police officer, I would jump up to a salary of $42,000. At the Post Office, as I mentioned, I was making $36,000. However, it would take me an additional five years employment with them to get into the mid-forties if I remained at the Postal Service. Furthermore, by my becoming a police officer my family would have free medical benefits. As opposed to the medical benefits I was currently paying a pretty penny for at the Postal Service. There would also be a good pension when I retired. Nevertheless, she just didn't seem to care. She was completely against the change and would constantly pepper me with demands.

"When are we getting a house?"

"I want out of this shithole apartment!"

"I need a new car. When are you buying me a new car?"

"Don't you love us? Don't you love your son?"

"Don't you care about us?"

It was a fucking nightmare. The downward spiral of the relationship had begun. The stress got to me so much at times that I thought of quitting the police academy and going back to the Postal Service, just to shut her up. When I tried to explain that we would be able to get a new house and a new car more quickly with the career change, she still wouldn't stop. Nothing I was doing was good enough. She hated her life, and she hated me. She blamed me for the way things were. We weren't poor, but we were living almost paycheck to paycheck. Both of us were still so young that was to be expected—except she didn't see it that way, and I received the brunt of it.

I was by no means innocent in all of this. I could say some nasty things, and at times have a nasty temper. I was never violent toward her, but I wasn't shy about slamming a door or two.

It (usually) takes two to make a relationship, and two to break it. However, I was trying to do the best I could with what little I knew about taking care of a family.

By September 1996, after I had been out of the academy and on the job for about four months, we split up for good. She began to constantly accuse me of cheating on her, even though I had not given her any indication that I was doing so. It seemed like it was just a reason to fight with me, I suspected. Her physical violence toward me grew, because she knew I was powerless to strike back. She knew that I would never jeopardize my career by laying hands upon her, and that I'm not a woman beater. The straw that broke the camel's back happened one day during one of our many arguments.

"You know what. Since you love this fucking job so much, how about I just get your ass fired!" She threatened.

She then walked over to me as I was packing my bag to leave the apartment until things cooled down. Once next to me, she slammed her hip into me, like a hockey player throwing a hip-check. She screamed aloud, as if she were performing for an audience.

"Oh my God, you just hit me!"

Then, she ran over and picked up the cordless phone, dialing 9-1-1. I heard her say to the dispatcher for the Bellmawr Police Department (at that time we lived in Bellmawr, right next to Brooklawn)

"My husband is a police officer, and he just hit me."

"Congratulations, you just got me fired." I told her, as she hung up the phone.

I was completely stunned she would sink that low.

For those of you who are not aware, for a police officer to be accused of an act of domestic violence is a nightmare. The officer is pulled from the street and placed on the "rubber gun squad." They are then subjected to a lengthy internal affairs investigation, whether they are guilty or not. An officer who is still on probation during their first year on the job (such as I was at the time) can be dismissed based merely upon the allegation, without any confirmation of the event actually having taken place. So, not only was I losing my marriage, my home, and my family, I was also getting dangerously close to losing my job.

As I turned my back on her so I could finish packing my bag, she suddenly smashed the cordless phone she was holding into the back of my neck, at the base of my skull. I instantly felt a shock wave go through both of my arms and hands, and I dropped my bag. I lost the ability to grip anything, and I crumpled to the floor as I became dizzy. After I hit the floor, she screamed and started crying. After a few moments, and as soon as I regained feeling in my arms and my hands, I jumped up, grabbed my bag, and ran out the door. I went outside the apartment building and sat on a curb, waiting for the Bellmawr Police to show up. I hoped to plead my case, and somehow keep my job.

Fortunately, an officer from the Bellmawr Police Department whom I had met on a previous occasion, arrived. We had met while I was doing some of my training with Brooklawn prior to my entering the police academy, and we had hit it off right away. He knew I wasn't some woman-beating asshole, or at least I was *hoping* he knew that.

"Chad, what the fuck is going on?" He began. "The report over the radio said you hit her. *Please* tell me it's not true!"

I told him everything that had occurred. I swore I never touched her, and that she had slammed into me with her hip on purpose. I also showed him the lump that was now on the back of my neck, and I told him about losing feeling in my arms and hands after being hit with the phone. He asked me if *I* wanted to press charges.

"No fucking way! I just want to get my stuff and go!"

The Bellmawr officer marched upstairs, and after a few minutes I could hear him yelling at my wife inside the apartment. I could hear her crying, I could hear our son crying, and I began to cry. While waiting outside alone, I began to think about how volatile my life had been up until this point. *How did things get this way? Why can't I just live a normal life?*

All I ever wanted was to raise my son how I had wanted to be raised, which was in a peaceful and loving home. However, once again I screwed up, when I made a poor choice for a companion. This was on me. After a few minutes the Bellmawr officer came down the stairs, and asked me if I needed a ride somewhere.

"What did you say to her?" I asked.

"Chad, please don't be mad. But once she admitted to doing everything just like you told me." He paused. "I told her she was a fucking dumb bitch because she could cost you the job, and then you guys would lose everything. Please don't be upset with me, bro."

*Upset?* As horrible as this sounds, I felt vindicated. I'm fully aware how stressful the whole situation must have been for her. A young new mom. Caring for our young son all day, alone. Her husband spending very few hours at home while he's away training at the police academy. And who was now working rotating shift work. Still, I can say without reservation, I truly did everything I knew of at the time to make the relationship work. I tried to make her happy, but it just wasn't meant to be. I was completely crushed. This meant one thing: we were over. We couldn't live together as a family anymore. I couldn't take the chance of her making any more allegations against me, and possibly getting me fired. I would no longer be living under the same roof with my son every day. He would now be a child of divorced parents, just like his mother and I were. That is something I swore I would never do to my child, and I felt broken. I felt like I betrayed this innocent little boy. I still carry that guilt around with me until to this day. I have never been able to fully get over it.

After our split, and after several months alone, I began *dating*, to put it civilly. Mostly, I was focused on trying to be the best dad and cop I could be. Still, I was a young man who had needs, and I fulfilled them as often as I could when Chad wasn't around. I want to apologize to any woman who dated me during this period of my life. Going out with me while I was in this scorned mindset could not have been a pleasant experience, for any of them. For that, I am truly sorry.

When I was younger, during my high school years especially, I noticed I had developed a horrible propensity of mistreating women emotionally. Just as I had witnessed my father's mistreating of my mother. I never struck a woman. I would never put my hands on a woman. However, I did play mind games with them. Sometimes I found myself enjoying the drama of getting them upset, or of making them jealous. Other times, it was just dumping them for no overt reason. I don't know why I did these things. You would have thought that with all the drama I had going on in my life, that I would welcome someone actually caring for me, and that I would conduct myself accordingly. Yet, it seemed like I couldn't be happy unless I was causing some sort of turmoil. Of course, and I didn't know it at the time, but much like the child of an alcoholic who becomes an alcoholic themselves, I found myself mistreating women and disparaging their feelings just as my father had done to my mother. Learned behavior.

My son Chad's mother was the first woman I made a conscious effort to *not* treat this way. However, and after the failure of our relationship, I was so damn bitter and angry that I fell into a mindset of just using women for pleasure. I didn't care about them or their feelings. I wasn't interested in developing a long-term relationship. The job became my wife. The women I dated became my conquests, and nothing more. I would never let my son see the revolving door of women in my life. There was no way I was going to expose him to the *flavor of the month*. To say that I had a bit of a *wanting to watch the world burn* mentality when it came to my relationships would have been a correct assessment. In my mind, if a girl fell for me and I later dumped her, well, that was *her* fault and not mine. Of course, I was conveniently ignoring my culpability in the whole thing.

When Chad and I were together it was him and I against the world, and no one else was allowed into that world. I would allow nothing or no one to come between us. On a couple of occasions after our separation, his mother and I spoke about reconciliation. Then she would find out I was "dating some whore" as she would put it, and that was the end of that. She began this tactic of keeping our son from me by not taking my calls when it was time for us to spend time together. Or, she would make sure they wouldn't be at home when I came to pick up him up.

Over my career I have seen hundreds of couples use their children as pawns, while they try to inflict maximum emotional damage upon each other. It is one of the vilest and most disgusting things a parent can do. I had to deal with it in my personal, as well as my professional life. Whenever my ex would use these tactics, I would turn toward my job to take my mind off things. I was wrapping myself up in the job more and more. I volunteered to work overtime whenever it came up. Sometimes for the extra money, but mostly just to bury myself in the work. It wounded me so badly and so deeply when she kept our son and I apart, that I had to throw myself into my work to keep myself from pure dread.

At the same time, I was very fortunate to wind up working with a great group of officers in the bordering towns. They turned out to be the perfect mentors for me, which helped to make me good at my job, and made me enjoy coming to work.

After graduating the police academy in May 1996, I had two weeks of agency training. Agency training is where you ride along with a veteran officer and begin to learn the job. This is where the rubber hits the road, so to speak. In police work, we always discussed how two sets of rules exist. There are the things that are in black and white, such as the laws, rules, regulations, and the other academic stuff you learn in the academy. Then there's the stuff of the real world, *the gray areas* of policing. Where what you do and how you do it seldom resembles what you were taught in a classroom. Agency training is where you have to begin to form your ability to handle the job in real time, and depending on how well you progress, will determine when you will be sent out on your own.

When you work 12-hour shifts, the two weeks of training is actually only seven or eight working days, depending on how many days are in that month. I received at total of seven working days, or 84 hours of training. After which, 1 was handed the keys to the squad car and was entrusted with enforcing the laws and protecting the lives of the 2,200-plus citizens of Brooklawn—*while doing it all alone.* And so it was, a twenty-three year-old rookie officer was solely responsible for the lives and the property of the townspeople of Brooklawn after only sixteen weeks of academy training, and a whopping seven days (84 hours) of agency training. Brooklawn, because it had only one officer on duty during a shift, depended on the neighboring towns for back-up utilizing what's called the Mutual-Aid Agreement.

Basically, the Mutual-Aid Agreement allows for municipalities to share police services, as well as fire and emergency medical services in some cases. The responsibilities are to provide the same level of service with the same lawful authority across town lines, while still being covered legally. In other words, I was as much of a cop in neighboring Bellmawr, Mt. Ephraim, Gloucester City, or Westville as they were when they came into Brooklawn to assist.

Being surrounded with good officers from other towns would be paramount to my success and growth as a police officer. If a rookie cop gets on a squad full of shitty officers, that rookie will often turn out to be a shitty officer as well. I was fortunate to be working with a great group of officers, from young go-getters to seasoned vets.

At the time, Westville and Brooklawn were so tight knit that they were almost like one department. Westville often had only one officer on duty as well. Therefore, our motto became, "Where I go you go, and where you go I go." We did this in order to watch each other's back, and keep each other safe. Westville had a great group of officers who taught me the ropes. They were a wealth of knowledge, and were at different points in their respective careers. Westville also had a group of dispatchers in-house (because they were self-dispatched) who were phenomenal. I learned a ton about the job from them as well.

In Bellmawr and Gloucester City, I was surrounded by a bunch of *old head* veteran officers—officers who tend to not look to get into anything proactively, since they've pretty much done their time, and are mostly *short timers*. Short timers are officers who don't have much time left on the job until retirement. Old heads are usually a wealth of knowledge (depending upon how good the officer was to begin with), and they sure as hell know how to handle stuff when it goes down. Gloucester City is known to be a working class-blue collar town, and this is where I mostly hung out during my teenage years. Gloucester City is also where I graduated from high school. With its bars in full swing on a Friday or Saturday night (or actually any night), Gloucester could be a rough and tumble town. It could also be a lot of fun! Gloucester cops knew how to handle themselves, without a doubt. My point is, I had no shortage of great cops and great people with tons of experience around me to draw from.

From 1996 until 2002, I patrolled the streets of Brooklawn mostly single-handedly. I got to do a million different things when it came to police work: pursuits, fights, domestic disputes, suicides, robberies, and even a couple of homicides. Along with being in patrol, I became our department's Investigator, and I got to conduct both long and short-term investigations. For a little town of less than one square mile, and with only 2,200 residents, we were busy. We were known as a transient town, meaning that most of the crime being committed was by criminals passing though. With our close proximity to Camden, New Jersey (one of the most dangerous cities in the United States), and just three miles from the bridge leading to Philadelphia, we got our share of crime. Tons of shopliftings, burglaries, theft, and more. I even had a male try to pull a handgun on me while on a domestic call.

Besides crime fighting, I also did many things socially with these officers, as I began to form close friendships. Overall, these were good years of my life. However, by 2002 my *boredom bug* showed up again, and I would make the first of many bad decisions for my career. Which would later come back to haunt me.

# CHAPTER 4

# *SOMERDALE*

"Frank, I want to transfer to the Somerdale Police Department."

This was a tough conversation. Not only had Frank given me my first shot at becoming a cop, he was my Chief, and more importantly, he was a friend. The Somerdale Police Department belonged to the same PBA union local as Brooklawn.

[Note: There are two dominant union organizations in the New Jersey area: the FOP (Fraternal Order of Police) and the PBA (Police Benevolent Association). The FOP is a national organization, whereas the PBA is more regional. Most of the PBA membership is located within the northeast corridor of the United States, particularly in the New Jersey and New York areas.

I am also aware there are departments which are non-union, particularly in parts of the south, west, and mid-west.]

Somerdale, Brooklawn, and a host of other towns belonged to the same union local, PBA Local 30. Each month, officers from various departments would gather together at our monthly meetings. I became friendly with some of the Somerdale officers from these meetings, and when a spot opened up on their force they asked me if I wanted to take advantage of the new Intergovernmental Transfer program, and come aboard.

The Intergovernmental Transfer Program was started by the State of New Jersey Civil Service Commission. The program permitted officers to transfer from one department to another, while keeping their vested time within the Police and Fire Pension System. The transfer program afforded an officer the opportunity to negotiate (to a certain extent) the terms and conditions of their transfer. Items, such as where they would fall within the pay scale, and a few other employment conditions could be open for negotiation. Of course, this depended on how flexible the new employer and the union were willing to be with the provisions contained within their current contract. The benefit of the program for police officers was that an officer could be getting a significant raise in pay, simply by transferring to another police department. The benefit to the department was they were getting a trained and experienced officer, one who could hit the street right away.

Because of the total years of service I already had on the job, I would be getting a $10,000 per year raise in pay just by my transferring to the Somerdale Police Department. This transfer was especially appealing to me financially, because I was still damn near broke from my divorce. [Note: Brooklawn was the second lowest paid police department in Camden County at that time, and I was topped out in the pay scale making about $44,000 a year.]

"Frank, it's the same type of policing, but I would be making ten grand more a year for doing the same job." As I tried to make him understand my needing to leave. "Plus, I might have a shot at being promoted. You and I both know there won't be any opportunities for me to be promoted here [Brooklawn] anytime soon."

Frank was understandably hurt and angry, but in the end I made the transfer to Somerdale in October, 2002. Financial issues aside, which I was looking to put behind me with the new raise, I had gotten married to my second wife, Suzanne, and we had a son, Jacob. I had finally gotten over my *screw them and forget them* mentality, and I started to place a value on finding a meaningful relationship.

I first met Suzanne while working in Brooklawn during my rookie year on the job, in 1996. Suzanne's family owned a restaurant in town, Weber's Drive-In. Weber's was a 1950s retro-styled drive-in restaurant, and Suzanne was a car-hop waitress and manager. She, along with her mother Lillian, and her sister Karen–ran the restaurant. They often worked twelve and fourteen-hour days seven days a week. Suzanne's father, Robert, would be there every morning to open up and resupply the restaurant. He would then take off to go run the family's miniature golf course they operated at Cooper River Park, in nearby Cherry Hill. With Brooklawn being a small town, and with them being a local business owner, Suzanne and her family wanted to get to know all of the police officers in town. I'd frequently stop by their restaurant during the day to check on them, and just to make sure that any undesirables passing through town weren't giving them any problems.

I remember the first time I ever saw Suzanne. She is Chinese-American, born and raised here in the states. Her father and mother emigrated from China before Suzanne or her two siblings were born. Being Chinese, I thought she had this beautiful-exotic look to her. When I first saw her I thought to myself *she is stunning*! However, I immediately thought she was out of my league. With her being a business owner, I felt that financially I would never be respectable enough to be with her. Suzanne drove very nice cars, and she seemed so classy. Me, I was barely keeping my head above water while driving my early 90s Chevy Beretta. Furthermore, there were the cultural differences. I had never really dated outside my own race or background. Growing up in Brooklawn and Gloucester City I wasn't exposed to other cultures. Gloucester, at the time, was a predominately White Irish-Catholic population. Hell, I wasn't even Catholic!

When I first met Suzanne, I wasn't even thinking of even asking her out. I was going through my divorce at the time, and I was moving from one woman to the next. However, and over time, Suzanne and I developed a friendship. I only saw her from the end of March until the middle of September, since the drive-in restaurant would shut down for the winter months. Still, with each new season about to begin I found myself looking forward to Weber's opening up. Originally, it was because it meant summer was coming—my favorite time of the year. Later, it meant that Suzanne and I would get to see each other again. I found myself thinking of her more and more.

During the summer of 1997, I had brought this girl I was seeing at the time to eat at Weber's. I actually didn't plan to bring her there. We were riding by the restaurant with another couple in the car, when both girls yelled out they wanted fries and shakes, which is what Weber's was famous for, along with their root beer. As we pulled into the parking lot, I remember seeing this look of disappointment on Suzanne's face. At the time, I didn't appreciate what it meant. However, while we were eating I could sense Suzanne acting differently toward me. She was still friendly, but being a bit standoffish. She was acting polite, while being condescending as well. At one point, she even *playfully* started throwing ice cubes at me. I knew she was a bit upset when I went to my car and got my sweatshirt for the girl I was with. My date said she was cold, so I went and got her my sweatshirt to keep her warm. I happened to catch Suzanne looking at us out of the corner of my eye as I put the sweatshirt on my date's shoulders. She had a look of, *Well, that was nice of him—Asshole!*

For the rest of the summer, and whenever I stopped by the restaurant while I was on patrol, I could sense Suzanne was still a bit put off by my having brought a date to the restaurant. Since she brought it up quite frequently.

"Did you bring her here to make me jealous?" She would playfully ask. "She's not that pretty you know. You just like her because she has big boobs!" And comments of the sort.

I started thinking—*maybe I do have a shot after all!*

CHAD HOLLAND

Suzanne and I started dating in April 1998, after I had split up with the girl I was seeing over the winter. We have been together ever since. She has been through it all with me. She embraced the fact I had a son from a previous relationship, and has cared for him deeply. Suzanne got over her concerns of my having been previously divorced, the cultural differences, since I am White and not Asian, and that I was a cop. I can say unequivocally, that without Suzanne and her love and support there would be no me. From day one her father has always treated me like a son. But her mom- Mom was a bit tougher to convince, to put it mildly.

One particular day, Suzanne's mom and I sat down together at one of the picnic tables at the restaurant, right after she found out Suzanne and I were dating. Mom then blasted me with both barrels with every personal question that you can imagine.

"Why do you want to date my daughter?"

"You're a policeman, and that job's too dangerous, and you don't make a lot of money."

"You are divorced, and you have a son. That's no good."

"Why are you divorced? Were you a bad husband? Were you a bad daddy to your son?"

"You're White! Why you want to date a Chinese girl?"

She fired away! I sat there taking every question and comment head on. I explained everything honestly to her, and in as much detail as possible. I answered everything truthfully, no matter how difficult or personal the question. If she sensed I was lying, or being hesitant in any way, Mom would have pounced on it in a second! At one point, Suzanne tried to stop her mom when she overheard one of her questions.

"Do you just want my daughter for sex?" She asked, as Suzanne tried to intervene.

I told her it was fine, and to let her finish. I knew if Suzanne and I were going to have a future I needed to get Mom to at least give me (us) a chance. In Mom's defense, cops had been coming to Weber's for years trying to "get with" Suzanne and her younger sister. There were always rumors that this cop "had her" or her sister. The truth of the matter was that none of the cops ever made any headway with either Suzanne, or her sister. So, they were spreading false rumors in order to make themselves look good. Suzanne and her younger sister, who is very attractive in her own right, were always walking around in their Daisy Duke Shorts and tight t-shirts in the summer heat, which attracted a lot of attention from cops and patrons alike. Needless to say, they received a lot of offers. Mom had protected them for years from these advances. So understandably, she was suspicious of my intentions. That is why I was willing to swallow my pride and submit to the interrogation. I was also deeply in love with Suzanne by this point.

We had "secretly" been dating for about nine months before her family found out. I was willing to do whatever it took to make this work, and to win her heart. After Chad's mom and I split, I never thought about finding "The One". I thought that true love was just a myth. It didn't take me long to realize Suzanne was The One. To this day, besides our children, I have never loved nor wanted to please someone as much as this woman. I can't imagine where I would be without her. After the inquisition with Suzanne's mom was over, I was able to overcome a lot of her skepticism. Mom finally accepted me into the family, especially after Suzanne and I gave her a second grandchild—and the first boy born into the family. Suzanne once told me, that it was during mom's questioning that she knew she absolutely wanted to be with me. Her thinking was that if I was willing to subject myself to the rash of very personal questions by her mother and still stick around afterwards, then she knew I would always be there for her, no matter what. Still, our greatest tests as a couple were yet to come.

# CHAPTER 5

# MY FIRST LESSONS IN POLITICS

You may recall earlier in this book when I wrote about how I would make a host of bad decisions regarding my career. Well, my transferring to Somerdale, or my leaving Brooklawn, however you wish to look at it, was the first.

At the time of my transfer, there was an Acting Chief of Police in Somerdale. An Acting Chief means that the previous Chief has retired or moved on, and the township has not yet appointed a permanent replacement. There may be some reason they are holding up filling the position, such as a prolonged search for a qualified applicant, or budgetary reasons. In a Civil Service department, where the testing for promotions is (mostly) mandatory (there have been departments who have gotten around the testing via political connections), the township is usually just awaiting the test results in order to appoint the new chief. Oftentimes, the ranking officer they anticipate will be the next Chief is usually appointed as the Acting Chief of Police in the interim. Basically, this permits the future Chief to get some on-the-job training. This way, they can hit the ground running when they are permanently appointed to the position.

My apologies for the long-winded explanation, but it sets the ground-work for what's to follow.

I transferred to Somerdale in October, 2002, and I immediately started in patrol. I was already a trained officer with six years of experience. I would be expected to enforce the same laws, use the same radio codes, and patrol in the same manner in Somerdale as I had in Brooklawn. I just needed to learn the layout of the town, the paperwork, and the ebb and flow of the department. That's all that should have been required, or so I thought. However, behind the scenes there was a power struggle going on which I had not been made aware of during my interviews, or at any time during the transfer process.

At the time of my transfer Somerdale had two Lieutenants. One Lieutenant was fulfilling the role of Acting Chief of Police. This Lieutenant seemed to have the inside track to being named as the permanent Chief, as he was close friends with the Mayor. The second Lieutenant had taken the test for Chief as well, and unbeknownst to anyone within the department at the time, this second Lieutenant was making power moves behind the scenes to get the Chief's job. The Acting Chief was not a "hometown boy," since he was from Bellmawr. The second Lieutenant was a Somerdale boy, born and raised. Somerdale was a very close knit community of about 5,000 residents. So, the hometown Lieutenant was working diligently behind the scenes trying to turn the tide toward him getting the position, by using his lifelong connections within the community.

It was announced the council would be appointing the permanent Chief during the next public meeting. The Acting Chief's family planned a party for him the night of the meeting. His relatives were coming from all over to see him being sworn in as the new Chief, as it was assumed he would be named Chief. It was going to be a grand moment in his career, especially since his older brother would be in attendance. His older brother was the Chief of Police in their hometown of Bellmawr, just a few miles down the road from Somerdale. But, it was not to be. Prior to the public meeting, and just hours before he was actually set to be sworn in, the Acting Chief was informed that he was not going to be named the permanent Chief. The council members were naming the second Lieutenant as the next Chief of Police. This was my first exposure to the dirty politics of policing and government. However, it would be far from my last, and now this mess was about to trickle down to me!

One night in early November, while I was working the overnight shift in Somerdale, the Lieutenant and former Acting Chief of the department (the one who was not made Chief), called me on my cell phone.

"Chad, the Mayor has requested you stop over his house tonight after midnight. Make sure you park the police car at the end of the block and walk down the street to his house, so that no one sees you."

"Why? What does the Mayor want to see me about?"

"I don't know." Said the Lieutenant. "But he insisted you come."

I arrived at the Mayor's house at a little after midnight, and the Mayor quickly ushered me into his darkened living room. The whole thing reminded me of one of those smoke-filled backroom deals you envision politicians are always involved with. Where the movers and shakers are making career and life-altering political decisions in top-secret closed-door meetings.

The Mayor seemed like an overall nice guy. During my interview process he was very respectful of the fact that I was a trained officer. I remember him asking thoughtful questions about me, both personally and professionally. Still, this meeting had a much different feel to it. This meeting had an ominous feeling from the moment I walked in his front door.

The Mayor began, "Chad, first off, I have to apologize to you. Due to no fault of your own you've gotten caught up in some political bullshit between myself, the Council, and the two Lieutenants."

"What do you mean, Mr. Mayor?" I asked, perplexed. "What the hell do I have to do with any of this? I just got here."

New Jersey is full of small towns with small-town police departments ran by small-town politicians. Even though the towns may be of similar size and demographics, they can differ in many ways. For example: the Chief of Police in one town could be making a salary of $100,000 to $150,000. Yet, the Chief of Police in the next town over of similar size could be making $85,000 to $125,000. The Chief in the town of Stratford, New Jersey, which borders Somerdale, was making significantly more than the former Chief of Somerdale, even though the Chief of Stratford had been on the job for a lot less time. The Lieutenant who had just been promoted to Chief of Somerdale was not looking to make the same mistake. He wanted to be paid comparably. This was the root of the problem I was about to be faced with.

"Chad, the new Chief has started contract negotiations with the Council." The Mayor stated. "And he wants to be paid like Stratford's Chief. Since he was the Council's choice over my choice, they're going to give him what he wants."

[Note: When the Council named the other Lieutenant as the new Chief it had stemmed from political payback toward the Mayor.]

The issue of the Chief wanting a significant raise in and of itself wasn't a big deal. The problem I faced was that there were some Council people who were against my hiring to begin with. They believed Somerdale already had enough police officers, and I, along with my $54,000 salary was an expense they felt was unnecessary. The new Chief was also in this camp. Apparently, it was suggested during his contract negotiations that if the Council were to lay me off (release me), they could then use the money from my salary to pay the Chief, and give him the large raise he wanted. The Mayor said this idea of letting me go was no longer being treated as just a suggestion. The council was actually looking into how to go about it, and what needed to be done to move forward in the process. The council was currently investigating the ramifications with Civil Service. However, because the transfer program was still so new no one knew what, if any, penalties would be assessed against the township for letting go of an officer they had just hired.

"Chad, please believe me when I tell you that I never would have let you transfer over had I known this shit was going to occur. I am so sorry!" Said the Mayor.

"Oh, I believe you Mr. Mayor. But with all due respect, what the fuck am I supposed to do now? I have two kids, one less than a year old. Brooklawn won't take me back. So what do I do?" I was getting very upset.

"Chad, I can't stop the Council from letting you go." The Mayor replied. "And to be honest, they'll do it just to get back at me at this point. So, I'm sure it's going to happen, if it can happen. But if you find somewhere else to go, I will absolutely help you get there!"

I left his house sick to my stomach. How could part-time small-town elected officials have so much power over the careers of full-time police officers? How could they kick a good cop to the curb, screwing up his life and the life of his family and trash his career over petty bullshit arguments and power grabs? How or why didn't matter. This was my reality. I had to move, and I had to move fast!

# CHAPTER 6

# AN OLD FRIEND TO THE RESCUE

"Hey, Chad, I heard you left Brooklawn. Where are you working now?"

Don was a Camden police officer. Remember earlier when I said cops often frequented Weber's Drive-In. Well, Don was one of those cops. Not because he was trying to pick up Suzanne or her sister—he just loved the food! When I was hanging around the restaurant on one of my off days so I could spend time with Suzanne, I noticed Don in his car. Actually, I noticed a Camden Police Department uniform shirt in a clear plastic dry cleaning bag, which was hanging from the hook in the back seat of Don's car. I walked over, introduced myself, and asked him if he was a Camden cop. We hit it off from there.

Whenever he came to the restaurant, and if I was there, we'd end up bullshitting about anything and everything. He'd tell me the crazy stuff that went on in "The City" as it was commonly referred to, and I'd share with him my small-town policing stories. Don was a *worker*, which in police parlance meant that he saw a lot of action. He was very proactive, and he got into a lot of stuff. Don wound up becoming a bit of a legend in Camden. By the end of his short career he would be involved in *five* separate shootings with suspects. The last one was filled with enough controversy that it drove him out of the job.

Currently, I'm sitting in a classroom at the Camden County Police Academy for the State of New Jersey Attorneys General mandatory update class. It's the middle of November, 2002, when Don walks in. Don and I would be attending the class together for the next couple of days. We hadn't seen each other in a while, but Don had heard through the grapevine that I had left Brooklawn. I took the time during a break to catch him up about my current predicament.

"Don, these motherfuckers are about to lay me off." I said.

"What! Why?" Don said, obviously stunned.

I gave him the background on what had happened. Don then made an offer that was about to change my life in so many ways, ways that I never could have imagined.

"Chad, Camden is taking lateral transfers through the Intergovernmental Transfer Program. I'm working in the training unit now. I'm on desk duty due to my most recent shooting, and I'm doing all the background checks. If you want to, give me your resume, and I'll blow out your background in a week. I'll package everything up nice and pretty, and get your package to the right people. We can get you over to Camden before Somerdale can lay you off. Fuck them!"

About two years before my finally leaving Brooklawn, and before I had considered transferring to Somerdale, I had briefly entertained the possibility of going to Camden. Mainly, because a buddy of mine from the police academy who was a Gloucester City officer at the time, was transferring over to Camden, and he had asked me if I wanted to go. This was the end of 1999, beginning of 2000. I would have had to take a pay cut to go to Camden, and I just couldn't do it, so I passed. But now, in 2002, my situation was different. It was desperate.

"Don, you'll be here in class tomorrow, right?" I asked.

He nodded in the affirmative.

"Well, let me talk it over with my wife, and I'll let you know tomorrow, okay?"

"Sure." Don replied. "But if you're interested, just make sure to bring your resume and your certs (certifications) with you to class. That way we can try to get you started in January."

I went home and laid it all out for my wife. She knew Don from his coming to the restaurant, so she knew I wasn't being fed any bullshit.

"Babe, you do what you think is best. You know I'm behind you." Suzanne said. "Besides, if they are going to lay you off, what choice do you really have?" She paused. "Unless, you think someone else would pick you up."

She was concerned about the dangers of my working in Camden. I had pretty much made up my mind from the time Don made the offer. I knew I didn't want to go to another small town police department, and I wasn't State Trooper material. As I didn't have the required college degree. So, my thoughts were something along the lines of, *Well, if I want to be a great cop, I need to go up against the best criminals!*

Don, as promised, finished up my background check in about a week. It really wasn't that difficult, since I had already been a police officer for several years. He shipped my package over to the Business Administrator's Office, located in Camden City Hall. I was told I would start right after the New Year–January, 2003. Then the start date was pushed back to February 2003, due to budget reasons. That date was subsequently pushed back again. Then, I was told around mid-February that I would finally be starting my new job in Camden during March of 2003. The entire process was a race of my moving to Camden before Somerdale could let me go. Fortunately, the contract negotiations between the Chief and the Somerdale Council were taking longer than anticipated. This gave me just enough time to make my move.

I met in secret with the Mayor of Somerdale in late November, 2002, and I told him of my intentions to transfer to Camden. The way the Intergovernmental Transfer Program works is, the transfer documents must be signed by the Appointing Authorities of both the transferring municipality and the receiving municipality. In each town, city, borough, village, and so on this Appointing Authority could be a different entity. For example: In Somerdale the Appointing Authority was the Mayor. Therefore, he alone could sign the transfer documents without the knowledge and consent of the Council, or the Chief of Police. In Brooklawn, the Appointing Authority is the Business Administrator, who acts on the advice and consent of the Mayor and Council. In Camden, the Appointing Authority was the Office of the Business Administrator, similar to Brooklawn. Nonetheless, because Camden was under state oversight at the time, they would require the signatures of a few other individuals who were in positions of power.

My biggest concern at the moment was if any of *the powers that be* in Somerdale found out I was trying to transfer they could attempt to block it, or at the least, they could try to delay it. They could even release me before I was able to transfer. If any of that happened, I would miss my window to get into Camden. It was literally a race against time, and I had to pull it off in secret. Another concern was that if the Chief of Police of Somerdale found out I was trying to leave behind his back he could make my life a living hell! Now, you're probably thinking—*why would Somerdale block my leaving?* Especially, since they would get to use the money from my salary to pay the Chief. Just as they wished to do. You're right, that would free them up to use the money from my salary as they wanted. But, one thing politicians hate is to lose control over a situation. So, the indications from the Mayor were that if they found out I was leaving with his help they would either block the transfer, or they would let me go right away, just for spite.

Needless to say, my stress level was at an all-time high while trying to get this transfer completed. The constant delays in Camden were nerve wracking. I was also getting worried that the transfer would never go through, as my start date kept getting pushed back month after month. Camden was notorious for fucking things up. That is why they were under state oversight in the first place. The longer I was in Somerdale, the closer I was getting to being cut loose. The closer the Chief got to the settling of his contract, the closer I was to losing my job. I was afraid word would leak out and Somerdale would drop me. Then, if the transfer to Camden fell through, I would be out of the job completely.

In late November, when I brought him the paperwork for my transfer to Camden, the Mayor signed it right away with no questions asked. He asked me if I wanted him to try calling Camden and speaking with the people in charge, hoping that it might help to speed up the process. I told him to have at it. In the end, I don't know whether he ever called, or if he did call if it had any impact. However, when I finally got the "drop dead date" from Camden in mid-February 2003, and was assured I would be starting my new job, I marched into the Chief's office to happily give him the news.

"Chief, you got a second?" I asked.

"Yeah, Chad, what's up?"

"Just wanted to let you know that I'm out of here! Here is a copy of my signed and approved Intergovernmental Transfer Agreement."

"What! What the fuck are you talking about? No, I didn't approve this."

"Well, Sir." I began. "That's the beauty of it. In this case you, or your approval, isn't needed or required. It's the Appointing Authority who has to sign it."

I watched his face begin to turn red as he started to process what was happening.

"Which is the Mayor, and the Mayor only." I added. "So, just consider yourself notified." I waited while he fumbled through the document.

"By the way Chief, let me ask you something." I watched as he furiously flipped through the pages of the transfer agreement. "Did you know I was going to be laid off so you could have my salary for your raise?"

He took a quick glance up at me, his eyes as big as saucers. The look on his face screamed, *Oh shit*! The look of guilt was evident. He quickly dropped his eyes back down to the paperwork on his desk.

"What–What!" He stammered. "Who–Who told you that? Where did you hear that?"

Never once did he deny it. That was all the affirmation I needed. I told the Chief my start date in Camden, and I promised him I would finish out my shifts in Somerdale over the next two weeks.

"This is bullshit!" He yelled. "I'm the Chief of Police. The Mayor can't just let my guys go whenever and wherever he wants. I'm calling the Solicitor!" (The Solicitor is the town's legal counsel.)

None of it mattered, I was gone. Camden, here I come!

# CHAPTER 7

# *CAMDEN*

My first day in Camden was Monday, March 3, 2003. I remember the exact date for a few reasons. First, March 3 is my mom's birthday. Next, that was also the day my youngest brother, Michael, was hired for a permanent position as a Sheriff's Officer with the Camden County Sheriff's Department. Their headquarters is also located in the city of Camden. We both started our careers in Camden, me with the municipal police department, him with the Sheriff's Department on the exact same day. Finally, I remember this date as it being the first time I was a member of a police department where another officer had committed suicide.

I arrived at the training unit for my week-long interoffice training at a little before 8 am. Interoffice training is used to go over the rules and regulations of the department, the paperwork, and the policies and procedures, along with other administrative aspects of the job. Camden did things much differently than Brooklawn and Somerdale. Even Camden's radio codes were entirely different.

Sergeant Sharp, a grizzled veteran of the department, and our range master, Sergeant Murphy, a military veteran and a hand-to-hand combat specialist, Officer James, a happy-go-lucky kind of guy, and my buddy Don arrived just after 8 am. Just as Don was introducing me to the other guys and giving them my background, Sergeant Sharp answered the ringing desk phone.

"What? No! No! No! Fuck! Are you sure? Fuck! We're on our way."

As he was on the phone, we had all stopped speaking. Whatever it was, it was *bad*!

Sergeant Sharp hung up the phone. Then suddenly, he slammed both of his fists down onto the desk, while letting his head hang low for what seemed like several moments. It was actually probably only a few seconds, but it felt much longer. Finally, Sergeant Murphy broke the silence.

"Sharp, what the fuck?" Sergeant Murphy said, with both a tone of empathy and annoyance.

Sergeant Sharp slowly looked up and said, "That was dispatch." He paused and swallowed hard. He then took a deep breath and tried to speak while he fought back the tears now welling up in his eyes. "Pine Hill police are at a reported suicide." He began to break down as he spoke. "Sergeant Tommy just killed himself!"

He was barely able to get the words out before he began to sob.

I learned that Sergeant Tommy was widely loved and respected within the department. After some more back and forth between the two Sergeants, everyone suddenly stopped what they were doing and began staring at me. Sergeant Sharp was the first to speak.

"What do we do with him?" He said, as he gestured toward me.

To take the discomfort out of the room, I quickly answered. "Guys, go do what you have to do. Don't worry about me." As I tried to assure them I wouldn't be a concern for them. "Just give me the materials I'm supposed to study, and just leave me here. Go do whatever it is you have to do."

I could sense their relief at my willingness to handle business myself. Don gave me the things I needed to study, and he told me to make sure I signed in at 8 am every day, and signed out at 4 pm (*wink-wink*). I sat in the training room all alone as I studied administrative documents, policies, procedures, rules, and regulations, while completely bored out of my mind. I didn't see Don or any of the other guys for the rest of the week. I learned it was the training unit's responsibility to plan and execute all funerals for current or retired members of the force. With Sargent Tommy's popularity in the department, it was going to be a large funeral to plan for. On Friday, Don briefly stopped by to give me some good news.

He had pulled some strings and gotten me assigned to the 2nd Platoon, 4th District in South Camden. I would be working for Sergeant Street. Sergeant Street was known to be a "cop's cop." He was an old-school street Sergeant who made sure his officers were taken care of. The following Monday, I arrived at the platoon just as we were to begin four straight working days of our 3pm to 1am rotation. The first person I met when I arrived was Sergeant Street. Sergeant Street was your prototypical street cop: uniform pressed, cigar in his mouth, loud, and fearless. Along with Sergeant Street, I met the officer who would be my training partner, and become one of my dearest friends, Officer Kevin Kyle. As we sat in the tiny Sergeant's office within the 2nd District house, Sergeant Street laid out what he expected of me and of the platoon. He liked the fact that I had been a cop for seven years. In his opinion, I was "probably way past all the rookie new guy bullshit." Sergeant Street hated breaking in rookies because of their unpredictability. The only concern he had about me was that I had been a "suburban cop."

Camden, being a rough city, had a habit of chewing up and spitting out suburban cops who tried to work there. They usually couldn't adjust to the fast pace, handle the violence, or adjust to the ebb and flow of a city. I told Sergeant Street that I had spent half of my childhood growing up in the city of Philadelphia, so I was familiar with the way a city operates. Sergeant Street laughed, then with a growl he said, "Well, that's good. But wait until you get a load of this place!" And with a broad smile proclaimed, "You'll wonder if you're still in America!"

*What the fuck did I get myself into*! As Officer Kyle and I rode around the city during my first night on the job, I was thinking that this place looks like a Third World country, and not a city in New Jersey. I knew Camden was bad. I had heard the stories through the police grapevine. Still, while I rode around the streets of Camden with Officer Kyle, I couldn't believe how each neighborhood, each block for that matter, was like a ghetto within the ghetto, if that makes any sense.

Officer Kyle had grown up in Camden in the Fairview section, or as it was affectionately called by its current inhabitants, "White Fairview." The White Fairview moniker was a reference back to when Fairview was the last remaining all-White section of the city. Officer Kyle is White, and I believe he was the only White kid in his Camden High School graduating class. Camden, at one time, had been home to many Italian, Jewish, and Polish families. Ironically, the section in South Camden I was assigned, Sector 403, was affectionately known as "Polack Town." Although, it had been quite a while since any Polish people had actually lived in Polack Town. Sector 403 was the Whitman Park section of the city. Whitman Park was known to be one of the most violent, drug filled, congested, and dangerous areas in Camden.

Officer Kyle wasted no time in showing me the ropes. He described the locations of the drug sets (an area, usually a street corner or a house where drug dealers have set up to sell their drugs to customers), showed me who the players were, and informed me of where past (and possibly future) homicides had taken place, or would likely occur. Officer Kyle was a wealth of knowledge and he is an amazing cop, as I would come to witness firsthand over the years. He understood the city and the department, which are two totally different animals. After a couple of weeks of training, and after he and I had gotten into a few *situations*, Officer Kyle began to realize I was not going to be the normal suburban cop transfer who failed to make the transition.

After one particular incident where we were involved, one in which I had anticipated many of the events before they unfolded, and while taking the appropriate actions, Officer Kyle gave me my first compliment.

"I'll admit it Holland, you picked up how the ghetto works pretty quickly. You got your ghetto pass pretty fast. Especially for a suburban cop."

Being a cop from the suburbs, and trying to win the approval and trust of your fellow officers while working in a place as dangerous as Camden, it is important to show them you can do the job well and show them quickly. Getting that kind of compliment from a seasoned Camden officer like Officer Kyle was a tremendous boost. He also spread the word that I was "good to go" to the rest of the platoon, letting them know that I was trustworthy as back-up. My approach to the job in Camden was much the same as while I was working in Brooklawn and in Somerdale, which was fearlessly, but not recklessly. Soon, I felt accepted by the platoon, which was a huge relief. I also felt like I understood the city and how to police it. Most importantly, I felt like I had finally become a *true street cop*.

In both Brooklawn and Somerdale officers always rode alone in their squad cars—just one officer per vehicle. In Camden, and Sergeant Street in particular, they believed in having as many two-officer vehicles on the road as possible. So, two officers per vehicle was how we rolled. We did have some loners on the squad, particularly those who lived in the city. They wanted to ride alone so they could go home for their meal break, or in order to go visit their loved ones during their shift. Because of this, they didn't necessarily want a partner with them, and Sergeant Street would accommodate them as much as he could. Sometimes a commander would tell Sergeant Street he wanted him to split-up a two officer unit, just so we could cover more ground. Sergeant Street would usually blow his top and start yelling at the commanding officer.

"Fuck these savages!" Sergeant Street would often say. "If they want to kill each other, fine. But none of my guys or girls are getting hurt. We're not splitting anybody up! This policing shit ain't real anyway. How the fuck are we supposed to police Beirut!"

Now, you may be reading that statement and thinking Sergeant Street's words are insensitive at the least, or even racist at the most. You have to understand, we didn't care about the color of someone's skin. Working in Camden, where you are working in a 99% minority city–race doesn't even come into mind; race doesn't factor into our thinking. It's behavior! In a city such as Camden, where day in and day out we witnessed some of the most horrific crimes imaginable being done to fellow human beings, crimes committed by Black on Black, Hispanic on Hispanic, Black on Hispanic, and Hispanic on Black when we are talking about people being *savages* we were talking about their *behavior*, and not their *race*.

Any fears I had of letting my new partner down as I learned to police in the city were soon abated after just a short time of riding together. Officer Kyle and I developed a great chemistry very quickly. It wasn't long before we would finish each other's thoughts and each other's sentences. We would see the same things happening at the same time, and we would begin taking the same actions simultaneously. It was the perfect situation. Officer Kyle and I would remain partners for the next five years, and we would get into a lot of crazy shit together along the way. Things I never could have imagined or anticipated.

# CHAPTER 8

# HE'S WAS ALIVE, AND NOW HE'S DEAD

Officer Kyle and I responded to a home invasion robbery in progress within the area of the Ivy Hill Apartments, which were located within the 1500 block of Pershing Street, Camden. The actual call for the robbery came from the 1300 block of Morton Street, which led right up the apartment complex.

When we arrived, we started to speak with the victims. The victims, a Hispanic male and his wife, stated that while they were watching television before going to work, a male suspect started kicking at the front door of their home, trying to break in. When the male victim went to the door to see what was happening, the suspect pointed a large-caliber handgun at him through the front window. The male victim ran from the window screaming for his wife to call the police. After a couple more unsuccessful kicks at the front door, the suspect ran away. The husband had gotten a good look at the suspect, even though it was dark outside, because of the light on the front porch. He provided a detailed description of the suspect, whom he described as a short and stocky Black male, wearing a white t-shirt and black pants, with a large-caliber black handgun.

After we put the description out over the radio, another officer from our platoon, Officer Atta, pulled up to let us know that he would be circling around the apartment complex to see if he could locate the suspect. While my partner and I were standing outside the victim's home speaking with him, he suddenly pointed over our shoulders, directing our attention behind us.

"There! He's right there." The victim yelled out. "He's right behind the corner of that building."

A Black male, wearing the clothing previously described, was standing maybe seventy-five feet away. He was peering at us from around the corner of one of the apartment buildings. Just for context, this call was occurring at about 4 am in the morning, so it's not like there were a lot of people on the street at this time. Officer Kyle and I started to run toward the suspect, while simultaneously calling it out over the radio.

"Suspect spotted! Corner of Pershing and Morton Streets. He just ran down the steps into the Ivy Hill Apartments Courtyard."

At the far end of the building where we had spotted the suspect, was set of concrete steps that led downward from street level at the corner of Pershing and Thurman Streets, and into the Ivy Hill Apartment's open courtyard. This is an outdoor courtyard that is completely wide open. There is no tunnel or overhead covering of any sort. Suspects would often use this path as a quick get-away when they were selling drugs up on the street. This route allowed suspects to traverse one block over to another in seconds. There was a multitude of places where they could disappear, and we lost many a suspect in this courtyard and complex.

"I'm going around the far side and heading into the courtyard from Thorn Street." Officer Atta said over the radio, with the roar of his police car's engine almost drowning him out as he accelerated.

Once Officer Kyle and I reached the bottom of the steps arriving in the courtyard, we saw Officer Atta's car. It was parked in the middle of the courtyard with the driver's side door wide open, and the car still running.

But it was empty. Officer Atta was nowhere to be found, and neither was our suspect.

"Atta, Atta, where the fuck are you, man?" I yelled.

"Officer Atta, where are you?" Officer Kyle asked over the radio, with no response.

We quickly secured his patrol car and started to look for Officer Atta, with Officer Kyle running off in one direction, and I in another.

"Kyle! Kyle! I think Atta is chasing him on foot. I think they just ran up the hill." I called out over the radio.

As I had turned the corner of one of the buildings, I caught a glimpse of Officer Atta as he was finishing his ascent up the grassy hill leading from the courtyard and onto Thurman Street. I was closer to the stairs which led up to the street than the hill I saw him climbing. So, I ran toward the stairs as fast as I could, hoping to catch up to Atta and the suspect. As I got to the top of the stairs I could hear yelling and commotion. As I cleared the last of the steps, I looked straight ahead down the sidewalk of the 1300 block of Thurman Street. I saw Officer Atta in a physical struggle with the suspect.

They were both standing upright, and were pressed against a parked vehicle–and were face to face. The suspect's back was up against the car, and Officer Atta was standing directly in front of him. I saw that the suspect was reaching into his waistband, as he was attempting to pull something from it. Officer Atta's free hand was on top of the suspect's hand which was reaching into his waistband, as he was struggling to keep the suspect from pulling the object free. Officer Atta's weapon was out, and was being held in his opposite hand. I heard Officer Atta yell, "Fucking drop it!" a pause, and then Boom! Officer Atta shot the suspect at point-blank range. I recall ducking when Officer Atta fired. I ducked because the shot made such a loud echo in the courtyard behind me that it sounded like a shot was being fired from directly over my shoulder.

I started running down the sidewalk toward Officer Atta and the suspect with my weapon drawn. I saw the suspect say something to Officer

Atta after he was shot, since he hadn't gone down. The suspect still had his hand in his waistband, and was still trying to get the object free. In an instant, Officer Atta pushed off and stepped back and away from the suspect as he fired a second shot into the suspect's chest–Boom! In the predawn hours it sounded like a bomb went off. Running as fast as I could I felt like I was running in slow motion, as if I was running in quick-sand. I had a thought of trying to take a shot at the suspect, because he still wasn't down after Officer Atta's second shot. The thought came and went in milliseconds. Out of the corner of my eye, and off to my right, I could see my partner-Officer Kyle. He had come from an alleyway in-between the apartment buildings, and was pointing his weapon and yelling commands at the suspect. Just as I reached Officer Atta and the suspect, the suspect dropped to the ground, landing right at my feet. He was dead, bleeding heavily from his two point-blank gunshot wounds to his chest. Still gripped in his hand, and halfway out of his waist band, was a black large-caliber handgun. It was a Bulldog .44 revolver.

"Atta, Atta, are you alright! Are you hurt?" I asked.

Officer Atta and I have a running joke about what happens next. He is an absolute physical specimen. Tall, muscular, powerful and well trained in the martial arts. Me. I was in great shape at the time, but I am 5'9" and 175 pounds. Not exactly a big guy. Just after shooting the suspect, Officer Atta started to lose it a bit. With all his strength he started shaking me–violently! He was throwing me around and shaking me so badly by my collar that my neck hurt for about three days afterwards, like I had gotten whiplash.

"Why!" Officer Atta screamed. "Why the fuck did this happen? Why the fuck didn't he just drop it. Why–Why!" He yelled, as he was punching me in my chest.

Our joke is that he made me look like one of those crash test dummies as it gets bounced around in a vehicle after it hits the wall, flailing about. I felt like a ragdoll as he tossed me around. Another unit arrived on scene, and I stuffed Officer Atta in the back of the police car and told them to take him to the hospital. He would need to be medicated in order to calm him down.

Sergeant Lover arrived on scene during the shooting. He was Officer Atta's Patrol Sergeant, his boss. When Sergeant Lover heard the gun shots ringing out he ran from his vehicle, and up the street toward us. The memory of Sergeant Lover running toward us with his "pimp limp," which was actually a wobble he walked with due to an old hip injury, was hysterical. We had nicknamed him "Pimp Limp" partly because of this limp, but mostly for his way with the ladies. Sergeant Lover was a smooth player!

"If he moves again, shoot him in his ass!" Sergeant Lover ordered.

When I think about him wobbling up that sidewalk and yelling to shoot the guy in his ass it still makes me laugh. Of course, it wasn't funny at the time. But later, when everyone was safe and we had time to reflect on the whole event, the gallows *cop humor* kicked in.

"Holland, what the fuck happened?" Sergeant Lover asked.

"Dude tried to pull a gun on Officer Atta. Officer Atta dropped him." I said, very matter of fact.

"Alright, you see that gun?" As he pointed to the suspect's gun. "You stand right here on top of it until Crime Scene collects it. I don't want that thing walking away."

I stayed with the gun (and the dead suspect) until the Crime Scene Unit and Medical Examiner arrived. Then I headed downtown to write my report. By the time I made it to our station I was completely spent. Camden had a ridiculous rule that in order to go home, you had to finish all your reports before you finished your shift. Even if something occurred at the very end of your shift when you were completely exhausted, and while you couldn't even think straight. I always thought that was a mistake. Its human nature to not only forget important pieces of information when you're tired, but to also rush through the reports. Many reports were kicked back for this very reason and had to be rewritten. It always struck me as a waste of time.

In this case, I had just witnessed my first fatal shooting. I witnessed my first death in the line of duty. I had seen dead bodies before, but it was the first time I witnessed someone alive one second, and then dead the next. Never had I before witnessed someone being killed, with their body now laying lifeless, and while oozing blood. Furthermore, I had damn near pulled the trigger myself when Officer Atta had fired and the suspect remained standing. I truly considered firing a shot for a fraction of a second as I ran toward them.

*Can I get a shot from here? Will I make the shot from here? Is Atta too close? What if the suspect gets that gun out and Atta doesn't fire again in time?*

These were thoughts I never had to previously consider, and I wanted time to process it.

I was so exhausted physically and mentally that I couldn't tell you to this day what I actually wrote in the report. It was all a blur. I wasn't even sure how I was supposed to feel. This was all new to me, and I wasn't sure how I was going to react. However, after a couple of days the shooting surprisingly never entered my mind again. I don't know why. I didn't purposely try to keep it out of my head. But it just seemed to pass very quickly. I wouldn't think again about this shooting and the vision of the suspect lying dead and bleeding at my feet until much later in my career.

There is a bit of twisted irony to this story. What I failed to mention at the beginning was that this was my first night back at work after having been out sick for the past two weeks. I was out sick after having had a vasectomy. The vasectomy wasn't the problem—the accompanying infection was. Two days after having the vasectomy I wound up with severe stomach pain, and my nuts looked like the size of two grapefruits when I awoke in the morning. While my partner Kyle and I were chasing after the suspect I blurted out, due to the immense pain now forming between my legs, "Kyle, if we catch this sonofabitch get the fuck out of my way. Because I am going to fucking kill him for making my nuts bounce around like this!"

I, of course, said this as a joke. Little did I know that within minutes the suspect really would be dead! I guess this is a case of watching what you wish for.

# CHAPTER 9

# THE ANGRY FRIED CHICKEN LADY

Camden had crazy things going on almost every night, and after a while it all seemed so normal. However, there is one thing I want to clarify before I get into any specific details about anything that went on in Camden.

I know a lot of what I discuss here pales in comparison to what other officers have seen, or have been through in their careers. In every ghetto across the country, and even in places where you would never expect to see such horrors, officers are exposed to some of the most appalling and unspeakable acts that a person can never un-see. I don't think I'm unique in this respect. My intention is not to "one up" anyone as far as *war stories* are concerned. I simply want to share some of my personal experiences, as I think these experiences, along with my failure to properly deal with them as they occurred, are what would lay the emotional groundwork for my susceptibility to PTSD and depression. If sharing my experiences can help just one person from making the same mistakes I made, then this was well worth it!

One of the more tragic things I witnessed while working in Camden was the killing of a little girl when she was ejected from her mother's car. I was actually on the scene of an officer involved shooting when this call went out. I left the shooting scene, and I arrived right after other units had signed out at this tragic event. This horrific event occurred after the little girl's extremely drunk mother took the child from the child's grand-mother's home at around 1am in the morning, and decided to drive while drunk in the pouring rain with the child in the car.

Already staggering drunk earlier in the evening, the mother had pre-viously tried to take the little girl from grandma's house, leaving the child's grandmother to physically fight off the child's mother in order to prevent her from taking the little girl. After everyone had fallen asleep, the intoxi-cated mother snuck back into the house using her key, and took the child out of her warm bed and into the cold-rainy night. She made it less than a mile down the road before she smashed into a curb, flipping the vehicle over, and hitting a telephone pole. The child's entire car seat was ejected from the vehicle, because her mother failed to properly fasten it to the rear seat of the vehicle with the seatbelt.

When we arrived on the scene, the child's car seat was resting in the street in the pouring rain, about fifty feet or so from where the car had overturned. The child's body was laying just feet away from the car seat. The small lifeless body was still clad in pajamas. That precious child, who just moments ago was sleeping in her warm bed, was now dead on a cold, dark, wet street in Camden, killed by the actions of her own piece-of-shit mother. That one has always haunted my memory. The vision of that child's broken body, wet and dead in her pajamas is something that will never leave me.

Another, almost surreal event that sticks out in my mind is that of the robbery suspect who tried to flee on a stolen motorcycle. He had just stolen the motorcycle during a strong-armed robbery, when he lost control racing down a city street at well over 100 miles per-hour. After he lost con-trol of the bike, he proceeded to bounce off cars and other fixed objects, as his momentum propelled him down the block. He lost various body parts along the way as he pin-balled about. Eventually, he hit a fence so hard that his body was sheared almost completely in half. His head, while still in the helmet, was hanging onto his body by just a thread of skin. We were left to search all over the block for his missing body parts. We even had to get down on our hands and knees to search under parked cars, porches, gutters and the like. It was a bloody mess! We required several body bags for all the severed body parts.

A call I still think of often is one I refer to as "The Angry Fried Chicken Lady."

While working the day shift (7 am to 5 pm) one beautiful spring day, I responded to a call for a domestic dispute on a small and almost forgotten about side-street, which runs right next to the Campbell's Soup World Headquarters. It was extremely rare to get a call on this street, since there were only about ten houses on the entire block. It was known as one of the very few quiet spots in Camden. As I arrived, I saw a female sitting on a chair on the front porch. She was eating what is a very popular meal in Camden—a three-piece box of Crown Fried Chicken. Crown Fried Chicken is a local chicken establishment, and the three-piece meal is by far the most popular meal they serve, since it is so inexpensive.

As I approached her on the porch, I noticed that she was staring straight ahead, like she was in some sort of trance. I also noticed she was eating her chicken while both of her hands were covered in blood.

"Hello, ma'am. What's going on? Are you okay—Are you hurt?" I asked, as I was trying to put together what was happening.

"I'm good, officer." Her voice was barely more than a soft whisper. "But I told him. I told him I wanted all three pieces this time. I keep paying for it, and he keeps bringing it back with only one piece left. I told him, if he come back this time with any of the pieces missing I was gonna cut him. So, I did."

While the woman was speaking, I noticed a blood trail leading from the porch and through the open front door of the home. It continued throughout the home and led to the kitchen, which was located at the back of the house. Peering into the home, I could barely make out what appeared to be the bottom of someone's shoes on the kitchen floor in the distance. As they were just barely peeking out from around the corner of a wall that separated the kitchen from the living room area. The shoes were facing toes down, and it appeared someone was lying face down on the floor. Just as the *Chicken Lady* was finishing her story, my partner Officer Kyle, arrived. We were riding separately that day because the department was short on staffing.

"Watch her." I said to Officer Kyle, as I made my way into the house.

As I got closer to the kitchen the blood trail grew in size. Once I made it into the kitchen, I observed lying face down on the floor with the telephone receiver lying next to him, an older male. He was lying in a huge puddle of blood—the largest puddle of blood I had ever seen. He was African-American in life, but was now ghost white, as the life had literally drained out of him. He died in that spot after he had dialed 9-1-1. We secured the female as she was placed under arrest, and we found the bloody knife lying underneath a chair. After she was read her Miranda rights and taken downtown, she gave a full confession of the homicide to the detectives. I am paraphrasing things because I don't have access to the actual transcript, but her recount of the incident went something as follows.

She had routinely been giving her boyfriend money to buy her a three-piece box of chicken from Crown Fried Chicken. But time and time again, he came home with a box of half-eaten chicken, and had spent the rest of the money on a 40-ounce beer. So, she couldn't buy any more chicken. The suspect warned her boyfriend that he had to come home with all three pieces of chicken this time, or she would "cut him." He didn't heed her warning. When he came home on this particular day and handed her the box of half-eaten chicken she was ready. As soon as she opened the box and saw there was only one piece of chicken left, she pulled out a knife and stabbed him. She didn't just stab him—she made sure she did things correctly.

While seated in the chair, and with her boyfriend standing directly in front of her, she had a clear shot at each of his legs, specifically his inner thighs. If you're not familiar, this particular area of the leg's anatomy is precisely where the main arteries run—the femoral arteries. Severing these arteries is like turning on a valve and draining a swimming pool. Everything pours out, and the victim dies in minutes. The female suspect made two perfect strikes with the knife. One into the femoral artery in his left thigh, and one into the artery in his right thigh. But she wasn't done.

As the victim reacted to her stabbing him in the legs, she stood up and stabbed him in his chest, and then his neck. He also had defensive wounds on his arms when he tried to block her further attacks. The victim was able to make it to the telephone in the kitchen, where he dialed 9-1-1 and then collapsed. It was estimated he died within three to five minutes of the first stab wounds, as both strikes completely severed both femoral arteries. It was like when a mechanic is changing the oil in your car, and they pull out the plug from your car's oil pan. We've all seen how quickly the quarts of used oil come pouring out of a vehicle, and how quickly it drains. The same thing occurred with the victim. All the blood in his body had literally drained out in minutes.

After stabbing him, the suspect sat down on the chair and began to eat the remainder of the chicken in the box, and that's when I arrived. The suspect admitted in the interview that both she and her boyfriend were long-time alcoholics who had been abusing each other for years. But neither one of them had ever bothered to ever call the police before today.

Camden wasn't all about tragedy. There were many aspects of the job that I really enjoyed. One of my fondest memories was when I was assigned to bike patrol during the summer months one year.

During that summer, my partner Bill and I rode our bikes through some of the roughest and most crime-infested areas in Camden. We made a lot of arrests, but we also met a lot of great people who were literally trapped in their homes and in their neighborhoods due to crime. There are so many wonderful people in Camden who simply lack the resources to leave the city, making them prisoners within their own household. As we rode around the city on our bikes fully exposed and unprotected, we gained a lot of respect from the citizens and the criminals, alike. They thought that if we had the balls to ride our bikes through the roughest areas of the city with nothing to protect us other than ourselves, then we must be crazy or brave or both!

The law-abiding folks in the community loved it! My partner and I got invited to more cookouts while we were riding around the neighborhoods than I can count. As we rode down the street, folks often started yelling to us and insisting we come to their yard to eat their barbecue. As more and more folks began to trust us, we started to get tips as to who was doing what, where, and when. We would make the busts, and the next day people were outside their homes and their kids were now playing in the street. We would get hugs and tears of thanks for our efforts. This really helped to reshape my views of Camden and the people in it. Most people, simply needed our help. We did our best to make these people feel safe, and we definitely messed with the drug dealers' heads.

We had the ability to just pop out of an alleyway or come up a one-way street the opposite way completely stealth like, giving the drug dealers no warning. It got so bad for them, that the drug dealers began to have their lookouts follow us on their own bicycles. This way, they could at least call ahead and let them know what area we were riding in. It was fun playing cat-and-mouse with the dealers and their mobile lookouts. It was such a rewarding time in my career, and I felt like I truly was making a difference.

If there was one thing I enjoyed the most about being a cop it was the pursuits—in a vehicle, on a bike, or on foot. The purity of it appealed to me. The bad guys are running away, and we are chasing them. Their goal is to get away, and our goal is to catch them. It's that simple. I liked anticipating their moves and of course, arresting them. I was very good at calling out the pursuits over the radio, always remaining very calm and cool. Pursuits in Camden were numerous and easy to come by. Still, there are two motor vehicle pursuits that stick out in my mind in particular.

Officer Kyle and I had just picked up our nightly coffee at a local donut shop (only coffee, we didn't do the donuts), and no sooner had we walked out of the coffee shop, when a report of an armed robbery in progress went out from dispatch. There was a description of a getaway vehicle broadcast over the radio, and as luck would have it we wound up behind the vehicle almost immediately. We chased the suspect vehicle all over the city. At one point, we wound up on the highways of Route 676 and Route 42, which are two major thoroughfares that intersect and run through Camden. We had gotten up to speeds of 125 miles per-hour while we continued chasing this suspect vehicle all over the place. However, and most importantly, I was driving with just one hand on the wheel, while holding my hot cup of coffee in the other. My partner, who was working the lights, siren, and the radio while I drove, was holding his coffee in his hand as well. Neither of us spilled a drop! We weren't about to waste a good coffee. At one point, we just looked at each other and started to laugh. There was no need for words. You know you're a couple of relaxed veterans when you are flying around in a police car at speeds that would scare the shit out of most people on a normal day, and your biggest concern is not spilling your coffee. The pursuit finally ended when the suspect crashed. We took him into custody and recovered the handgun used in the robbery. Later, as we recapped the whole event, we laughed our asses off at our nonchalant approach to the whole thing. Although very relaxed, we never let our guard down tactically. Although, I am sure there are those who would disagree.

The next pursuit I remember fondly because it is a point of pride for me.

It was a daytime pursuit. They were robbery suspects who had committed a robbery in nearby Cherry Hill, and had attempted to purchase drugs from an undercover officer with the proceeds from the robbery. After they were observed trying to buy the drugs, they had tried to run down the undercover police officers from the Cherry Hill Police Department who had swooped in to make the arrest. The Cherry Hill officers then pursued them into Camden. It was a pursuit in the middle of the day time that went all over the city, which is never a good thing. Daytime pursuits offer several obvious, as well as not-so-obvious, challenges.

First, the obvious. They are inherently more dangerous because there are more people out and about, which increases the probability of an innocent person being hurt or killed.

Another, and less obvious issue, is the number of bosses around. You had better do everything by the book or the bosses will have Internal Affairs up your ass before you can even start the paperwork. Especially if something bad happens during the pursuit, and things go south.

This particular chase had been going on for several minutes, when the pursuing units were cut off in traffic and lost the suspects. I located the suspect vehicle and I picked up the pursuit in front of Cooper University Hospital, which is in downtown Camden, in the center of the city. This is by far the most populated area of the city at that hour, especially during a weekday workday, which is when this chase is occurring. I had been monitoring the chase on the radio, and I started taking short cuts via backstreets toward the section of the city they were heading. I had a sense these suspects were from out of town, mostly because of the randomness in their direction of travel. Suspects from the city (for the most part) have specific patterns and head toward specific areas in order to get away. These suspects were driving around like a couple of lost tourists, and I assumed they were trying to get back to the highway.

When I finally caught up to the suspects, I watched as they smashed into just about every vehicle in their path. As the pursuit continued, they hit more cars and several parking meters. They jumped the vehicle over curbs, struck fences, and drove down sidewalks—you name it, they did it! The driver was a White male, with a White female passenger. I don't know if he was doing it on purpose, or if he was just that shitty of a driver, but he would constantly hit other vehicles as he tried to flee. He would then suddenly come to a complete stop, and would start doing 360-degree burnouts–for no logical reason. While he was doing these 360 burnouts, I would just stop my vehicle and watch and wait until he was done. Then, he would take off again in some random direction. He drove over medians, over more curbs, and down various sidewalks in his attempt to shake me off his tail. This guy was driving like a complete lunatic, and there was no real skill or logic to his methods of eluding.

I chased the suspects from North Camden, to East Camden, and back to North Camden again. When we finally got back into North Camden, the driver lost control and smashed into a retaining wall on the Rutgers University College Campus, thus ending the chase. Both suspects were then taken into custody. However, there was a bit of a dust up afterward. Right before the suspects smashed into the wall, I was cut off by about six or seven other police units soaring in from my west. I slammed on the brakes and let them get ahead of me. Otherwise, I was sure they were going to smash into me. Once the suspects' vehicle hit the wall, the officers in those units ran up to the smashed vehicle and pulled the male suspect out of the car. They then gave him a bit of an ass whooping before cuffing him.

The reason for the ass kicking was because those officers lived in the city, and this scumbag had sailed past their kids' schools, rode up onto the sidewalks in their neighborhoods, and in one case, smashed into a car belonging to one of the officer's family members. Consequently, the officers administered a bit of street justice. The video from the assisting Cherry Hill Police vehicle that had been recording my pursuit had recorded this ass kicking, and it wasn't long before Internal Affairs opened an investigation. Fortunately for me, I hadn't witnessed any of the beating. By the time I pulled up to the scene, it was over. So, even with Internal Affairs grilling me with questions about the pursuit itself (especially when one of our officers appeared to ram the suspect vehicle on video—a big *no-no* in New Jersey), when it got to the part about the beating I was able to tell Internal Affairs to *screw off*, because I hadn't witnessed any of the assault.

The reason I consider this pursuit a point of pride is the video and the accompanying audio demonstrated that I had called out the pursuit calmly and clearly, and was on point with my locations and directions of travel. I had even anticipated many of the suspect's moves and changes in direction prior to him making them. My anticipation helped assisting units shut down roads where there were pedestrians and motor vehicle traffic, and before the suspect had a chance to endanger them as well. I kept the proper distance, speed, and complete control of my vehicle the entire time, even when an assisting unit almost forced me to smash into a parked vehicle, causing me to make a pretty cool evasive maneuver. The pursuit was complete chaos, but I had kept it under control. The department would later use the video and my radio transmissions as a teaching tool, and to show what an officer *should do* during a pursuit. I had always prided myself on my ability to remain calm and clear on the radio during times of high stress. This made me feel like I had done something to help other officers become better at their jobs.

There is one last job I will speak of, and one of which I think is a perfect demonstration of the challenging relationship between law enforcement and the communities they serve. This will offer as a good example of how even when the police do something right, they are still often viewed as the enemy.

It was a brutally hot August summer night. The heat and humidity had everyone out of their homes and onto the streets. For most folks who lived in the city, it was cooler to sit outside when it was 90-degrees and humid, even at 1:30 in the morning, than it was to sit in their homes. Especially, since so few homes in Camden were air conditioned. The cops were dying from the heat when we were out on the street while wearing our full uniform and body armor. The brief ride between calls for service in our air conditioned vehicles being our only relief. While I was meeting up with the Patrol Sergeant I was working with that night for log check (Log check is when you meet with your Patrol Sergeant so they could collect your reports for the shift and check over your patrol log), he and I heard a series of gunshots ring out from just a block or so away. Boom!-Boom!-Boom!

"Damn Sarge, that's close." I said. "Sounds like a shotgun."

"Yeah Holland, it sounds like it's just a block or two over. You head down Jackson Street, I'll head around to Sheridan Street and come up that way." The Sergeant directed, as we formulated a quick plan.

I took off from our location and started to head up Jackson Street, where it sounded like the shots were coming from. I drove the wrong way up the one-way street with my lights off and my vehicle "blacked out" for tactical advantage. Just before I got to the corner of Louis and Jackson Streets I could see that the block, which had been filled with people just moments earlier, was now completely empty.

"Hey Sergeant, head over to Louis and Jackson, I think this may be where they were firing." I said over the radio, as my sixth sense was telling me this was the place.

I parked and exited my vehicle, and began to walk to the corner of the intersection. Just before I got to the corner, I heard someone crying out.

"Yo, Cop! Here–I'm here. Help me, Cop. I'm shot!"

The Patrol Sergeant had just turned the corner (he was on foot as well), and he also heard the voice call out.

"Sarge, it's coming from down the alleyway, right here." I said, as I gestured toward an alleyway that ran between two homes just before the end of the block. "Sarge, I will go down the alleyway, you hang back here at the entrance and cover me, just in case it's a setup."

Very cautiously, I began to walk down the dark and narrow alleyway. I didn't want to use my flashlight because my natural night vision was pretty sharp. I figured I stood a better chance of not tipping them off if I wasn't using my flashlight, if this was in fact, a trap.

"Help me Cop! I'm hit. I'm shot!" The male called out.

I could tell it was a young male from the lack of maturity in the voice.

"Cop, hurry. I'm bleeding, man. Hurry!" He repeated.

What I couldn't figure out as I creeped down the alleyway was, *how the hell did he see me from all the way down here in the alleyway in the first place?* He started calling me when I was still at the street corner, and a few hundred feet from the alleyway. How the hell did he even know I was there, let alone know I was a cop? How could even he see me? Perplexed, I carried on. I was about a third of the way down the alleyway, when I came upon a burned out garage behind one of the houses. The garage had a smell like damp-old burnt wood. It had obviously been burned down a long time ago, but the humidity that night made the burnt wood smell come alive. I was now covered in sweat, and the mosquitoes were starting to feast on me. While I was standing by the garage fighting off the bugs, and debating how much further I was willing to travel down the alleyway, I heard the voice I had been tracking call out to me once again. However, this time it was coming from directly above me!

"Cop, here. I'm up here!" The male called out.

As I looked up, I saw lying on top of the burned roof rafters within the garage the male who had been calling for help.

"Dude, what the fuck!" I said, as I saw him lying precariously across two charred roof supports.

"Cop, you gotta help me! They shot me. Them boys shot me in the back!"

Seeing him up above, I realized how he had been able to see me on the street. It was because he was perched up high, while lying on top of the burned out remnants of the garage.

"Sarge, I found him. Start EMS, he's shot!" I shouted.

I let out a sigh of relief as I thought about how grateful I was that this wasn't a set-up. If it had been a set-up he could have easily blown me away, since he was positioned high and above me. I was squeezed into the tiny alleyway with nowhere to go. It would have been like shooting fish in a barrel. As I tried to figure out a way to reach the victim, I couldn't believe he had gotten up there and not fallen through. This garage was filled with trash and other debris. There was an old burned-up car in the garage, but it was buried under mounds of trash and fallen wood from the previous fire. It looked like there was no safe way up and onto the rafters the victim was lying upon. But I had to figure out how to get up to him, since he was possibly dying.

"Hey, Sarge. He's up on the garage roof. You better start the fire department as well. We're going to need a ladder."

"He's on the fucking roof!" The Sergeant replied with disbelief.

"Cop-Cop, you gotta help me man, help me!" The victim begged.

"I am. Help is coming. Hey, how the hell did you get up there in the first place?" I asked, as I tried to figure out a way to get up to him.

"I just ran as they were shooting at me and I came up here to hide." The wounded young man replied. Then he said something that brought me grave concern.

"Cop, I feel sleepy. I feel like I'm going to sleep."

*Dammit! He is dying. I have to get up to him and see if I can stop the bleeding.*

"Sarge, he's hurt bad. I got to get up to him or he's not going to make it!"

"Okay, be careful!" The Sergeant replied.

I began to climb around on the debris in the garage. After slipping and almost falling a few times, I was able to bridge myself between the retaining wall and a charred beam. I then swung up and onto the beams the victim was lying upon, and I literally crawled over to him. Otherwise, the beams would've probably collapsed.

"Hey man, you with me?" I asked, as I made it over to the victim.

He was a kid, no more than fifteen or sixteen years-old.

"Chad, EMS and the FD are on the way." The Sergeant advised.

"Jesus Christ, Chad! How the fuck did *you* get up there?" The Sergeant asked quizzically. As he saw me now perched on the beams.

I didn't have time to explain, not with the kid possibly bleeding to death.

"Hey, where are you shot?" I asked.

The young male was wearing a long black t-shirt and black shorts. As I slipped my rubber gloves on, I began to check around his back for wounds. Since he said he had been shot in the back.

"Here man, they got me right here." As he pointed to the right side of his back.

His black t-shirt was sticking to his back when I tried to lift it. At first I thought it may be from sweat, but after touching it with my light blue colored rubber glove and shining my flashlight on it, I saw that my glove had become covered with blood. He had taken a shotgun blast to the back. The suspects had shot him as he had run down the alleyway. Fearing if he kept running in a straight line they would finish him off, the victim jumped into the garage, bounded up the wall, and ended up on top of the burned beams. He said he had watched as the suspects had run up and down the alleyway looking for him, but they never noticed him lying up on the beams. Just as I hadn't noticed him when I was standing in the alleyway below.

"Cop, I'm starting to see funny lights." The young man mumble.

"Do not go to the lights!" I said firmly. "Stay with me, dude. You're not allowed to die! You understand me? You're not allowed to die! I won't have it."

"Alright Cop. I don't want to die. But I'm sleepy."

I applied pressure to his wounds and kept him awake by talking with him. He was shot in the lower right portion of the back, his right hip, and right buttock. It took several minutes to get him down once EMS and the Fire Department arrived. It was a tight spot we were in, so it was hard to get any equipment to us. Furthermore, the beams he and I were lying on were creaking and cracking. I thought that at any moment we were going to hear–SNAP! And we would go crashing down into the pile of debris below. Luckily, were able to get both the victim and myself down without any further damage to either of us.

"Holland, you did a good job up there. You saved that kids life." The Sergeant said to me, after we had wrapped up the scene.

"No biggie Sarge." I replied. I really didn't look at it as a big deal. Just another day working in Camden.

The next night in roll call, the Sergeant gave me a "shout out" in front of the whole platoon. I was kind of embarrassed when he emphasized how much empathy and compassion I had shown toward this kid. The Sergeant told everyone how I had spoken with him and kept him awake, and such. It just didn't fit with the hardcore exterior we try to keep as cops. Silently, I did appreciate his recognition for a job well done.

About two years later I would see this kid again. I never knew what had happened to him. After my report was written and turned over to the detectives, I never heard another word about the shooters, or the victim. Until one day, I received a subpoena to appear as a witness for a trial. I didn't recognize the names on the subpoena, so I just showed up at court figuring the prosecutor would bring me up to speed. It was for the kid who had been shot. They were able to eventually identify the shooters, and there was now going to be a trial.

I walked into the courtroom right before court was in session, and even two years later, I was able to recognize the kid right away. He was sitting in the first row just behind the prosecutor's table. I walked over to introduce myself, genuinely happy to see that he was still alive and well.

"Hey, man, how you doing?" I began, as I stuck out my hand to shake his.

The kid looked up at me and gave me a nasty look. Then he said with an air of disgust in his voice, "Do I know you, Cop?"

"Yeah man, I'm the one who was up on the roof with you that night."
I replied.

"How you doing, man? You look good!" I said, as I was truly happy
to see he looked well.

He had obviously grown, and he didn't look any worse for the wear.

"Pssssstttt, yeah, whateva!" He said dismissively, as he brushed aside
my outstretched hand while turning his back to me.

I was completely shocked. "Dude, what the hell!" I was stunned.

My eyes met the prosecutor's, who had turned in his seat to witness
our exchange. The prosecutor gently turned his head side to side, as a sign
to let me know that I wasn't going to get anywhere with the kid.

This is what I spoke of earlier. How a cop can do everything right,
but the code of the streets takes over, and even a person whose life you may
have saved, now treats you like trash. He was part of the streets. The code
of the street doesn't let you embrace the police–no matter what. Knowing
I had helped to save the kid's life would be all the thanks that I would be
getting from him.

# CHAPTER 10

# THE GOOD GUYS ARE THE BAD GUYS

U.S. Attorney: "Officer Holland, you just read the report of the incident as written by Officer Fabio to the members of the jury, correct?"

Me: "Correct."

U.S. Attorney: "Now, Officer Holland. What Officer Fabio wrote in this report, is this how you recall the way the incident took place?"

Me: "No, sir. This report is not reflective of how the incident occurred."

Twenty-seven officers were assigned to the Elite Supplemental Patrol Squad. Our job was to be a proactive unit. We didn't answer radio calls or normal calls for service, like most police patrol units do. Our job was to go out and put ourselves in harm's way by being proactive and arresting drug dealers, and by making gun arrests. In the City of Camden—one of the poorest cities in America and consistently one of the top ten most dangerous cities for crime—drugs, guns, crime, and criminals were plentiful. This unit was made up of what were considered to be the best officers within the four-hundred member department, and our job was a dangerous one.

In order to attack drug trafficking and gun violence we employed numerous tactics. We had undercover officers pose as drug users and purchase drugs directly from the dealers. Unmarked vehicles would float around the area as roving back-up, while the officers in plain (civilian) clothes would roam around the various drug sets. They would look for active deals going down, as well as try to identify anyone who may be carrying a weapon. The old police adage of "Where there are drugs there are guns" is extremely accurate, and violence usually isn't far behind. Our goal was to catch some of these drug dealers with their guns on them— and *before* the violence had a chance to occur. We had a group of five officers on this squad who were considered to be the best of the best. These five officers were always in plain-clothes, and they seemed skilled at coming up with the big busts of guns, drugs, and cash. These five officers, "The Fab Five" as I will call them, would receive award after award each month for their activities. These guys were known to have a great eye and a great feel for the street.

The Fab Five could usually look at a drug set and pick out right away the different players and their roles within the drug trade. A typical drug set would consist of lookouts, slingers, the money man, and the muscle. The lookouts could be on foot, on bikes, in vehicles, or any combination of the three. The lookout's job is to warn the slingers (the guys who are selling the drugs), and the money men when the police, or even rival drug dealers, were approaching. The muscle would deal with anyone who got in the way, and with whatever force was necessary.

These five officers were making numerous gun and drug arrests because of their sharp skill set. It appeared they had a knack for it, or at least so it seemed. Our bosses would often communicate to the rest of the squad that we should, "be more like them (the Fab Five), and that if we would all work as hard as them we would absolutely drive down crime." The Fab Five were held up as model by the bosses of what police officers should be.

I was very rarely in plain-clothes. My partner, Officer Jay, and I were usually assigned to the arrest van, and we worked while dressed in our full uniform. Jay and I were both fairly fast runners, so we would swoop in to help the plain-clothes guys take down the drug dealers when they wanted to effect an arrest. Sometimes we'd wind up in a foot pursuit, and since Jay and I were fleet a foot they liked having us around. After we took down the bad guys, we would transport them downtown to Central Booking for processing. The Fab Five would meet us downtown, where they would be responsible for processing their prisoners and inventorying the evidence. Which usually consisted of guns, drugs, money, or all of the above. After a while, Jay and I started to notice a pattern.

Usually by the time the Fab Five called for us to take down the suspects, they had already done so on their own, and long before we had arrived. They would call out the location, and we would show up with the arrest van. But by the time we had arrived, the drug dealers they were targeting would already be in handcuffs, and seated on the ground. The guns, drugs, money, or whatever else they had on them would already be in the Fab Five's possession. We started to get the sense that they had been out there for a while with the suspects, and possibly long before they called for us to come and assist them. Jay and I didn't think much of it at the time. These guys were pretty secretive and guarded when it came to how they liked to go about their business. It was almost like they were territorial in their methods, and they didn't want to share their tricks of the trade with anyone. We had assumed they were able to take down the suspects without incident. Jay and I were only there to "clean up the trash," so to speak.

"That shit ain't even mine! Y'all planted that shit!"

To hear a suspect claim that a cop planted drugs on them wasn't uncommon. Suspects were always coming up with ways of trying to deflect blame. So, to hear one proclaim their innocence by accusing the police of putting drugs on them usually didn't raise any red flags. Not immediately, anyway. The problem was, the various suspects that the Fab Five were arresting were uttering the same claim–over and over and over again. Finally, a wrongly accused suspect went to Internal Affairs and gave them an incredibly damaging statement about the Fab Five. This statement was unique in that it said something to the effect of, "Look, I'm out there hustling [selling drugs], I ain't denying that. And you guys have caught me dirty [with drugs] before. I admit that. But the day these guys [The Fab Five] said I was dirty, I promise you I wasn't. As a matter of fact, I was out of product that day."

You may be thinking to yourself, *what's the big deal*? This guy admits that he's a drug dealer, and that he's been caught in the past. So, what does it matter if he was "dirty" that day as opposed to another day? Since he is obviously a criminal. The obvious issue is that when you have drug dealers coming to Internal Affairs who know they are guilty of past crimes, but are now just pleading for an opportunity to be caught legitimately, and by not being set up illegally, then there is a larger problem afoot. It's called several things: fabrication of evidence, wrongful imprisonment, entrapment, perjury, violation of civil rights, and official misconduct to name just a few. The Fab Five was dirty, and it was all about to come crashing down.

The Fab Five, which consisted of Sergeant Mo, Officer Parks, Officer Stoddard, Officer Fabio, and Officer Lloyd were put on trial. In the cases of Sergeant Mo, Officer Parks, and Officer Stoddard–plea deals were struck. Sergeant Mo, Parks, and Stoddard each served between one to four years in federal prison after taking their deals. Officer Lloyd, who was put on trial along with Officer Fabio, was found not guilty. Officer Fabio, who lost at trial, took the biggest hit. He was sentenced to *ten years* in a federal prison. The Fab Five had been planting evidence (drugs) on suspects and stealing their money. They were also keeping some of the drugs, after they had arrested suspects with drugs on them. They would keep some of the drugs out of evidence, so they could use the drugs to set up the next dealer they wanted to take down. And so on and so on.

Why would they sacrifice their careers, their lives, and the lives of their families along with their freedom for some lousy drug money? There is no one answer. Each had their own reasons and motivations. For Sergeant

Mo, it was a financial decision. Even though he was making great money as a Sergeant, he recently had gotten divorced. To top it off, he had just had another child with his new girlfriend. So, between the child support and alimony he was paying to his ex-wife, he was getting crushed financially. To him, taking money from drug dealers was an easy and a tax-free way of making some extra income. In his mind he was just taking money from the bad guys. Drug-dealing criminals who were walking around with wads of cash in their pockets, while he was struggling trying to make an honest living. He felt that since he was "one of the good guys," and the dealers had gotten their money by doing their dirt, he was entitled to just take it.

For Officer Stoddard, it was as much a financial decision as it was related to ego. Officer Parks simply followed Stoddard's lead. Same with Officer Lloyd. Lloyd was partnered with Officer Fabio, and he just went along with him. I suspect Lloyd was afraid to come forward, out of fear of what the others would do to him. I knew Officer Fabio had financial issues due to a divorce, along with having a new child with his new girlfriend, much like the situation of Sergeant Mo. But ego also played a role with Fabio. From the time he started on the job, he had always wanted to be one of the guys others looked up too. He wanted the respect and admiration of his peers, and I think he found that by being part of this group.

I am not afraid to admit, one of the scariest days of my life was when the FBI and U.S. Attorney showed up at my front door with a subpoena. After a few minutes of intimidation, they confirmed that I wasn't a target, and I hadn't done anything wrong. However, it still didn't put my mind at ease. Even though I knew I had done nothing wrong, I didn't know what the Fab Five may have tried to do to implicate me. Nor, how I was being associated with their mess. After all, I had helped them take down and transport many of their suspects—suspects who were found to be completely innocent and were now cooperating FBI witnesses. Besides, you can go from not being a target of the FBI to being a target of the FBI with the stroke of a pen. I was subpoenaed to testify about one specific job that involved the Fab Five.

U.S. Attorney: "So, Officer Holland. Can you tell the members of the Jury [Grand Jury] how you recall the incident taking place?"

I proceeded to recount the incident in question. So as not to make this a long and drawn-out explanation, I will do my best to keep it brief and to point out the major differences in the details.

My version of this particular incident was that Officer Jay and I had responded to Officer Fabio's call for assistance at a home located on Spruce Street in Camden. Officer Fabio wanted us to assist him with searching the home of a drug suspect. When we arrived, several people were already in handcuffs, and they were sitting both inside and outside of the residence. Officer Fabio showed Jay and myself a Consent to Search form, which was signed (allegedly) by the homeowner, and had granted the police permission to enter and search the residence.

A Consent to Search form is basically a quasi-search warrant, but without the hassle of having to fill out an affidavit and get it approved by a judge. It is a useful tool *if* the homeowner (or the owner of whatever property you wish to search) gives their full consent without feeling as though they were being threatened, or being put under any duress, or receiving false promises. The lawfulness and validity of a Consent to Search form is that in order for it to hold up in court, the person giving the consent must be made aware of and know they have the right to refuse the request, and the right to stop the search at any time without any repercussions.

Once Fabio showed us the form, he said, "I need you guys to help me search the upstairs, especially that back bedroom."

Officer Jay and I went to the upstairs in the stifling hot house, along with Officer Fabio. After just a few minutes of us being in the home we were completely drenched and dripping with sweat. Jay and I were getting close to the end of our shift, and it was the end of our four-day tour. Which meant we were going to have the next three days off, and we had already made plans for that night. So frankly, this end of the shift cat-and-mouse bullshit was a bit annoying to us. And with Officer Fabio it always seemed to be that way. He seemed to make mountains out of molehills in his never-ending pursuit for individual glory.

Jay and I started searching the back bedroom. After just a few moments, Jay opened up a stand-alone closet and found a rifle tucked away inside. Officer Fabio pounced on it!

"Whose gun is this?" Fabio yelled.

He went downstairs and began to berate the handcuffed folks who were still seated downstairs in the living room.

"Who's this gun belong too, huh?" No one answered. "Oh, so no one wants to fess up. Fine! Then you're all under arrest."

Jay and I were standing outside of the room in the boiling hot hallway as we waited for Officer Fabio's next move. Officer Fabio walked right past us, and he immediately looked underneath the bed. He then reached under the bed and pulled out a shoebox. When he opened the shoebox, it was filled with drugs.

"Got it!" Officer Fabio declared.

Jay and I just looked at each other perplexed. Jay asked him the question we were both thinking. "How did you know that was there, Fab?"

Officer Fabio just stared at us, and without saying a word returned to the living room. Not once did we hear anyone tell him there were drugs in the house, let alone exactly where to find them. Officer Jay and I just looked at each other with a, *what the fuck was that* look on both of our faces. Stupidly, we chalked it up to Officer Fabio having some information we weren't privy to. Jay and I then transported a few people downtown for Officer Fabio and the rest of the Fab Five, and we left for the night. Looking back on it, and especially after the news broke about them being dirty cops, I knew there was something about this particular job that bugged me at the time. With examples like this job being their norm, I felt very stupid and made a fool of after finding out how much they played us with their lies.

The following excerpt is paraphrased based on my memory of what Officer Fabio had written in his report about this incident. As you will see, the differences between what occurred, as compared with what he wrote are glaring.

Officer Fabio had written that he chased one of the suspects on foot, after he observed the suspect dealing drugs on the street. The suspect fled up the front steps of this particular house, with Officer Fabio giving chase. Officer Fabio said he chased the suspect through the front door of the residence, and that he was "right on the suspect's heels." He wrote that as soon as they entered the home, "right there in plain view, in the foyer, was a rifle." He was referring to the same rifle we would find in the upstairs bedroom, hidden, within a closet.

Officer Fabio further states, "That he chased the suspect into and throughout the house." and claimed that, "As they entered the living room, and lying in plain view on the living room table was a shoebox full of drugs." He was referring to the same shoebox full of drugs he would pull from beneath the bed in the aforementioned bedroom. It didn't take a genius to see the problem here. Officer Fabio's whole report was a complete and utter fabrication. Total bullshit!

Over the coming months and years, we would find out the breadth and depths the Fab Five went too in order to rob, steal, and frame their victims. One day, shortly after the corruption story broke, I became extremely angry when I realized how much danger these assholes had actually put us in. Not only did they risk our livelihood and our freedom by getting us tangled up in their sick and twisted little game, but they placed us in tremendous physical risk as well.

For example: One of the framed drug dealers had told the authorities during an interview that while he was sitting in one of his stash houses (a house where drugs, money, and often guns are kept), he saw the Fab Five coming up the street toward his drug set. He recognized their unmarked vehicles, and he had just recently gotten out of jail after having been set up by the Fab Five during a prior arrest. This drug dealer had sat in the county jail for thirty days until he was able to post bail. Having already been victimized once by one of their fraudulent arrest, he wasn't about to go back to jail. Nor, was he going to let them rip him off his drugs and money again.

As the Fab Five came up the street in their undercover vehicles, the drug dealer picked up his AK-47 military grade assault rifle and took aim at the lead car. He decided that if they stopped at his drug set he was going down fighting, and was going to open fire. Fortunately, and for all parties involved, the Fab Five bypassed his drug set this time. However, later that same evening this same drug dealer saw them driving by yet again. This time, the Fab Five were being followed by the arrest van with "the two White boys in the van" as per the drug dealer's statement. The two White boys in the arrest van were Officer Jay and I. When he saw our van following the Fab Five he thought for sure we were going to take down his drug set.

Again, he picked up the AK-47 and took aim. Except this time, he decided the uniform cops in the van "would go first." Luckily, we continued on and didn't take down his drug set for whatever unknown reason(s). It was only by the grace of God that the Fab Five decided to not go after his drug set that night. Otherwise, this dealer would have opened fire with that AK-47, taking out Jay and myself first. That's how close we came to getting killed, and without us even knowing it. It was all because these assholes wanted to set-up and rob drug dealers.

In interview after interview with the FBI and U.S. Attorney's Office, what the drug dealers said bothered them the most wasn't getting caught dealing drugs. They understood they were *in the game*. Previously, and when I had arrested drug dealers, they would acknowledge the fact that getting caught was all part of the game. On more than one occasion, they'd say to me,

"Officer, I get whatcha doing. It's all in the game. I appreciate you respecting me, and not doing me dirty."

In the case of the Fab Five, what bothered the dealers the most was their lack of respect. The Fab Five had a lack of reverence for the rules of the game, and that pissed off the dealers. The drug dealers had finally had enough of being disrespected, and they went to Internal Affairs to complain. They didn't do it because they were innocent. They did it because the Fab Five were violating an unwritten code—the code being that drug dealers know that when they are dirty, and if they get caught, it's all part of the deal. It's just part of the inherent danger of being a drug dealer. However, when you start setting them up and robbing them and lying about them being dirty, well, now you have broken that unwritten code. You have disrespected them, and disrespected the game. And The Fab Five had to pay!

Some of the most respectful and cooperative criminals I ever locked up were drug dealers. Why? Because no matter what happened out on the street, I still treated them with respect. Unless, of course they took things in a different direction. Still, even guys I fought with would treat me with respect, and I would treat them the same. I never took it personally. They ran, we chased. They fought, we fought back. And even during times when an ass kicking needed to be given—once it was over, it was over!

There is a dirty little secret in policing; in fact, this secret extends to anyone who is in charge of policing or governing anyplace that has a ghetto. It's a secret that isn't politically correct to speak of, and politicians, police brass, the media—no one wants to admit it. But, the fact is, that the drug trade employs a lot of people. Like it or not it's what keeps the ghetto from falling into total anarchy and imploding.

With a poverty rate approaching 30%, with struggling schools, absentee parents, fifth and sixth generation welfare recipients, teenage pregnancy run amuck, and a huge lack of jobs for underqualified and undereducated persons–drug dealing, and all of the existential jobs that it creates, is the only thing keeping Camden and many of its residents propped up. If the drug trade were to be quickly extinguished in Camden there would be total chaos. The drug trade employs ex-cons, single moms, single dads, dropouts, delinquents, runaways, the abandoned, and many others that society would have no use for otherwise. Before I get too far off the rails, I am in no way advocating for drugs or drug dealing to remain a staple in our society. I am simply explaining how this illegal activity is sustaining a huge part of our poorest and most vulnerable. So, what's the remedy? Sorry, I'm not even going to pretend I know how to solve this problem.

After their convictions, the damage from the Fab Five would remain a huge stain on the Camden Police Department for some time. The wrongful arrest and violation of civil rights lawsuits by their victims came pouring in against the city, the department, and against the individual Fab Five members. Needless to say, everyone in the entire unit had been investigated by the FBI and the U.S. Attorney's Office. The department eventually disbanded the unit. The Chief would use this incident to help justify disbanding the police department, *the entire police department*, in 2013, under the guise of reform. However, I was about to face some problems of my own.

# CHAPTER 11

# *AND SO, IT BEGINS*

I made yet another bad decision in my career trajectory while I was working in Camden. The decision of my getting involved in the FOP (the Fraternal Order of Police) union turned out to be a huge mistake on my part. On the surface, it wouldn't seem like a big deal to join the union, and at first, it wasn't. I had been an executive board member for the PBA (Police Benevolent Association) while I was working in Brooklawn and Somerdale, and there were never any repercussions for my choosing to do so.

For those of you who may not be familiar with unions, the main function of a union is to ensure the CBA (Collective Bargaining Agreement), otherwise known as the contract, which is negotiated between the employer and the rank-and-file police officers, is adhered to. There are certain rights and privileges each side enjoys within the framework of the contract. One of the functions of being on the board of the PBA or FOP is to assist in the negotiating of a new contract when the time comes. That was my main purpose for joining the union. I wanted to be a part of the contract negotiation committee the next time the contract was up for renewal. I felt there were some things in our current contract that could be improved upon for both sides. I simply wanted a seat at the table.

I first joined the FOP as a Trustee, and I was later elevated to Treasurer. Eventually, I rose to the position of Second Vice-President. However, my main focus, and my more important role was that of chairman of the grievance and negotiation committee. This is a position that is usually created within each union's local, and under various and differing titles. It was my acting in this capacity that would put me right in the crosshairs of the new police administration.

After the new Chief took over the department, a whole litany of contractual violations took place. Now, I know there are a lot of folks who believe that public sector employees, such as Police, Fire, EMS, and even the teachers in our public schools should not be entitled to collective bargaining rights. And by no means am I a blind supporter of unions. There are many things unions do and say that I completely disagree with. We can debate the merits of that argument another day. Still, and for the purposes of this writing, we are going to work off of the understanding that these rights were already in place. For those of you who do not support or understand unions, please know that what a union is NOT meant to be is an impediment in the running of a department or business.

Disrupting the day-to-day operations of the department was not our intent. As a matter of fact, we operated under the premise that it was their (the city's and the Chief's) department, and they could pretty much run it however they wished. Yet, we did have a legal and binding contract, and we wanted to be a partner in the discussion of any major changes that were going to come down from the new command staff. Especially, if these changes were going to affect the rank and file officers directly. The rank-and-file police officers had a valid contract in place with the city of Camden. But, the new Chief and his administration were now violating those duly negotiated rights and privileges contained within the contract at an alarming pace.

Our thoughts were that if any of these changes they wished to implement were in danger of violating the provisions of the contract, then let's sit down and figure out a way to make it work, like a true partnership. But the new Chief and his administration were having no part of it. It was their way or the highway. If you crossed them, or otherwise ran afoul of them, you had better watch out! Guess what? I ran afoul of them—very afoul. This is not something I say with any sort of pride. I never wanted to be in anybody's crosshairs. Especially, when they came after me with fire and brimstone.

In my capacity as chairman of the grievance committee, I started to file grievance after grievance when the Chief refused our overtures to discuss the numerous issues that were piling up. [Note: A grievance is a formal complaint that a specific provision within the contract has been violated. A grievance consists of various steps for remedying the issue, starting with a meeting with the Chief at Step One, then ending at arbitration in order to resolve the issue if required.] The Chief often ignored our request to meet, or if we did talk, he'd promise to "look into it," but he would never take any corrective action(s). At one point, the Chief and I were on the phone trying to work our way through some of the issues when he said to me,

"Chad, you have filed like over a hundred grievances. This is ridiculous!"

"You're right, Chief." I replied. "It is ridiculous. You and I have better things to do. So, can we meet like a couple of men and get this straightened out?"

"I'll get back to you."

Of course, he never did. There was one time he did meet with the FOP President and I in his office. It had nothing to do with a grievance, per se. One of the Chief's new strategies was what they called directed patrols. These patrols were supposed to "account for blocks of time," as the administration liked to describe it. Here is how the directed patrols were (allegedly) supposed to be carried out.

The city was divided up into patrol sectors. The administration would use crime reports to map where crime was occurring in the city, along with *who*, *what*, and *when* the specific categories of crimes were taking place. Additionally, what methods and weapons the criminals were using to commit these crimes (i.e., guns, knives), along with the description of the suspects (occasionally) would be included. They would use this information to come up with a directive of where to focus our efforts, and where specifically we were to conduct the directed patrols. Once directed to an area, an officer was supposed to "engage" the members of the community in order to ascertain *valuable crime information*. It was this *engagement* requirement that led to our complaints.

What started out as a good tactic, turned into our being required to approach folks and compel them to speak with the police, but without any justifiable reason for doing so. At least that was how it was being passed down via the chain of command. We were ordered to ascertain their personal information—again for no real reason––other than the supposed "intelligence gathering." Another thing that troubled us was, not only were we required to obtain their personal information, but we were required to obtain *a certain number* of these stops, and record the interactions. Officers started to face threats of discipline from superiors for failing achieve a certain number of these citizen encounters. The number became a constant moving target, with the upper echelon of the department denying that such a number even existed. I could literally write an entire book on the whole directed patrol fiasco. However, for the sake of expediency, I'll summarize it more simply.

Essentially, the directed patrol concept was nothing more than a numbers game.

With hindsight being 20/20, it acted as the nexus to get rid of the entire Camden City Police Department, and replace it with the "new" Camden County Police Department. In other words, *the powers that be* wanted to rid themselves of the current rank-and-file's union and the union contract that was in place. The simplest way to do that was to lay off and disband the entire police department, which they eventually did in 2013. The force was later reformed with a (originally) non-union police force.

[Note: The term "lay off" as used in this writing means to lose employment, as opposed to a temporary furlough or RIF (Reduction in Force)]

Eventually, things got to a point where Officer Jay, FOP President Wallace, and I filed a lawsuit against the department and the administration on behalf of the rank and file. We believed we were being given orders that violated the civil rights of citizens in order to meet these specific directed patrol numbers. On its face, the directed patrol concept is, in fact, a good tactic. However, it was the nefarious motives below the surface of the entire operation that made it suspect. We went to trial on this matter ten years after filing the original lawsuit, and we lost in a jury trial. The reason(s) I believe we lost the trial is the same reason I'm not going to waste hundreds of pages trying to explain the whole directed patrol concept. I believe that for the jury, the directed patrol concept and what violations we alleged had occurred, was just too complicated of an issue for them to fully grasp. Not only did the nuances of the concept seemed to fail to resonate with them, but I felt the jury never fully understood what was actually wrong with the directed patrol expectations. I don't fault the jury. They could only base their decision on the evidence being presented, the testimony provided, and the limited explanations we were able to provide of what we believed were the administration's sinister motives.

Our biggest obstacle in proving our case occurred even before the trial ever began. The pre-trial rulings by the court as to what evidence we could present was so devastating to our case, that it was practically eviscerated from the start. The court decided that such a large block of our evidence was inadmissible from the very beginning, and for a variety of reasons. What we were left to work with in presenting our case to the jury was a complicated mess at the least, and completely baffling at best. The rulings ruined our case. It changed the ebb and flow of how we could prove the time line of events, and we couldn't demonstrate how every one incident continue to build upon the other. By taking away the evidence, the judge basically set the table for an easy win for the defense.

The trial took place in Camden County, and quite frankly we felt "the fix was in" from the get-go. We were going after some very powerful and connected people within Camden County with this lawsuit. Basically, we were going after the people who run Camden County. The Chief was their handpicked Golden Boy. So, if we made him and the rest of the administration look like they were violating the civil rights of the citizens of Camden, well, let's just say that wouldn't have played well in the public eye. This lawsuit would also become part of my "constructively terminated/whistleblower" lawsuit, which I will explain later.

What bothers me the most about this whole thing is that, in a sense, we were ahead of the curve as far as bringing the issues of police and community relations to light. Issues that existed between the police and the community, like those we are seeing today. This lawsuit took place before Ferguson, and before all of the other incidents that have recently taken place. As a matter of fact, and as I am writing this chapter the murder of George Floyd has taken place about a month prior. So, when we filed our lawsuit back in 2010 we were actually bringing up the issues of police and community relations, and questioning the lawfulness of the direct orders from our superiors regarding our interactions with citizens long before there was a national outcry. Imagine how differently things may have been had we been taken seriously.

Some of the evidence that was tossed out by the court was what we alleged the administration had done to me personally, and when they came after me—relentlessly!

While working in patrol, I had filed for time off under the Family and Medical Leave Act, because my mother was fighting breast cancer. I'm not going to get into all the legal particulars of what the protections are under the law when utilizing the Family Medical Leave Act.

What I had filed for in particular was what they term *intermittent family leave*. This particular provision of leave permitted me to take time off *as needed* in order to care for my mother. It afforded me time off so I could take her to her doctor appointments, radiation treatments, etc. I was supposed to be able to take off without the fear of being disciplined, or charged with abuse of sick time. But that was far from the case.

Internal Affairs showed up at my house whenever I took off. They said it was in order to make sure I was at home caring for my mother. They wrote me up for abuse of sick time anyway, and ordered that I be disciplined, despite my legal protections under the Family Medical Leave Act. I suffered various forms of harassment. Everything from phone calls to letters of reprimand, surprise home visits, and so on—all while not knowing if my mother was going to make it through her battle with cancer.

As I am writing this, it has suddenly occurred to me how many of you may be reading this chapter and thinking how I was just some kind of malcontent, or some sort of a troublemaker. That I was just a guy who didn't want to do what he was told, and I was just rebellious. That maybe I just got off on trying to buck the system. I will tell you this—at first, the answer to all of the above was a resounding *no!* I realize I confessed earlier as to how I often despised authority. Still, I was actually hoping the new young chief would energize the department when he took over, and we would be able to cut through some of the antiquated ways we were still doing things. My hope was that he would bring some innovation to the department, and I looked forward to making rank and being a part of it. However, it didn't take long to see that his intentions were nothing but self-serving. He was looking to make himself shine at any cost to those who served for and around him. So, was I purposely busting his balls? Yes—Yes I was—as things proceeded in the wrong direction.

On one particular occasion, and after having been written up for abuse of sick time, I questioned the Lieutenant when he called my house for a sick check. I was friendly with this particular Lieutenant, so I know he would shoot me straight.

"Chad, its Lieutenant Leu." He began. "I'm checking to see if you're home, because you called out sick."

"Lieutenant, with all due respect, you know damn well I didn't call off sick. I'm on family medical leave. I just took my mom for her treatment today, and she is sick as a dog. So why are you calling me?"

"Chad, you know it's by order of the Inspector. You know damn well he's not going to stop until he has your head. You pissed these guys off. He [the Inspector] and the Lieutenant in IA [Internal Affairs] are coming for you."

After many months of trying to jam me up and being unsuccessful, the administration's *coup d'état* to do me in came in the form of a videotape. How they tried to set me up is going to be a bit of a long-winded and complicated explanation, but please, stay with me.

# CHAPTER 12

# SETUP TO FAIL

I had just started out on my patrol shift, when I radioed to dispatch that I would be heading to "The 206 Sector to conduct a 10-43." (Directed patrol). A few moments later, the dispatcher came across the radio and redirected me to a totally different part of the city, and far from the area I was assigned to that evening.

"216, conduct a 10-43 at 7th and Kaighn." The dispatcher directed.

Although a little confused as to why I was being diverted to that particular area, I headed over, nonetheless. I drove west on Kaighn Avenue, then turned north onto 7th Street. As I turned north onto 7th street, I saw one of our marked patrol units parked in a dirt lot across the street. The front of the vehicle was facing away from me, so I couldn't see who the officer was seated within the vehicle. There was a large female leaning up against the driver's side door, who was standing outside of the vehicle. She had one arm on the top of the door along the roofline, and the other hand on her hip. I could hear both the officer and the female outside of the vehicle speaking, as they were laughing and joking around. No reason or cause for concern.

One of the unique things about Camden is that many of our officers (at the time) grew up in the city. Even though the entire city is only 9.8 square miles, several of our officers still had relatives living in and around Camden. This interaction between the officer and the female looked and sounded to me like a very friendly conversation between two people who knew each other, and nothing more.

After turning onto 7th street, I pulled over to the side of the road and parked, as I radioed to dispatch that I was on location. Just ahead of me there was an apartment complex well known for drugs and violence. Next to this apartment complex was a liquor store. As I was pulling my vehicle onto the side of the road, there was a lot of movement at the front of the liquor store which had caught my eye. It was the sort of activity that indicated there was some drug dealing going on, along with other degenerate doings, such as prostitution. I sat in my vehicle observing for a few moments, as I was trying to get a feel for what was going on, and to pick up the vibe on the street. It is amazing how you can just watch people congregate in an area, and after a short time pick up the ebb and flow of exactly what is happening.

While I was watching the corner, I would occasionally look over at the officer who was parked across the street and still involved in the friendly conversation. Both the officer and the citizen were still laughing and joking. Nothing seemed to be amiss. However, after a few more moments had passed, I looked over at them once again. This time, I saw the officer hand the female what appeared to be a paper summons. This struck me as odd, for the simple fact that I never heard the officer sign out with anyone in the area over the radio. Normally, if an officer is taking an official police action, the officer should have called it out over the radio and reported it to dispatch. This would have alerted me (and others), that the officer was involved with someone in the same area I was being sent to by dispatch. If the officer had signed out on the radio, I would have known this was going to be a back-up situation, and not what simply appeared to be a casual conversation between two friends. Something was wrong with this picture.

I threw my car into drive, made a U-turn in the middle of the street, and pulled up beside the passenger's side of the officer's vehicle. I sat next to the officer for a minute or two before Officer Courtney, a female officer who had been on the job for about seven or eight years, realized I had pulled alongside her. Actually, she only realized I was there when the female outside her vehicle said to me, "Hi, Officer Handsome. How ya doin hunny?" Which made me laugh.

Officer Courtney, now realizing I was there, lowered her passenger-side window and asked, "Hey Holland, what are you doing here?"

"Officer Courtney, I was about to ask you the same question." I replied. "What's up?"

"Oh, nothing." She began. "There was just a bunch of people out here drinking, but they bounced out." [Meaning they left the area]. Officer Courtney continued, "She [the female next to her vehicle] was drinking in public, and she was a bit slow putting down the beer when I told her to dump it. So, I wrote her a summons. I know her from back in the day, and we're actually cool [friendly]. We were just talking about old times and people we both know and what happened to them." She paused. "Why you out here anyway?"

"Good question." I began. "They sent me out here to do a 10-43, but they didn't tell me you needed back up. I didn't hear you sign out on the radio. Did you call this out?" I asked, as I tried to put the pieces together.

"No, I didn't call it out." Courtney replied. "They told me to 21 dispatch."

[Twenty-one means 10-21, which is a code to use the telephone and call dispatch, instead of broadcasting over the radio].

Officer Courtney explained, "When I 21'd them [dispatch] they told me the Inspector wanted me to come out here and write up some people for drinking in public, but I was not allowed to call it out over the radio. It didn't make any sense to me, but whatever. You know how they do, all fucked up with their bullshit and all." Officer Courtney asked, "Holland, you said they sent you out here to do a 43. Why? I was already here."

"I don't know, Court." I said, as my mind began to spin. "But something doesn't seem right. Anyway, are you good?"

"Yeah, I'm good. Hey Holland, you know these guys are assholes, right? You know that, right?" Courtney said.

"Oh, I know it." I replied. "You'll get no argument from me on that. Since you're okay, I'm outta here."

I pulled away with a sick feeling in my stomach. Something was up. Especially with the Inspector giving her the order to not call it out over the radio, which is so inherently dangerous. What if she had been attacked by the people who had been drinking? What if she was fighting for her life? No one would have known where she was, or what she was doing. Why send an officer out on a job via the telephone so no one can hear her, or know where she is? Why send her to the location all by herself? Something was very wrong. My senses were tingling. I filed this day away in my head as one to remember.

# CHAPTER 13

# *TIME FOR ME TO GO*

I've always had a sixth sense of when things are about to go bad for me. I think it comes from my childhood. I could always sense when shit was about to go down with my father, or bad things were about to happen at home. Whenever something was about to pop up in my life that would cause me some type of grief, I seemed to know when it was coming.

Over the last year while working in Camden, I began to get this same feeling. I suspected more and more that my days as a cop were numbered. Especially, since I was getting constant warnings from the higher ranking officers in the department that the administration was making the cutting off of my head a priority. They were so pissed off that I had been filing grievances and challenging them. In their minds, I was screwing up their grand plans—whatever they may be. Still, I was a good officer, a clean officer. So they couldn't find anything legit to try and charge me with. Every time I sensed they were moving in on me, I would pivot away from whatever it was they were focusing on, and somehow turn it around on them. Then they would have to start all over with trying to build some half-assed case against me. They were clearly getting frustrated.

I would often use their own rules and regulations against them when they tried to punish me, as well as their conflicting orders. Largely, because they were issuing new and contradictory orders and directives on a daily basis. It was so bad that middle managers (i.e. Sergeants and Lieutenants) couldn't keep the orders straight. An order they would read at roll call one day, would be completely changed by the next. That is no exaggeration. I was using this internal chaos against them, as they tried to jam me up. Internal Affairs would try and charge me for disobeying a new directive, but then I would pull out copies of conflicting orders and directives. Which were often issued on the same day--and sometimes, even by the same commander.

"What was I supposed to do?" I would ask. "Which order did you want me to follow?"

This would drive them crazy! How can you put the screws to somebody when they were showing you in black and white that their own bosses didn't know what the hell was going on? Still, this game was becoming mentally, emotionally, and physically exhausting. It is tough enough to battle the criminals in a place like Camden, let alone having to battle the administration on top of it. Furthermore, I was still caring for my mother. Whose battle with breast cancer, and her outcome, was still far from complete. While all of this drama was taking place I decided to start looking for a way to leave Camden. I surreptitiously started to look for a way out.

The original nexus for me beginning my search for a way out of the Camden Police Department didn't start with the fact that the Administration and Internal Affairs were coming after me. It started as a result of a conversation with the incoming Mayor of Camden. This conversation occurred during a meeting with the newly elected Mayor and some of the Mayor's team. The negotiation committee I was chairman of, was in the process of trying to negotiate a new contract for the police department. We, (the committee) thought that we could catch the incoming Mayor during "the honeymoon period" that newly elected officials often enjoy. It is during this honeymoon period that officials tend to be more agreeable and approachable, and before the job and the politics takes its toll on them. If we could get to the new Mayor during this period, the Mayor-elect may be more likely to give us what we are asking for in our new contract. Since a good relationship with the police department is usually a vital component to any successful mayoralty. However, we were wrong. During a very short but very contentious meeting with the Mayor-elect and the Mayor's team, we were given a laundry list of give-backs that they were demanding. They made it clear we were to accept their offer, or suffer the fate of not doing so.

The Mayor-elect stated, "I don't care if I have to lay off every member of this police department, you *will* accept this new contract we are offering, give-backs and all. Or, you all will be looking for new jobs."

The FOP President Wallace, who was seated to my left at the table, laughed directly at the Mayor-elect's face. Then, the FOP President replied, "Is that right Mayor-elect. You're going to lay off the entire police department your first day on the job? Well, we will see about that. We will see."

We then stood up from the table and walked out of the meeting. After we left the room and got onto the elevator, I turned to President Wallace and said, "The Mayor-elect is serious. That wasn't a hollow threat. That was a clear declaration. That was a statement. The Mayor-elect has marching orders from someone."

"Chad." President Wallace began, "We work in the most dangerous city in the United States of America. How the fuck are you going to lay off cops! We need more cops. Lay off cops–Please! The Mayor-elect is fucking crazy."

As I stated earlier, I have a sixth sense about these things. The Mayor-elect had orders. If we didn't accept the contract offer, which was preposterous to say the least (It was basically a give-back of every provision we had in our current contract, as well as a cut in pay), the Mayor-elect had permission to crush the department. The Mayor-elect was a political hack to begin with, and was bestowed the position by the powers that controlled

Camden County. So, there was no doubt the Mayor-elect was speaking from a position of authority.

Don't ask me how I knew for sure, but I somehow believed that the threat from the Mayor-elect was completely legit. I took what was being the said as the Gospel. Thank God I did, because it is what ultimately saved my career. Between the Mayor-elect's threats, along with the way the department was coming after me, I knew my days in Camden were numbered. The writing was on the wall. It was time for me to go. But my problem was, *where could I go? And how quickly can I get out before they get me?*

It was now going to be a race to the bottom for me and my career.

# CHAPTER 14

---

# *TALE OF THE TAPE*

"Look at this blatant cowardice! How dare you leave that officer to fend for herself while she was surrounded by thosecriminals."

A few weeks after the incident where I witnessed Officer Courtney handing out the summons to the woman who was drinking in public, I was summoned to Internal Affairs. I brought the FOP President Wallace with me as my Union Representative.

[Note: Anytime an officer is summoned to Internal Affairs for a disciplinary matter, they are entitled to having a union rep sit in on the meeting. They are entitled to legal counsel if necessary as well.]

At this meeting with Internal Affairs, I was told that I was being charged with *five* departmental charges. Furthermore, I was being charged with intent to dismiss (fire) me. To be charged with five departmental charges without having done something so shocking, or something so heinous to warrant such a heavy-handed reaction is unheard of. It's the equivalent of $500,000 of punishment for a $5 dollar crime!

"Why am I being charged? What did I do?" I asked.

"We have a video of you failing to back up an officer—an officer who was surrounded by a group of dangerous and intoxicated suspects. You failed to come to her aid."

"Oh, I can't wait to see this." I said, as the investigator pulled out a video tape. "Let's do this!" With a look of surprise at my cavalier attitude, the Internal Affairs officer started the video tape. The tape displayed the following.

The Internal Affairs (IA) officers are filming the area of 7th and Kaighn Avenues, while they are seated within a vehicle. This was the same area I was being sent to by dispatch to conduct a directed patrol, as I indicated in the previous chapters. The IA officers are parked facing toward the east on Kaighn Ave. As the officers are taping, Officer Courtney arrives on scene and pulls into the dirt lot, where I will later see her seated within her vehicle. This lot has a tree within it, and seated underneath the tree are about five or six males and one female. They are sitting under the tree on stacked milk crates and old chairs, while openly drinking beer.

After Officer Courtney pulls into the lot, everyone who is drinking suddenly stands up from their chairs and the milk crates. Some of the group starts to wander off, while others start tossing away their beers. Officer Courtney exits her vehicle and walks toward one of the males who did not toss his beverage, and she begins to speak with him. Her back is turned to the rest of the group. In the meantime, the rest of the group begins to gather around her from behind and on all sides, now completely surrounding her. All the while, the Internal Affairs officers remain seated within their vehicle. They are parked across the street, approximately 100 to 125 feet away, and they make absolutely no effort to exit their vehicle and back her up. Even though they are commenting on the video about how poor they felt her tactics were, and how they could see she was being surrounded. Anything could have happened in a fraction of a second. And all the Internal Affairs officers would have been able to do is watch and capture it on film, since they were seated so far away. Too far away to help, for certain.

Officer Courtney appears completely unaware that there are people all around her. Honestly, her situational awareness left something to be desired. But the Internal Affairs officers never moved. They sat in their car, watching. Not once do they suggest that "maybe" they should go and back her up. It's all about trying to get the "gotcha" moment. With me as the target.

After a few moments, most of the members of the group start to walk off in different directions while dumping out their beers. Officer Courtney walks back toward her police vehicle. As she is being seated within her vehicle, the large female (who I will see her speaking with upon my arrival), is now standing at the front of Officer Courtney's police car, with her beer still in hand. She eventually makes her way to the driver's side door after Officer Courtney motions for her to approach, and winds up dumping her beer. This is where they will remain while Officer Courtney and she have their aforementioned conversation.

After several more minutes had passed, I arrive. I turn the corner and you can see me look over at Officer Courtney's vehicle. Just as I turn the corner, you can see both Officer Courtney and the female laughing on the video. They are captured on video laughing several more times. After a few moments, I pull over and park next to Officer Courtney. This is when Officer Courtney and I speak. We eventually pull away at roughly the same time, leaving the area.

"Holland, you are disgusting!" the Internal Affairs officer began. "You just sat in your car across the street while she was completely surrounded and in danger. Look at this blatant cowardice! How dare you leave that officer to fend for herself while she was surrounded by those--criminals."

President Wallace and I just looked at each other in complete shock. President Wallace was the first to speak.

"Wait a minute." Wallace began. "We all just watched the same video, correct? Where your officers [Internal Affairs] are sitting on their asses when she is surrounded. And you are telling us that you are accusing Officer Holland of neglect of duty?"

"That's right!" The Internal Affairs officer spat back. "He just sat there while Officer Courtney was engaging a suspect for drinking in public. Officer Holland just sat in his car across the street, way too far away to help Officer Courtney if things went badly. Officer Holland is a lazy and dangerous officer. He is a disgrace! He must be punished."

It felt surreal. What video were they watching? Finally, I spoke.

"Gentlemen." I began very calmly. "The video you just showed us, this video right here. You are correct. This video clearly demonstrates neglect of duty. The lack of concern for that officer's safety while she is surrounded by possibly intoxicated individuals is heinous. The only problem is, the neglect of duty is being committed by the *Internal Affairs officers*. It does not demonstrate any neglect or negligence on *my* part."

I paused to let it sink it.

"What are you talking about, Holland?" The lead Internal Affairs officer began. "How dare you! You're not turning this around on us. No fucking way! You are wrong here, not us."

"Okay." I began. "Let's run back the tape to where Officer Courtney is surrounded." We rewound the tape. "Okay, now stop! She's surrounded right now." I pointed out, as we paused the tape and noted the time. As well as the fact that I'm not yet present.

I had asked for the corresponding radio transmissions as well. That way, we could coordinate the time on the tape with the time I was dispatched, compare it to the time of my arrival, and so on. Conveniently, they were not able to produce the audio tape at this time.

"Let's watch it further." I said. We watched the tape for a bit longer. "Stop!" As we stopped the tape once again. "Right here." I began, as I directed my ire at the Internal Affairs Sergeant. "Right now, while Officer Courtney is surrounded, your Internal Affairs officers are just watching, and they're about hundred or so feet away. What are they going to be able to do at that distance? Why aren't they putting themselves in a better position tactically to help her? Why aren't they aborting the taping of the video, and moving across the street to back her up? Particularly, since she's surrounded and in such imminent danger, as you clearly stated."

I continued. "Right now, the only good your Internal Affairs officers could do at that distance is maybe be good witnesses to her assault. Or, maybe they'll catch her murder live and on video!"

I could see they were fuming. But I wasn't done yet.

"Look at that!" I pointed out, as the tape again began to roll again.

We watched as I arrived, and long after the group had already left the area.

"How long was that before I arrived?" I asked. "How long until I arrive, but *after* the group has already disbursed? Look! There's Officer Courtney in her car having a casual conversation with the female. Boy, it sure doesn't appear there's any danger by the time I get there, now does it. Let's face it, it was never that dangerous to begin with, right? How could it be? Particularly, since the commanding officer in dispatch, *the Inspector*, specifically instructed Officer Courtney to not call it out over the radio in the first place!"

I wanted them to know I was aware of that little piece of information.

"It couldn't have been that dangerous if he sent that officer out there all alone, without any backup, and without her being permitted to tell anyone over the radio where she was."

I paused. My voice was rising as I was getting pissed. But I didn't want to lose control.

"We all know that an officer not being permitted to sign out with a subject over the radio is a complete violation of our policies and procedures, and of our rules and regulations. But apparently that doesn't matter to the Inspector or Internal Affairs, now does it?"

I was livid now, and I kept going.

"Did you guys pull the radio transmissions? Did you listen to her calling out with this group? No, of course not. Why would you! Especially, since you already knew she was instructed to not call it out over the radio– by the Inspector."

It was time for us to wrap up their bullshit investigation.

"Gentlemen, we all know the only time Officer Courtney was in any danger was when she was surrounded by the group. Which is precisely when the IA officers were sitting in their car, and on their fat asses, videotaping. That was the *only time* she was in danger. And long before I had even arrived."

They were dumbfounded about what to do. I could see it in their body language. They knew they blew it! In a matter of minutes we had shredded their entire case against me. The lead Internal Affairs investigator began, "Holland, you can say what you want. But you're clearly a danger to other officers." He proclaimed, and as he tried to save face. "We're not going to serve you with the charges right now. We're going to talk to the Lieutenant first. But you will be hearing from us, soon!"

"Wallace, I'm done." I told the FOP President after we had left the Internal Affairs office. "If it's not this, it will be something else. It'll be anything they can come up with to try and get me. I'm transferring back to Brooklawn Police at the end of next month. I just need to get through November and December."

Wallace was the first person in Camden who I told that I was leaving.

# CHAPTER 15

# FROM MY PAST EMERGES MY FUTURE

In the beginning of December, on my birthday actually, I was summoned back to Internal Affairs. FOP President Wallace was out of town, so I went alone. I thought to myself while sitting in the waiting area, *the hell with it. I'm leaving. What can they possibly do to me in a few weeks' time?* I was leaving effective January 1, 2010.

I had mentioned earlier that I started to look for a way out of Camden when things just seemed to be getting worse for me. I was looking for somewhere, pretty much anywhere, to go.

Well, as fate would have it Brooklawn, the very first place I had worked as a police officer, was looking to hire an additional officer using a Federal Grant. They reached out to me to see if I was interested in coming back. I had stayed in touch with the officers in Brooklawn, and they knew the shit show that Camden had become. So, when the opportunity opened up, they asked me if I wanted to come back.

The process of my transferring back to Brooklawn started in late September/early October, 2009. I basically had the green light to go through with the transfer, since I had already laid the groundwork to leave

Camden. But the truth of the matter was, I still loved policing in Camden. The thought of going back to small-town policing crushed me. At this point in my career, I had gone up against some of the most fearsome criminals. I had been involved in some of the most dangerous situations you could imagine, and I had held my own. Over the years, I was in more scraps, fights, and tussles than I could count. I had my uniform ripped apart on more than one occasion, and had my blood spilled more than once. But I still enjoyed the rush of working in the city.

I loved the constant crackle of the radio on a Friday or Saturday night in the summer time, when it was scorching hot outside, and the city was completely off the hook with violence and mayhem. It was a pit of a place to work, but I loved it just the same. I loved policing in a city—a city of chaos. I always felt like I was meant to police in a city, and Camden had proven me right. How could I give this up? How could I leave, when I knew this is what I was meant to do! When I put on that Camden uniform, I literally felt like I was putting on armor and going to war. I know that's a mindset which isn't looked upon kindly by the PC Police. Nevertheless, that is how working in Camden felt, like we were going to battle on our every shift. After all, our vests are called *body armor* for a reason.

The thought of leaving the *major leagues* of policing and going back to the *minor leagues* crushed my soul. Furthermore, I had just taken my first Sergeant's exam after fourteen years on the job (I told you my timing and career decisions were horrible). I was fairly confident I had done well on the test. At the time, I was making about $75,000 a year without over-time. Sergeants were making about $85,000 per year, minimum. Most of them got a shitload of overtime, and were making well over $100,000. So, I was looking at a nice pay bump should I make rank. Additionally, it had always been my dream to become a street Sergeant.

A good street sergeant is where the "rubber hits the road" in a police department. A good street Sergeant is always thinking about the well-being of their officers, first and foremost. Their duty is to act as a buffer, as well as an advocate for their officers when dealing with the upper ranks within the department, and when dealing with the public. Additionally, a good street Sergeant has proven themselves in battle, and they're able to make quick decisions under immense pressure. Most importantly, a good street Sergeant has to be willing to *go to the wall* for the officers under their command. It is probably the hardest, and yet, the most rewarding job in a police department. At least in my inexperienced opinion. I felt that I would check all of those boxes if given the opportunity. I knew that if I went back to Brooklawn, my dream of becoming a street Sergeant was dead. I had no hope of, nor would I have any opportunity for a promotion in Brooklawn. A return to small-town policing would effectively end my career. However, at this particular moment I'm back in Camden Internal Affairs, and I am about to be threatened with my entire future.

The Internal Affairs Lieutenant, who was a smug sonofabitch if there ever was one, walked into the room. "Look Holland, its real simple." He began. "We're going to fire you! There is no ifs-and-or-butts about it. You pissed off the Chief. You pissed off the Inspector. You pissed me off. You made my guys [IA Investigators] look stupid with the video tape thing. You just have to go!"

I had been laying the groundwork for the transfer the past couple of months without the command staffs knowledge. It was only after I secured the assurances of the folks in the administration of Camden City Hall, as well as of that of Brooklawn, that I informed the Chief of Camden that I wanted to leave. I remember that meeting well. I walked into the Chief's Office and I told him I wanted to transfer back to Brooklawn, so I could be closer to my ailing mother. In his usual dramatic fashion, the Chief paused for a moment after I told him of my intentions. Then he began, "Well Chad, you know we have a *crime emergency* right now. So we're not letting anyone transfer out. However, I know your case is a special circumstance. So, this is the one time I'll permit someone to leave. Good luck to you. I hope your mom gets better soon."

The Chief wasn't doing me any favors. He already knew I had all of the permission I needed to leave. He was just trying to save face. Fortunately for me, I had a great relationship with the city administrators in Camden, as well as the woman from the State of New Jersey Department of Community Affairs who oversaw the City of Camden's Municipal Government. I went to them behind the police administrations back and I asked them to help me get my transfer through. Everyone knew the Chief would try to block it. Fortunately for me, these folks were no fans of the Chief. So to be a part of something that would surely piss him off seemed to appeal to them. These folks helped me to get everything in place so I could leave. However, there was just one catch with my ability to transfer, and Internal Affairs was about to play that card.

"Now Chad." The Lieutenant began. "Before we go and fire you, we know you're planning to transfer in a couple of weeks back to Brooklawn, correct?" He asked.

"Yes, I'm out of here. You guys won. I'm done." I said, as I was feeling defeated.

"Well, maybe not." He said, as a smirk spread across his face. "You see, what you don't know about the Intergovernmental Transfer Program is that it states you cannot transfer from one department to another while being held in '*bad standing*' with your current agency. You didn't know that, did you?" The Lieutenant asked. Now with a huge grin on his face.

Ah! Here it was. Now it all made sense. Once they got word that I was leaving they decided they were going to charge me, so I couldn't leave, and in order to exact their revenge. If I couldn't leave that freed them to not only charge me, but to also fire me, and end my career.

Being held in bad standing meant that you were under some type of discipline by your current employer. The framers of the Intergovernmental Transfer Agreement anticipated that there may be times when a *bad apple* may try and jump ship, and before their current employer could discipline them. This provision was inserted to prevent just that sort of thing from happening. Camden's Internal Affairs was going to use that provision against me.

"So, what do you want?" I asked, putting all my cards on the table. "Is that how you guys are going to do me?"

"Well, that's how I wanted to do you." The Lieutenant said, confidently. "However, deep down I believe the Chief actually likes you. He respects you, and he thinks you're very smart but just misguided in your loyalties and your efforts. Me, I think you're a piece of shit cop and a piece of shit person! I'd fire you right now if I could." The Lieutenant said, as he was obviously enjoying this. "But, The Chief decided he's going to let you keep your career. On one condition! If your transfer goes through, we won't serve you with the five charges. Therefore, you won't be considered to be held in bad standing. However, if for whatever reason you don't transfer, we will take these five charges, and whatever other charges we can come up with, and we will drop them right on top of your thick fucking head like a hammer! Your ass will be fired so quickly you won't know what the fuck hit you. Got it!"

They actually had me fill out and sign what is called a *special report*. The report stated: "I understand if I should not have transferred out of the Camden City Police Department by January 1, 2010 I will be charged and fired on that same date."

I waved the white flag. I was done. I wrote the special report and left there praying they would just let me go. My career was effectively over. I would never be promoted. I would never work in Camden again. I would now go back to small-town policing for the remainder of my career. I felt sick.

# CHAPTER 16

---

# *BACK WHERE IT ALL BEGAN*

I returned to Brooklawn eight year's older, eight years wiser (maybe), and with eight more years of police experience. Then again, I was completely worn out. I was now a bitter and burned-out cop.

Not much had changed in Brooklawn since I had left. On my first day back I walked into the station, filled out some paperwork, grabbed the car keys, and started out on patrol again on my own–just like before. The only thing that changed was the in-house computer system, along with some minor policy and procedure changes. Otherwise, it was business as usual. And that was the problem. Not only was I back to doing something I had left behind out of boredom years before, but I now had to do it for a shitload of less money. I had left Camden making about $75,000 per year. In order to come back to Brooklawn, I had to accept the maximum salary that was covered under a three-year grant Brooklawn had received from the Federal Government. That salary was $54,000 per year. I took a whopping $21,000 pay cut!

On one hand, I was grateful to still have a career. On the other, I was a miserable bastard. I was just starting my fifteenth year of policing, and I was now working for less money than I had made during my seventh year of policing. Plus, my career was at a dead end. I started to think about what I wanted to do next with my life. I would be forty-three years-old by the time I had twenty years on the job, when I would first become eligible to retire. My plan when I got into to police work had always been to work at least twenty-five years. Once at the twenty-five year mark, and depending on what position I was in at the time, I would either decide to stay or go. Now, I was considering getting out at twenty years. I started to seriously think about what I would want to do in my *second life*.

"How about a Physician's Assistant (PA)?" My wife said to me one day. "I think you would be great at it."

I had been taking classes at Drexel University majoring in Psychology, just because I thought psychology would be interesting, and I was doing really well. At one point, I had a 4.0 GPA and had made the Dean's List. I had received a call from my Psychology professor, who was also the Dean of the Psychology Department. When she called me, one of her first questions was to ask me what other degrees I already had.

"I don't have any other degrees." I replied, a bit puzzled by the question. "This is the first time I have been in a university. Prior to Drexel, I only had a couple of semesters at community college."

"Well, Mr. Holland." The Professor began. "I just thought you should know that the papers you have written are at a doctorate level. I have used your papers in my courses on campus to demonstrate to other students in my doctorate classes what I expect out of their writings. You should be quite proud of yourself. If you ever have the time, I would very much like to meet you."

I was blown away! I had never received such high praise. I was working really hard in my courses, and I tried to make sure my papers were good. I was getting straight A's, so I knew I was on the right track. But doctorate level? Never in my wildest dreams did I ever think I could achieve something that lofty. The Professor went on to tell me that if I did pursue my Master's or PhD in Psychology, she would be honored to write a letter of recommendation on my behalf. I'm not ashamed to admit that after that phone call, I cried. I felt like I had finally attained something meaningful. After the Camden nightmare, it was nice to feel appreciated.

My wife had planted the seed about my becoming a PA. Since I was doing so well in my courses, I actually started to believe I could do it. We scheduled a meeting with the Dean who oversaw the PA Program at Drexel University's College of Medicine. I wanted to gauge her thoughts on a forty-three-year-old becoming a PA—my age when I would retire from policing. And how they felt about an "old guy" entering the PA program.

* * *

"Chad, I love the fact that you are a police officer." Said the Dean of the PA Program, and quite to my surprise.

She was a thin older woman, with long gray hair, glasses, and a wonderful extroverted personality. She was so warm and friendly. I was immediately happy we decided to meet with her.

"I love the fact that you know how to handle people, and you won't have the fears of bedside manner that so many of our younger PA students do. These young kids are very bright." The Dean continued, in a hushed tone. "But, they just don't know how to handle people, or how to talk to people. When you're ready to apply I want you to reach out to me directly, and we will see what we can do. But, no promises!" She said, with a wink.

I was ecstatic! This was going to be my second career. I actually felt like I was intelligent and disciplined enough at this point in my life to make it through the rigorous courses that were to follow. I now had my plan in place. I would finish my police career with twenty years of service, and would take the early retirement. Which would provide me with a 50% pension (but no health benefits), and I would become a PA. In the meantime, I needed to complete my undergrad degree in Psychology. I was on my way. Everything was finally falling into place.

Or, so I thought.

## CHAPTER 17

# *HOW I STOPPED BEING SUCH A DICK!*

I was incredibly miserable when I had to work my shifts in Brooklawn. I hated the rotating shift work, and I just hated being there. Fifteen years of working around the clock was starting to take its toll on me mentally, and I was completely unhappy. Physically, I was in great shape. Probably the best shape of my life. But emotionally, I was feeling the stress of the job.

My experience with the administration in Camden had ruined me. I saw the ugly side of policing. Where the bosses become politicians, and were willing to *eat their own*. Ruining the careers of good men and women for nothing more than to further their own ambitions. Admittedly naïve to how politics worked in my profession, I had labored under the idea that since we were all cops, we were always on the same side. Now, I was completely scorned. I kept reflecting on my time in Camden, and I would beat myself up about how I let things get so far out of control. I punished myself mentally by ruminating over what *coulda, shouda, woulda* been had I just kept my mouth shut and went along with the program.

*Why didn't you just do what they asked? Why didn't you just play ball? You would have been a Sergeant by now. Why did you challenge them?*

*Especially, when no one really gave a damn anyway. Why you? Why did you have to join the union? Look at what it got you-nothing!*

These thoughts would play over and over in my head. I knew I had effectively committed career suicide and I couldn't forgive myself for it. To rub salt in the wound, Brooklawn was getting ready to make their first promotion to Sergeant in something like twelve years. They hadn't made a promotion in all that time. That would have most likely been my promotion, had I not left the department years before. However, and since I did leave, I would have no shot at it.

As a matter of fact, as part of my transfer agreement I had to agree to *not* seek a promotion for at least three years. Which automatically kept me from this opportunity. I knew there would not be another chance at my being promoted during the remainder of my career. This realization caused me to become the typical bitter, burned out, and disgruntled cop. The kind of cop I swore I would never become. I also became a completely arrogant jerk.

After having worked in the "big leagues" of policing, I felt as though this small-town policing was beneath me. It felt like I had been a pro, and now I was sent back to play in the minors. As I said before, I started to butt heads with the other officers in the department. It started with the attitude that my skills and knowledge were superior to theirs. I became a cocky, arrogant douchebag. At the same time, I felt like I couldn't help myself. The fact that I was doing so well in college and getting so many accolades, which I had let go to my head, certainly didn't help matters any. It just reinforced my overinflated sense of superiority to everyone around me. To the other officers, I was becoming unbearable to work with. Looking back, I can't blame them one bit for feeling that way.

I now hated dealing with the public as well. I detested it when the radio went off and it was some "bullshit" job, such as a couple fighting, or something I thought of as trivial. I was miserable and bitchy toward every-one around me–often for no reason. Even little things about the job began to annoy me, such as how the other cops on the street would respond to calls.

For example: In the suburban towns like Brooklawn and the surrounding areas, the citizens, our bosses, and even the local governing bodies expected police response times to be very quick. If a citizen called the police in Brooklawn, a town of less than one square mile, and a cop wasn't at their door in five minutes or less they wanted to know why. It didn't matter how minor the complaint. They wanted a prompt and immediate response. So, when "hot calls," such as fight calls or domestic disturbances (fights between couples or family members) came in, the cops in Brooklawn and the surrounding towns would go flying to those calls with their lights and sirens blaring.

Even as a rookie police officer I remember thinking that the danger of responding to the calls in this manner seemed to outweigh the end result. There was this idea floating around that if we got to the fight or domestic dispute in progress as quickly as possible, we could stop further violence from occurring. I'm not talking about the call where the caller is still on the line with 9-1-1 and is screaming for help. Police have arrived on scenes such as those and stopped further assaults from occurring. However, the reality is it normally takes anywhere from two to four minutes from the time a person dials 9-1-1 until the call is actually dispatched. Add in another three to five minute response time (or more), and the call is already five to maybe ten minutes old, if not older. Most people aren't beating the shit out each other for ten minutes.

What I'm talking about is when the complainant tells the call taker that they are having a verbal argument with someone, and one party simply wants the other party to leave, but no violence has actually occurred. Yet, this call is dispatched as a domestic dispute, which makes it a hot call. The truth is, usually by the time the police arrive on scene one party or the other is already gone. Or, the incident has somehow been resolved. We are usually there to just take a report. So, and in my opinion, flying to these calls at warp speed didn't make much sense. Another, and a much more cynical thought I had developed upon my return to Brooklawn was–*who really gives a fuc*k! Why do two grown adults need another grown adult to come to their home, and to tell them to either play nice, or to get the hell away from each other? Why should I risk my life and limb driving at high speeds and going to these calls in a hurry, just because these idiots don't have enough common sense to either get along, or get the hell away from each other!

This was the logic we applied in Camden. We responded to these types of calls at a normal speed, and without using our lights and sirens. In Camden, the fight or domestic call was rarely a "fresh call." We were usually so backed up on calls, that by the time it was dispatched (because short of a weapon being used it was such a low priority call) it was already several minutes, if not several hours, old. In addition, these calls always seemed to be originating from the same callers, and from the same locations. Even our dispatchers knew to make these calls a non-priority. If I had a dollar for every time a cop in Camden said, "I hope these assholes finally kill each other! We've been there three times already this week." I would have been set for life.

We had so many repeat customers for domestics in Camden that we could actually predict what day and time they would call. Usually, it was the first of the month, when the government assistance checks came out. It got to be so commonplace, even our bosses began telling us to take our time going to these calls.

"Look, I'd rather have you guys out there taking a murder-suicide report for these assholes, then have you cracking up a police car, or getting hurt." They would say in roll call.

One day, the Chief of Brooklawn said to me, "Chad, some of the guys are saying you're the last one to show up at the domestics in your own town. That the Bellmawr, Gloucester City, Mt. Ephraim, or Westville guys are beating you to your calls. What the fuck is that about?"

"Chief, most of these fights are over by the time we get there." I replied. "Or, they wait until the person has left before they even call us. Besides, do you really want me risking cracking up a car to get to a domestic that's usually over before we get there?"

I was trying to use some of my *Camden logic* on him.

"I mean seriously." I went on. "Who gives a damn? Let these assholes kill each other if they want too."

I had gone too far. I was now as bad as the criminals we were trying to stop. My Chief looked at me with a look of total anger and disgust on his face.

"You know what I think, Chad." He hissed through clinched teeth. "I think Camden fucking ruined you! You were a good cop. Why don't you try being a good cop again, and do your fucking job!"

He was right. I needed to snap out of this—and fast!

What I didn't realize at the time was, that I was exhibiting the classic signs of burnout, depression, and anxiety. Ironic, isn't it? Here I was studying psychology, and yet I couldn't even recognize I was having mental health issues of my own.

I had been working in Brooklawn just over a year and a half, when one day while working a dayshift, a woman walked into the police station to report her fourteen year-old daughter as missing. Fortunately, and just as I was a taking the report, the mom received a call that a family member had located the missing girl. They were bringing her to the police station to reunite them. There is nothing remarkable about this incident. Unfortunately, kids run away every day, but most are found safe and sound. What made this job different was my conversation with the mother, and the profound effect it had on me and my shitty attitude.

After the child arrived at the station, she and her mother started to go at it pretty good. At one point, the girl said to her mother,

"Why should I listen to an HIV-infested drug addict whore!"

I could see the mother was instantly crushed, and I couldn't help but intervene. I started yelling at her daughter.

"Knock it the hell off. This is your mother you're talking to, goddammit!"

"No she's not. She's an AIDS-infested pig!" The daughter spit back.

The relative who had brought the daughter to the station took the girl outside, so I could speak to the mother alone. Who was now in tears.

"I'm so sorry. I'm am so-so very sorry!" The mother said to me in between sobs.

"Ma'am, what are you sorry for?" I asked.

"I should have told you before." She began. "She's right. I used to be a drug addict. I was a prostitute a long time ago, when I was addicted to drugs. I don't even know who my daughter's father is." She said, as she was visibly falling apart. "I have HIV. I should have told you. I am so sorry. But I was afraid to tell you, because now I know what you're thinking."

"Listen to me." I began, and as I tried to calm her down. "I don't give a damn about your *medical condition*. I don't care what you did in your life. I'm not here to judge you. My job is to help you, and your daughter."

As soon as I told her I didn't care about her "medical condition," she stopped crying. She looked at me with these solemn eyes that seemed to suddenly brighten. After a long moment of silence she said to me, "Did you just say to me you *don't care about my medical condition*?" She emphasized those last few words.

I panicked a bit. I didn't want her to think I was some calloused jerk. I didn't want her thinking I didn't care about her being diagnosed with HIV. That is not what I meant. What I meant was, that it didn't matter to me simply because it had no bearing on the issue at hand.

I quickly began to correct myself, and I was fumbling for words.

"No–no. I'm sorry! I didn't mean it how you think. I just meant that it doesn't have anything to do with how I want to help the both of you."

She sat there staring at me for what felt like forever. Then, she suddenly burst into tears again. All I could think at this moment was, *Oh shit! What did I just do? Jesus, Chad. You really need to think before you speak. You dumbass!*

Just as these thoughts were running through my mind, the mother suddenly jumped up from her chair and ran around the front of the desk I was standing behind, flinging herself toward me. She threw her arms around my neck, and began to hug me very tightly, as she started sobbing–again.

"Hey–hey–hey! Are you okay?" I asked. I was completely stunned at what was happening.

It felt very awkward–us standing there with her arms around my neck with her crying. So, I began to hug her back. She was sobbing so heavily that hugging her was the only thing I could do to help her to calm down. After we held each other for a few more moments, she stepped back and looked at me, a bit embarrassed. After she composed herself, she said, "I'm so sorry Officer. I didn't mean to grab you like that." She paused, as she was trying to get herself together, and while she was still weeping. "But no one has ever called it a 'medical condition' when they find out I have HIV."

A bit perplexed, I asked, "Well, what else would you call it?" I honestly didn't grasp what she meant.

She stood there quietly for a moment. Her hands were trembling, as she was tearing little pieces of paper from a tissue she held in her hands, while dabbing away the fresh tears that spilled down her cheeks. I looked at her while she stood there. I could see that she had probably been such a beautiful woman at one time. She had crystal blue eyes, and a dark olive complexion. She had long raven dark hair, and it was obvious she once had a great figure. But now, from the years of hard living and drug abuse, along with her illness, she was thin, frail, sunken, and looked old beyond her years.

Once composed, she began, "When people find out I have HIV they never refer to it as a medical condition. She stopped talking and wept some more. "They say, "You have *HIV!*" and I can hear the disgust in their voice. And the way they look at me as they say it—like I'm scum." She became silent again. "Officer, you are the first person to ever call it a medical condition." She barely got the sentence out as she broke down again. "You're the first person in a long time who has made me feel respected, and the first person that made me feel like I'm still a human being since I was diagnosed with this disease."

I was in shock. I had no words.

She continued. "Please, and I mean no offense by what I am about to say. But, the last person I thought that would be showing me any respect would be a *police officer.*"

I was speechless. I felt ashamed. Mostly, I felt terrible about not recognizing the impact I/we/us (the police) can have on people. I also felt mortified about my shitty attitude toward everyone and everything. This woman gave me the jolt I needed to snap out of my self-pity and self-misery. This provided me with the wake-up call I needed to get my shit together, and to stop being such a selfish and self-righteous dick!

As you're reading about this conversation you may be thinking this whole exchange was not that big a deal. That there is nothing remarkable about treating someone with respect. You're right, and I get it. Still, I wanted to demonstrate for you how much of an impact treating someone with respect can have not only on how *they* feel, but also on how *you* feel. You really would've had to understand my mindset at the time in order to appreciate the profound effect this had on my psyche. Unfortunately, my recounting of this conversation will never fully translate the impact it had on me. Because of this otherwise unremarkable moment, I completely snapped out of my *woe is me* attitude. I realized I was in a position to have a huge impact on people's lives, and I needed to take that seriously, once again.

# CHAPTER 18

# A TIME TO KILL

On April 26, 2012, I was working alone during the overnight shift (7 pm to 7 am), as was most often the case. It was a fairly warm Thursday night, and it was the last night of my two-day tour. It was a little over two hours into my shift, just after 9 pm, when I heard a call go out over the radio in the neighboring town of Bellmawr. The nature of the call was for an ambulance being dispatched to the Bellmawr Manor Apartments for a male threatening suicide by unknown means. Whenever someone is threatening to kill themselves, and the method of how they plan to do so is unknown, red flags are immediately raised. A whole host of questions immediately come to mind. Such as:

Are they going use a bomb and blow up the whole place?

Are they going to lie in wait for the first responders to arrive, and like a sniper start picking them off one by one?

Will they set the house ablaze as the police and ambulance personnel arrive, burning everyone to death?

These are just some of the many horrible ways one could plan their own demise, while desiring to take others with them.

The Bellmawr Police Department had four officers working the street that night (including their Sergeant), but most of the officers were tied up on some type of industrial accident, which had occurred about an hour ago. The Bellmawr Sergeant (Sarge) responded over the radio that he would be heading over to meet the ambulance at the location, but that he would be responding alone. I was about a mile south of the apartment complex at the time the call went out. You never want an officer going to this type of call alone for the reasons I stated above. Someone who is threatening suicide is obviously an unstable individual. And you don't know if they're planning to go out in a *blaze of glory*. I advised dispatch that I would head over as the Sergeant's back-up.

The Sergeant and I pulled up to the complex at the same time. I knew this particular Sergeant from when I had previously worked in Brooklawn. He was always a good dude, and was known to do things by the book-straight as an arrow. The Sergeant had the ambulance stage (stand-by) down the block for the safety of the ambulance crew, and until we knew what we were dealing with. The Sergeant and I began to walk up the pathway towards the building where the call was reported to have originated from. The apartment where the call originated was a second-floor apartment. These particular apartment buildings have a brick exterior, and each building housed four separate apartments, two upstairs and two downstairs. The doors for each apartment are lined up four across at ground level, with each apartment having its own individual door for access in and out of the main building.

We banged on the door of the caller's apartment a few times, but with no answer. Looking up at the second-story window, the caller's apartment appeared dark within. We could barely make out the flickering light of a television emanating through the window. The Sergeant got on the radio and requested that dispatch try to reestablish contact with the occupants of the apartment, since there was no answer at the door. While we were awaiting the dispatcher's response, we wandered the outside perimeter of the building. Eventually, we took up a position in a grassy area located directly in front of the building, and just atop a small hill. A nice breeze started blowing, and the night was quiet, as it was now dark outside. We tried using the height of the small hill to get a better visual inside the second-floor window of the apartment. However, it was too dark to see, even when using my flashlight, and the hill wasn't quite high enough to help our vantage point. After a few moments, dispatch came over the radio. The dispatcher had a sound of concern in her voice.

Dispatcher: "Unit 404."

Sergeant: "404, go ahead."

Dispatcher: "Sarge, on the callback we got the caller's voicemail."

The dispatcher paused.

Dispatcher: "The voicemail had the following message."

The dispatcher paused again.

Dispatcher: "This is Mark W., and I am now deceased."

Sergeant: "10-4."

"Shit-shit-shit!" The Sergeant muttered. Without a need for an explanation, I knew we were going to be required to make a forced entry into the apartment. However, and just to make sure we were on the same page, I stated the obvious.

"Looks like we're going in, huh Sarge."

With a sigh he replied, "Yeah Chad, let's go." As we walked toward the front door of the apartment, again.

You may be wondering right about now why we are entering the apartment in the first place. I have often been asked why we made entry into the apartment. In a situation like this, when someone is threatening suicide, with no answer at the door, and taking into account the ominous message he had left on his voicemail—-we are duty bound to make forced entry.

The idea being that if the person inside is bleeding to death from having just slit their wrist, or if they just popped a bottle of pills, or maybe just hung themselves––they could still be alive.

We have to do our best to try and save their life. Therefore, it is our job to get in as quickly as possible, and to render aid if the situation dictates.

The door itself was made of wood, and had several separate small panes of glass. After the Sergeant tried the doorknob (it was locked), he tried breaking out one of the panes of glass with his set of hinged handcuffs. The Sergeant wasn't wearing any gloves, and fearing he would cut his hand once the glass broke, he only tapped the glass slightly. He would hit the glass, but then pull his hand back too quickly, and before the glass had a chance to break. After three unsuccessful attempts I asked him if he wanted me to give it a shot. I always carried a long flashlight—either a long thin flashlight called a Stinger, or a larger flashlight called a Mag-light. And I always wore gloves. I wore either leather or rubber gloves, depending upon the situation. When you constantly come into contact with people who are bleeding or covered in God knows what, you want to be prepared.

The Sergeant said, "Be my guest." As he stepped away from the door.

I took out my flashlight and I smacked the glass one time, watching it break. It was so quiet outside that the breaking of the glass echoed throughout the apartment complex. I reached into the apartment, and with my left hand unlocked the door. I turned the knob and pushed the door open while simultaneously drawing my weapon (a Glock Model 22 .40-caliber) with my right hand. I had put my flashlight in my back pocket, and I decided to use the flashlight that was affixed to my weapon. I often made entries this way. By switching to the flashlight on my weapon, it permitted me to always have one hand free. Just in case I had to push or grab someone, or something.

Once the door was opened I was faced with a set of stairs with about twelve steps leading upward. The first thing I noticed upon opening the door was the overpowering smell of cigarette smoke, as it hit me directly in the face. I have always had a bad reaction to cigarette smoke. My sinuses slam shut, and I instantly get a headache from it. This time, the headache started almost immediately. (As I was typing this sentence I had a full-blown flashback. Eight years later, and I can still smell the cigarette smoke in my memory as if I were back in the apartment at this very moment.)

Scanning the apartment from the bottom of the staircase, I noticed it was very dark throughout the apartment. Except for the aforementioned light originating from the television, the only additional lighting I could detect was a dimly lit bulb. Which I could see emanating from deep within the apartment. To make matters worse, it was extremely loud in the apartment. The television's volume seemed to be turned up to full blast. From the threshold of the doorway I was unable to see onto the main floor of the apartment itself. I had no way of knowing if someone was lying in wait to ambush us as we entered. This situation seemed to be getting more foreboding by the moment. The living room was elevated, and sat approximately six feet above the entranceway of the apartment. Besides the height disadvantage, my view was completely obstructed by a couch that was pushed up against a wrought iron railing. Which ran along the staircase leading into the apartment.

"Police-Police! Anybody here-Anybody home-Anybody need help?" I called out, as we entered the apartment. No one answered.

"Hello! It's the police." I yelled above the roar of the television.

With my weapon still drawn, I was trying to scan the area of the living room from my limited vantage point. I would need to climb higher and further up the stairs if I wanted to get a full view of the interior of the apartment. I had taken about three more steps up the stairway, and was just about to take another step up, when a man literally *jumped up* from the far end of the couch. He scared the living shit out of me!

"What the fuck are you doing in my house?" He screamed. "Get the fuck out of my apartment––you fucking cops!"

At least he realized we were cops.

He appeared to be unarmed, since he didn't have anything apparent in his hands. Still, he kept waving his hands around, which was making me nervous. I didn't know if he was concealing a weapon, so I pointed my weapon at him and began to give him verbal instructions.

"Show me your hands!" I yelled. "Show me your fucking hands-Now!" As I was hoping he'd stop flailing them about.

After a few tense moments, he started to comply with my directions. He got down onto the floor, kneeling at the top of the stairs, and just onto the landing area. A Bellmawr officer who had arrived on scene, quickly squeezed past the Sergeant and I on the staircase and took the person into custody. I continued to hold the subject at gunpoint while the officer cuffed him.

"Are you hurt?" I asked the male as the officer secured him.

"I'm fine." He replied, somewhat more calmly. "What the fuck are you guys doing here?"

I picked up a slur in his speech, like he had been drinking. I was about to reply to his question when suddenly, another voice began shouting from deeper within the apartment.

"Yo-Yo!" The male voice called out. "That's my brother. I'm in here! Leave him the fuck alone. I'm in here!" The voice boomed.

Before I could ask the man in custody who it was that was shouting at us, the officer led him out of the apartment. The Sergeant had squeezed past me on the staircase, and proceeded to the top of the stairs and just onto the landing area. He then positioned himself behind a wall for cover. After the stairway was clear, I made my way to the top of the staircase and onto the same landing as the Sergeant. This was the first time I was able to get a full view of the interior of the apartment. What a goddamn shit hole! Every single inch of the floor was covered with trash. Lying on the floor were empty pizza boxes, empty beer cans, used paper towels and napkins, newspapers and magazines, empty two-liter soda bottles—you name it! It looked like these assholes never heard of a trash can.

I noticed that the Sergeant was peering around the corner of the wall and was looking further into the apartment, as he tried to locate the other voice. I did a "quick peek" over his shoulder to make sure it was clear. I then cut across the living room and into a small dining area. The only noticeable pieces of furniture in the apartment were the large sectional couch that was pushed up against the railing, and I believe there was a chair in a far corner of the apartment, if memory serves me correctly. A television sat on an entertainment center in the living room, and was up against the wall opposite the couch.

After making my way across the living room and into the dining area, I came to rest against a wall. This vantage point allowed me to look down a very short hallway and into a bedroom that was off to my right. Just overhead was the dimly lit bulb I previously described.

The bulb was casting just enough light into the bedroom for me to see about three or four feet into the room. The room had a mattress lying on the floor, which was strewn with trash. Seated on the floor in a cross-legged position, was the male who had been shouting at us.

He was a large White male with long-straggly hair and a bushy beard. He was wearing a white undershirt tank top (aka the "wife beater"), a pair of blue jeans, and socks with no shoes. In his right hand was a very large and very sharp looking knife. If you have ever seen the movie *Crocodile Dundee* (I know, I am showing my age), the main character in the movie, Nick Dundee, played by actor Paul Hogan, had carried the exact same knife. It is what is called a Bowie or Buck knife. It was a total of 14-inches long, with a 10.5-inch blade. In other words, it was a *big fucking knife*! The man had it gripped tightly in his hand, as he was twisting the point of the knife into his right knee. He was not twisting it hard enough to break through his pants, or cut his skin. Rather, he was twisting it like one would do with a pencil on a piece of paper when they are deep in thought. In his left hand he was holding a lit cigarette.

Even though he was seated on the floor, I could tell from his build that he was a large man. I was having trouble putting his proportions into proper context, because the shadows that were being cast into the room by the light in the hallway were distorting my perception. I had my weapon in my hand with the flashlight trained on him. That is when we began our dialogue.

"Hey, what's going on tonight?" I asked softly, while trying to break the ice.

"You're going to have to kill me. That's what's going on." He calmly replied.

"Kill you? I don't even know you. Why would I want to kill you? Why would I want to do something like that?" I asked, innocently.

"Because, I'm going to leave you no choice." He responded--and quite foretelling.

"Now–Fuck you!" He suddenly screamed, angrily. "You're not talking me out of it. You're going to have to kill me, and that's it!"

"Listen." I began gently, as I was trying to keep this from getting out of hand quickly. "Just tell me what's going on. I'm here to help. The last thing I want to do is hurt you."

I never had any formal training in how to deal with people with mental health or emotional issues. Very few cops did at the time. De-escalation training wasn't mandatory or mandated during this period. It wasn't until after multiple incidents ended in "suicide by cop" did the rules, regulations, and training change on how to deal with people in crisis. However, those changes still won't occur for a few more years, and well after this incident. I also did not have a Taser or body camera, since they were not yet a part of our options. The extent of our training was what you learned on the street, and from your experience. Or whatever additional training you may have sought out on your own. I had dealt with suicidal people in the past, and I was able to get the situations resolved without any issues. I had no reason to believe this time would be any different.

After some coaxing the subject eventually told me his name—Mark. Mark and I began a conversation in which he shared with me how his life was basically a disaster. Mark told me he had kids, but that he hadn't seen them in quite a while. He said it was because he was no longer with their mother, and that he was severely behind in his child support payments. So, she wouldn't let him see the kids. Mark told me he couldn't find, let alone keep, a job. He described his frustration about having no employable skills. He told me how he had no money, and most ominously, how he believed he had no future. Mark had just recently been dumped, and was kicked out of his home by his girlfriend. On top of all his other issues, other than crashing at this apartment, he had no place to live. Mark was basically at his wit's end.

(It was later revealed we were in his brother's apartment.)

"I just want to see my kids!" Mark said, half-sobbing. "She never lets me see my kids. I love my kids. I want to get a job and turn myself around. I want to do the right thing. But, I just lost my job, and now I lost my girl. My parents are dead..." He was now in a full-blown cry.

As I listened to Mark's story about his train wreck of a life I truly felt sorry for him. I genuinely felt empathy and compassion toward him. Specifically, when he had mentioned about not seeing his children, it really hit a nerve with me. I had been through similar circumstances with my ex-wife, the mother of my oldest son, as I earlier discussed. Therefore, I had an understanding of what Mark must be feeling, and I connected with him on that point. I'm not excusing him for the fact that he hadn't made his child support payments. Still, we far too often see how money determines relationships, and that makes for a sad state of affairs. At one point, I tried used my being divorced to get him to lighten up a bit.

After Mark and I had been talking for about ten minutes or so, and with my feeling as though we weren't making much progress, I was looking for something, *anything*–to break the impasse. He was very upset and crying when I heard him say, "I've never even been married."

From my previous experience, I knew that humor usually gets folks to lighten up. Laughter has a great way of calming people down. So, I saw my opening.

"Wait." I began. "Did you just say you've never been married?"

"Yeah, why?" He stopped sobbing, and appeared to be perplexed by the question.

"Then what the hell are you so upset about?" I said, in a most light-hearted way. "If you've never been married, well, then that means you've never been divorced. And that, my friend, goes into the win column!" As I tried to say it most jovially. "See." I continued. "Shit can *always* be worse."

Then he laughed. Mark laughed! He really gave a good hard chuckle, and a big smile instantly came across his face. In that instant, I began to relax. I thought to myself–*Gotch*a! In my mind I thought, *once they laugh, it's over*! I mean, no one is going to attack someone who just made them laugh, right? No one is going to want to hurt themselves, or anyone else for that matter, once someone has them smiling and laughing. At least that's what my experience had been in the past. This assumption would lead me to my first mistake: Relaxing too soon. As I began to mentally check out of the conversation.

Tactically, I felt I was in a strong position. I was concealed behind the wall. I had my weapon trained on Mark, and I was in a position where I could move quickly if necessary. I even eyeballed a little path through the mounds of trash on the floor that I could take without tripping over any-thing, if it became necessary for me to move fast. Still, once Mark laughed, and with the benefit of hindsight, I realized I was no longer in the game. I was no longer really tuned into him. In my mind, the moment he had laughed basically ended this situation. Now, it was just a matter of "when" and not "if" he was going to abandon his suicidal plan.

However, after a few moments Mark stopped laughing, and then he completely shifted the entire dynamic of the situation. I had just fin-ished telling Mark that it was time to end this, and for him to come on out.

Mark proceeded to lean over from his seated position and in one motion, grabbed the door by its edge and slammed it shut! Prior to him shutting the door my attitude had become something along the lines of, *Okay, this shit is over. You're laughing now. Let's hurry this up. Time to wrap things up.*

Now, completely stunned, I thought, *what the fuck just happened? Why would he slam the door? Everything was going so well. He laughed. He had laughed! What went wrong?*

I tried to get my mind around what just happened. Why would he shut the door? Was he about to kill himself? Is he going to slit his wrists now? Is he going to end his life now, because he hasn't been able to get me to do it? I was completely taken off my game. At this point, the only thing he should have been doing was surrendering, or at least that's what I thought.

Reflecting on the situation, I'm sure Mark sensed that I had checked out on him. He must have somehow picked up that I no longer considered his desire to end his life as a serious request. Especially, after he had been making statements about how he wanted to live. Yet, I had failed to acknowledge them. Statements Mark made, such as: "I wanna see my kids." And "I wanna get a job and do better."

These are not the words of someone who wants to *die*. They are the words of someone who is looking for reasons to *live*. I failed to pick up on these clues, or to pursue them. I simply kept up my steady mantra of asking him "to put down the knife" or "to just come out" etc., etc.

I believe my failure to listen to him and to acknowledge him was the beginning of the situation taking a turn for the worse. Mark must have felt like he wasn't being heard or being taken seriously, and that I didn't respect his threat of him wanting to end his life. This turn of events shook me. It shook my confidence in my ability to talk to him. I had always been a great judge of people, or so I thought. I took pride in my being able to talk almost anyone into pretty much anything I needed or wanted them to do. But not this time.

You may be thinking that his closing the door wasn't that a big of a deal—that I should have just regrouped and tried to reengage him. All I can say is, it wasn't that simple! Mark shutting me out completely changed the momentum and the dynamic of the situation. Much like when a football player completely shocks the opposing team and the fans by returning a punt for a surprising touchdown to win the game, he shifted any momentum I had going in my favor. He took complete control of the situation with this one act. Looking back, the reason I was so taken aback was that he forced me to realize in that instant, that I was completely and totally wrong in my understanding of the situation. The reason I was unable to just shake it off was, that I didn't know what to do next. I had no idea how to reengage him, nor did I know what to say once I did. For the first time in my career I truly didn't know what to do. I felt powerless!

"Sarge, he just closed the door. It's a barricade situation now. You'll want to notify the negotiator and the tactical team."

I couldn't believe those words had actually come out of my mouth. The Sergeant started to make the call for the negotiator and the tactical team over the radio. However, because it was so loud in the apartment from the television's volume, he must have thought the wiser of doing so over the air, and he decided to make the call via cell phone. The Sergeant ran down the stairs and out of the apartment to make the call. I was now alone in the apartment with Mark.

Alone with Mark and just my thoughts, I was trying to get my head around what had just happened. At the same time, I started looking for a place to take up a position of cover. I wanted to keep my eyes on the door, just in case Mark decided to come out. I left my position on the wall near the bedroom, and backed into the living room.

One thing I hate is a loud television. It's a pet peeve of mine. I don't understand why people have to listen to a television with the volume turned up so loud they cannot hear each other speak. It annoys the shit out of me. An OCD quirk I suppose. While I was looking for a cover position to keep watch on the bedroom, I was also searching for the television's remote. There was so much trash and junk around the apartment, including around the television in the entertainment center, that not only could I not find the remote, I couldn't even get to the off button on the TV. Nor, could I find the plug to unplug it. Reluctantly, I gave up. I decided the best (and only) place for me to take up a position of concealment, was on the far side of the entertainment center.

I squeezed myself between the entertainment center and the wall. This way, if Mark did emerge from the room, I was hoping that the light being emitted from the television wouldn't illuminate me, and it might even mask my position. Those extra few seconds of concealment might give me the added time I would need to get my sights on Mark, and fire. Should it come to that. While I was squatted down in the tight little space behind the entertainment center in this hot–stinking dump of an apartment, my mind started to wander back to what went wrong.

*How did I lose this guy? I had him. I had made him laugh. What did I miss?*

After a few moments I became conscious of the fact that I wasn't focusing on the task at hand. I snapped myself out of these thoughts and I put them aside, as I tried to refocus. The heavy cigarette smoke and the screaming television, along with the heat in the apartment had given me a full-blown pounding headache. I was also getting dehydrated. It was so hot in the apartment, and with my adrenaline pumping, I was now pouring sweat under my body armor. I was dressed in a full uniform, so I was wearing about twenty pounds of gear. I could feel the tee shirt underneath my vest sticking to my body every time I moved. Since I was squatting down, I had to keep shifting my weight from one leg to the other so my legs wouldn't cramp, or my knees lock up. I could feel the sweat on the back of my legs beginning to form, as my pants began to stick to me. I was also getting frustrated as the minutes ticked by.

*What the hell was taking the Sarge so long? Where the hell is everyone? Why am I in here alone? For Christ's sake, this isn't even my town!*

As these thoughts were running through my head, I began to hear Mark's voice coming from the bedroom. He was shouting. But since he was about fifteen feet away from me and behind a closed door, and with the television being so loud, his voice was completely drowned out. After a few more moments, Mark shouted again. I still couldn't understand what he was saying. Then he shouted again. And then again. He was getting louder each time. Finally, he yelled loud enough that I could understand him over the constant roar of the television.

"Yo!" He shouted. "Is anyone the fuck out there?"

I wasn't sure what to do. I was no longer confident in my ability to negotiate with him. He had really thrown me through a loop when he rejected my attempts to settle him. He yelled a couple more times while I was contemplating what to do. Mark was getting more agitated each time he hollered and there was no response. I didn't know what think or what to do. I started to have conflicting thoughts. *Was he just trying to figure out who was out here so he could attack?* I was becoming concerned he would burst out of the bedroom and I would be left to face him alone. I had a quick vision of this scenario happening. Mark armed with the giant knife in hand, and me with my gun. It was a scene I was willing to deal with, but one I was hoping to avoid. Finally, I decided to respond.

"I can't hear you!" I called out.

Mark yelled a reply, but he was still too muffled for me to hear him clearly.

I repeated, "I can't hear what you're saying, Mark!"

Finally, in his booming voice, and just as there was a lull in the noise coming from the television, I heard Mark clearly state, "I'm opening the fucking door!"

*Shit! This is it. This motherfucker is going to attack me!*

I never understood why I made my next move, nor could I ever explain it. But, at the same moment Mark yelled that he was going to open the door, the Sergeant had started back up the stairs and into the apartment. Without even thinking about it, I jumped up from my position behind the entertainment center and ran toward the bedroom where Mark was opening the door. As I ran past the stairs, I put my hand up–signaling for the Sergeant to *Stop!* Which forced the Sergeant to stop his ascent up the staircase. I returned to the spot on the wall where I had been standing previously, but I hesitated for just a split second as the door opened. I hesitated because, even though I knew Mark had a knife, I still didn't know if he also had a gun! I didn't want to rush back to my previous position right away, just in case he came out shooting. After I reached the spot where I had been standing throughout this ordeal, I looked back and saw that the Sergeant had taken up his previous position behind the wall. *Good! The Sarge is safe.*

At the time, I didn't realize why I ran from my cover position behind the entertainment center and toward the bedroom where Mark was opening the door. Later, I realized I was simply acting on instinct. It was certainly not the most intelligent move to make tactically. However, I was simply putting myself in a position to protect the Sergeant, without even my realizing why I was doing so. Smart tactics is everything in a situation like this, and for so long I was unable to reconcile why I took such a risk. It was just that instinct to protect taking over.

Mark opened the door. He was seated on the floor, still in the same position, as he continued to hold the knife. However, now that the door was open I quickly realized that I was looking at a completely different person. It was still Mark, but he had a different look about him. He looked more aggressive–more agitated–*fiercer!* The apartment suddenly had a different feel to it as well. Even the air in the room had a different sensation to it. The air *tasted* electric! I know that sounds strange, but I cannot describe it any other way. I could actually feel and taste the heaviness in the air as I was breathing it in. It was like I was chewing on a piece of metal, and almost as if I was inhaling some animate object, instead of just air. There was a new edge in the environment. It's so hard to describe in words how things felt at this moment that it's frustrating for me. The best way I can define it is, that I was acutely aware there was about to be a finality to this situation.

"Hey bud, what's going on?" I asked, and as gently as I could.

With my confidence in my ability to calm him down completely shaken, I was trying to tread lightly.

"I want my brother! Where's my brother?" Mark asked, but in a very agitated voice.

"Who is your brother?" I replied. I was purposely playing dumb in order to keep him talking, and to stall him.

*Where the hell is the damn tactical team! Where is the freaking hostage negotiator?*

"The guy you took out of here before. The guy I told you guys to leave alone. Where is he? I want my brother! Where the fuck is my brother? I want my fucking brother, now!" Mark shouted.

"Listen to me. Before you can see your brother I need you to put down that knife." I pleaded.

"Fuck you!" Mark screamed. "I'm not putting down shit. I already told you, you're going to have to fucking kill me. Now get my fucking brother!"

This train was going off the tracks, and fast! He was becoming increasingly agitated as the moments passed. I felt overmatched. I didn't have the skills I needed to get this conversation back on track. I thought my best course of action was to simply focus on getting him to put down the weapon. I was praying for help to hurry up and arrive, since I felt as though I didn't have the tools to handle this situation any longer. I needed to be relieved from this position–pronto!

"Where the hell is the goddamn negotiator?" I whispered to myself aloud, as I tried to keep myself calm. My "thought voice" as I like to call it, told me to *just keep him talking. Keep him talking and everything will be okay*! So I tried to focus on keeping the dialogue going.

"Mark. I told you before. I'm not going to kill you. Now, listen to me." I said sternly, as I tried to reassert some semblance of control. "If you will just put down the knife—"

Cutting me off in mid-sentence Mark roared, "Fuck you–Fuck you–Fuck you! I'm not putting down shit. I fucking told you already. You are going to have to fucking *kill me!*"

There was a pause that seemed to hang in the air forever. I didn't know what to say. I was in way over my head. I had nothing to come back with. Nothing to counter with. Just as I was caught in this mental abyss, I heard Mark say, "You want a knife? Here. I'll give you a fucking knife!" I watched as he turned and reached to his left.

I believed he was possibly reaching for a gun, so I backed off the wall changing my position slightly. I prepared to fire my weapon. Mark, still seated, spun back toward me. Just as he threw a six-inch steak knife at the spot where I had just been standing seconds ago. The knife hit the other side of the wall with a thud. It bounced off the wall, and landed on the floor right next to my left foot. *Great! He's got more weapons after all.* Now, even if I get him to give up the big knife, I won't know how many more knives, guns, or other weapons he may still have concealed in the bedroom.

"Mark." I began, my throat now completely dry. "How many more knives beside the big boy you're holding in your hand do you have?"

"I don't know. A bunch. Like five." Mark replied, very matter-of-fact. "Now, where is my fucking brother?" He thundered again. "I want to see my brother, right now!"

"Listen, Mark." As I tried to keep calm. "How do I know you don't want to hurt your brother?" I was hoping this bit of logic might trigger him to pause for a minute and continue talking. "How do I know it's not your brother that may be causing you to be so upset, or who may be causing you to be so angry."

My attempt at reasoning with him didn't work.

"I want my fucking brother, now!" He shouted.

Mark's mantra stayed the same over the next several minutes, as he got worse with each passing moment. Mark seemed to be impervious to any logic, and he was becoming less and less willing to listen to any semblance of reason. He would repeatedly cut me off as I tried to speak. I was losing complete control of the situation. Not that I had much control to begin with. My confidence was now plummeting. It got to the point where I was afraid to speak, for fear of saying the "absolute wrong thing" that would set him off completely. I desperately needed help.

Just as I was about to speak, I heard a familiar voice coming from the area where the Sergeant had been stationed during this ordeal.

I had turned down the volume on my radio while I was speaking with Mark. One reason for my turning down the radio was that I didn't want to be distracted. The other was, I didn't want to take a chance of Mark overhearing any of our transmissions. Such as when the tactical team arrived, or any other info that might set him off. I don't know if the Sergeant radioed for someone to bring him back inside, but Mark's brother was now within the apartment. He was standing on the landing with the Sergeant and another officer, about eight feet away from me. Mark's brother began to speak, and his words were not going to be helpful. Not in the least.

"Yo, Mark. What the fuck!" Mark's brother called out. "What are you doing, Mark?" His speech was still slurred. "You've got all these fucking cops here, man!"

As soon as I heard Mark's brother's voice my heart sank. First, I felt as though we had just given up the only bargaining chip we had left to get Mark to surrender. We gave him what he had been asking for—his brother. In other words, we had just rewarded his noncompliance with his exact demands. Never a good tactic. Next, and what I felt to be the most foreboding reason: *Why does he want to see his brother so badly? Why is he*

*demanding to see someone he could have spoken with as much as he wanted
prior to us getting here?*

The only conclusion I could come up with was the one I didn't want
to consider.

"Mark, Jesus Christ! What the fuck are you doing?" Mark's brother
continued in his drunken speech.

I looked at Mark, and I saw him perk up the moment he heard his
brother's voice.

"Brian, [the name of Mark's brother] shut up! I'm trying to tell you
something." Mark shouted.

"Mark, this is fucking stupid!" The brother continued.

"Brian, would you shut the fuck up! I want to tell you something."
Mark repeated, cutting off his brother.

I could literally feel what was coming. The brother, the Sergeant, and
the officer were standing at the top of the stairs and just onto the landing.
Mark's brother was facing toward me. The Sergeant was standing directly
in front of and facing toward the brother, with his back facing me. The
other officer was standing directly behind Mark's brother, and just a few
steps below him on the staircase. Neither the Sergeant, nor the other officer were looking directly at me. I wanted to get their attention. Because
with each word Mark and his brother shared, it clearly had this situation
heading down a path of no return. I had figured out what Mark wanted to
say to his brother, and I didn't want him to get the words out. I didn't want
him to have a chance to say it. Because once he did--I knew what would
come next.

I was frantically waiving my arms toward the Sergeant and the other
officer, while trying to get their attention. I was even hoping the brother
might take notice of my gesturing toward them. Maybe just enough for
him to stop talking. You may be wondering why didn't I just yell out and
tell them to shut Mark's brother the up? Great question! The short answer is

I have no idea why I didn't do exactly that. Even though I didn't want Mark talking with his brother, for some reason I felt that shouting out at that particular moment was the wrong thing to do. I can't explain it. I assume I felt at the time that it might inflame Mark enough to make him commit to doing something I was still hoping to avoid. I also didn't want Mark to focus his attention on me at that moment. With Mark's brother trying to draw his attention to my presence, I didn't want Mark to focus on my being there. It wasn't fear. It was just—I really don't know how to explain it.

"Mark-Mark!" The brother continued. "Look at that fucking cop Mark. (Meaning me) That cop. He's got a fucking gun pointed at you, Mark. And he is going to *fucking kill you!*"

Those words seemed to just hang in the air. Almost like when you feel yourself falling in slow motion, and there isn't a damn thing you can do to stop it. That's how those words felt. They just stayed suspended in mid-air.

"Brian-Brian! Listen to me." Mark began.

I wanted so desperately to keep him from finishing what he was going to say. I knew in my bones what he was about to say, and what was about to happen. But, there was nothing I could do to stop it.

"I just want to say–I love you." Mark paused. "And–*goodbye!*"

As soon as Mark uttered those words they hit me like a punch in the gut. It felt like all the air inside of me had just been sucked out. Not just the air inside of me, but the air inside the entire room. There was an eerie moment of silence after he uttered those words, as we all processed what Mark had just said. Mark had won. He got to say his goodbye. It was absolutely the last thing I wanted. Whatever was about to come next was going to be out of anyone's control, but Mark's. It must have registered with the Sergeant what had just happened. Because he quickly had the officer standing behind the brother usher him down the steps and out of the apartment. I watched as Mark literally changed, as he transformed before my eyes.

As soon as he uttered his goodbye to his brother he seemed to flip a switch. In his left hand he was holding a freshly lit cigarette; in his right hand, the knife. I could see him readying himself. He began to smoke the cigarette more rapidly. *Puff-puff-puff-puff*, as he continuously took drags off of the cigarette. His grip on the knife tightened to the point that I could see his knuckles were turning white, even in the darkened room. His legs, although he was still seated cross-legged on the floor, began to bounce up and down at the knees. He was flexing his shoulders, pumping up his chest, tilting his head side to side to stretch his neck, flexing his arms and his hands. He was priming himself. Readying his body to move. This was a runaway train going down the tracks with no brakes. And I was standing right in front of it!

"Mark-Mark, let's keep talking." I said softly.

I began to shift my weight backwards and off of the wall, anticipating his movement any second. "Let's keep talking Mark. We were doing fine!" I tried desperately to reengage him in conversation.

A few more puffs of the cigarette.

"Mark, let's just be cool. We were doing fine. Let's just keep talking."

I could feel myself beginning to tremble with the new flow of adrenaline.

Then suddenly, Mark shouted, "That's it!"

In one fluid movement he jumped up from off of the floor, and was out of the bedroom and into the hallway. Mark was now standing just a few feet in front of me. I started to back up instinctively. I can remember calling out, "He's coming out!" just as Mark sprang to his feet, and as I backpedaled.

This was the first time I saw Mark standing completely upright. He had appeared to be a fairly big guy while he was seated on the floor. I could see he had broad shoulders, and he was thickly built. Now, standing directly in front of me in the narrow hallway of this tiny apartment he looked enormous! He looked larger than life. I began to walk backwards through the dining room, and toward the living room, praying I didn't trip over something.

As soon as Mark had entered the hallway he had switched the knife from his right hand to his left hand. My eyes were bouncing back and forth between Mark's eyes and that huge knife. Up close and with my eyes fixated on it, the knife looked like it was the size of a machete! Mark is now walking toward me with the knife at shoulder-high level, his elbow bent. He is holding the knife just how Jason Voorhees, Michael Myers, or a host of other Hollywood horror film murderers would hold the knife as they stalk their hapless victims. Except, I am not a helpless victim. I am a trained police officer. I have my duty weapon in my hand, locked and loaded and ready to fire. Still, I am more terrified than one of those horror film victims would be, because this is *real life*. No one is going to be yelling, "Cut!" (No pun intended). I have this wild-eyed suicidal man coming at me with a real weapon. The stakes don't get any higher than this. It is a moment of reckoning. One of which there is no avoiding.

My senses are off the charts. I am dialed into this moment like nothing before in my life. I continue backing up. My gun raised, my sights on him, with my finger on the trigger.

I alternate from yelling and ordering to pleading, almost begging him to put down the knife.

"Just drop it, Mark. Please! Just drop it. Just drop the knife, Mark. We were doing fine. Let's just keep talking."

I was aware of the fact that I didn't want to kill him. I wanted to help him. I was here to help him. Nevertheless, he is continuing to come toward me with the knife. Fourteen inches of shiny hardened stainless-steel clasped in his hand. The knife looks larger and larger as he's getting closer and closer. I look into his eyes. They have a blank thousand-yard stare in them. I feel like he's looking through me, as if I wasn't even there. My heart is pounding. I am now screaming at the top of my lungs at him. My throat is getting sore from being dry as sand. I am screaming so loudly, that I will later learn that people could hear me clear across the apartment complex. I am trying to somehow snap him out of this trance-like state that he seems to be in. Still, he isn't listening to me anymore. Mark's mind is made up.

*Oh my God! Is that a smirk on his face?* I can see he has a smirk, or a half smile on his face. *How can someone in this situation be smiling! Has he completely lost his mind?* This whole thing seems so surreal.

Mark's steps are labored. He is almost staggering as he walks, as he drags one foot behind the other as continues forward. I recall being so overwhelmed with the enormity of the moment that I felt like a little kid again. When you're so young and so small that you have to look up at all the adults around you, and it feels like you're surrounded by giants. That's how Mark appears to me at this moment—like a giant with a giant knife. I am still backing up. I'm using shuffle steps as I back up, so I don't trip. The apartment is a darkened and dank shit hole. This is not a place someone should want their life to end. *Why does he want to die here? Why would anyone want to die in this dump?* This death will be in a place not fit for a rat to die, let alone a human being. It won't be a peaceful or quiet death either, like many of us wish for. It will be a loud and violent death.

*Why does he want to end his life in a place that completely reeks of cigarettes and stale beer? Why does he want to fall among the trash that is tossed about in this shithole?* Oddly enough, these are just some of the thoughts that are racing through my mind in this moment.

I can sense I am running out of room. I can feel the wall coming up behind me. My senses are so sharp at this moment, that I literally feel everything around me. I can even smell sweat. However, it's not my sweat that I smell. Even though my sweat is pouring down my back and chest under my bullet-resistant vest in buckets. It's Mark's sweat! I can smell it, even with him standing almost six feet away from me. It was one of the strangest realizations I have ever had. My heart is pounding in my chest so hard it feels like it's about to come through my vest. My body is tense and tight. The sweat is now running down my forearms to my hands. I tighten my grip on my weapon, as my palms are becoming wet. I practice combat breathing. Breathe in for a four count-hold for four-exhale for four-hold for four-repeat. I feel fear. I feel terrified. But I also feel very much in control. It was quite the paradox of emotions.

Thoughts are racing through my head in milliseconds. Some of these thoughts I am conscious of. Others are just training and reaction. It's so hot, and the air is so very thick that it's hard to breathe. I start to feel light-headed. I'm so dehydrated. I'm continuing to shuffle backwards when suddenly, my back foot slips! I almost go crashing down to the floor. *Oh shit!* I feel a sudden surge of fear and panic race through me. Just like when you look up and hit your brakes right before you're about to smash into the car in front of you. And you get that warm surge and tingling of adrenaline that rushes through your body—that's what I felt.

My heart is hammering so hard it feels like it's about to burst. My legs feel weak, and rubber-like. If I fall down, Mark can be on top of me in a fraction of a second. He could start stabbing away at me with that huge knife. He could kill me with a single blow! I have a quick vision of this scenario playing out, and I feel a shudder of fear run though me.

*No! He is not going to kill me. I won't let him kill me!* I hear the thought voice in my head shout. Suddenly, I have another thought. *I will always come home.* That is the promise I made to my wife. I will not let Mark or anyone else keep me from fulfilling that promise. *I will always come home.*

It was at this exact moment when this whole thing felt so vividly real and completely dreamlike, all in the same instance. I remember thinking, *I can't believe this is really happening. I don't want to die. I won't die! So I need to focus.*

"Jesus Christ, just drop the fucking knife, Mark!" I scream.

My voice is different now. It's more forceful. I am beginning to feel a new feeling besides fear–*anger*. Not anger toward Mark per se. But anger that this was happening in the first place. This was all avoidable. I was angry because this shouldn't be happening.

"Just drop the knife! Drop the knife. Drop the fucking knife!" I scream repeatedly and rapidly.

After I slipped, and when I nearly fell down, I made up my mind that I wouldn't try to back up anymore. I couldn't risk falling and being stabbed to death. I remember my thought voice saying, *this is your Alamo. You can't back up anymore. You're done.*

But Mark is still coming toward me. The distance between us is closing with every new step he takes since I am no longer backing up. He has passed the kitchen area off to my right. I am standing just in the middle of the living room, less than six feet away from him. I'm now backed into a corner, with nowhere to go. The Sergeant is still behind the wall at the top of the staircase. Where he has been throughout most of this ordeal. But now the Sergeant is crouching down low to the floor. Mark is just on the other side of the wall, just opposite the Sergeant. *Does the Sarge have his weapon out?* Dammit, I can't see it. It's too dark. Another couple of steps forward and Mark will be practically on top of the Sergeant.

"Mark, stop!" I beg him. "Please-Please. Don't do this!"

I knew if he came forward any further he was going to be too close to the Sergeant, literally less than three feet away, and I was going to be out of options.

"Please, Mark. Drop the knife." I suddenly became angry again. "Goddammit Mark! Drop the fucking knife!" I screamed, in one last effort to get him to listen.

Just as Mark leaned forward to take another step, he paused. I watched as he turned his head and looked toward his left. He has caught sight of the Sergeant behind the wall. Mark then turned his head again, now looking back at me. He then shifted his gaze back toward the Sergeant. The best that I can tell the Sergeant can't see Mark. Or, he doesn't realize Mark is now standing just a couple of feet away from him, and just on the opposite side of the wall. Mark looks toward me again. I realize in that moment what he is planning to do.

"No, Mark!" I yell. "Don't do it!" The words feel futile at this point. "Don't you fucking do it, Mark!" I shout with all my might.

Mark is leaning backwards, as he transfers his body weight onto his back foot. He then turns and pivots his body into a bladed position. His chest is now facing the wall toward his right, which is on my left. He takes the knife and switches it from his left hand, passing it around his back, and grips it in his right hand. Mark again brings the knife up to a shoulder high level, with his elbow bent. He then pushes off of his back foot, springing his body forward and directly toward me. However, as soon as his feet make contact with the floor again, he quickly turns, pivoting toward his left and toward the Sergeant. Mark is turning, and is about to be standing directly over top of the Sergeant with the knife in his hand, cocked back, and ready to strike. As soon as Mark started his pivot toward the Sergeant I fired two shots from my weapon in rapid succession.

Boom! Boom!

I didn't see the first shot make contact with his body. However, I clearly saw the second round I fired strike Mark. While this sequence of events is taking place, I am conscious of so many different thoughts which are running through my mind in this moment.

I remember thinking to myself just as Mark leapt forward, *I don't want to die!* My next thought was, *Why isn't the Sarge firing his weapon? The Sarge has to see him by now. Why hasn't he fired yet?*

Finally, I recall vividly hearing the sound of my weapon firing. Or rather, the *lack* of sound of my weapon firing. When I fired my weapon, you would have thought that a .40-caliber Glock with hollow point ammunition going off in that tiny apartment would have sounded like a bomb going off. Still, all I heard was a low, dull, and very faint–*Pop! Pop!*

I remember my thought voice saying: *Wow! That wasn't very loud.*

I had fired two shots in total. I knew I struck him at least once. Because when the second shot was fired, I saw it strike him in his abdomen in the area of his liver. His white t-shirt instantly started turning crimson red. There was so much blood. The force of my shots striking his body spun Mark to his left. He took a stumble-step backwards, pivoted toward me, and then fell forward and onto the floor. Mark dropped down onto one knee as he crumpled to the ground. He then placed his left hand on the flooring, and was holding his upper body and torso off the floor. I am still screaming. "Drop it-Drop it! Drop the fucking knife-Drop the fucking knife!"

What happens next still haunts me in my dreams. It was so unbelievable and so surreal, I still cannot believe it happened. Mark, who now has both of his hands on the floor in order to hold himself up, took the knife from his right hand, and shuffled it across the ground in front of him, pushing it over toward his left hand. He then picked up the knife with his left hand, and placed his right hand on his right knee, which he has brought up into a 45-degree angle, as if he is in the marriage proposal position. Mark then pushes himself off of the floor, and back up and onto his feet, with the knife clasped in hand.

*This can't be happening*! I'm not sure if I said that aloud or if it was just in my head. In an instant, all these new thoughts are flooding through my mind. Both rational and irrational.

The irrational: *Did I miss him-Did I really fucking miss him? Did my gun not work-Did my gun not fire correctly?*

The rational: *But he's bleeding. Jesus Christ, he's pouring fucking blood! Look at all that blood. I had to hit him. How can he be standing? How is he not dead?*

The realization that Mark was standing upright and in front of me was undeniable. He was about a quarter of the way into the dining area at this point. I am standing about six to eight feet away from him, by my rough estimate. His white tee shirt is turning darker with blood by the moment.

"Drop the knife–Drop the knife–Drop it–Drop it–Drop it!" I am screaming over and over again.

Mark is swaying. He is staggering in place–like when a person is drunk and is trying to stand upright as they try to keep their balance.

"Drop the fucking knife!" I shout once again.

"Noooooooo!" Mark shouts back at me.

This cannot be happening. I am in complete shock and horror!

*Did this man who is dying, did he just say no to me?*

I couldn't put my mind around what was going on. I seriously started to think I was dreaming. This is the kind of thing you see in the movies, or on a television show, not in real life.

While I was trying to process this incredible turn of events my training kicked in. Ironically, it was my old training methods that came flooding back into my mind.

For years, when we went to the shooting range to qualify with our weapons, we were taught to shoot two rounds to the center of mass of the target, then finish them off with a third shot to the head. This became known as, "Two to the chest, and one to the head." And that was how we remembered to execute it. However, studies had found that when the third shot was fired it usually missed the target. This was often because the first two shots had already put the suspect down; or they had at least buckled the suspect enough that they were bent over, and facing at a downward angle. This led to the conclusion that when the third shot was being fired it was flying "down range," and without the officer knowing who or what it was going to hit. The firing of this third round to the head greatly increased the risk of injuring or killing an innocent person. So, they changed our training.

Our most recent training methods at the shooting range taught us to "double-tap" (fire two shots) into the center of mass of the target, and then reassess before firing again. This double-tapping is exactly what I had done when I fired at Mark initially. I double-tapped (fired two shots) into Mark's center of mass (his body), and then I reassessed. Just as I was trained to do. However, since he hadn't stayed down, and he was still armed with the weapon, my old training habit of "putting one into the head" was rekindled. I heard my thought voice say, *Okay, it's time for lights out!* This was my way of telling myself it was time to take the head shot and end this.

Mark actually tried to take a step forward, and he was able to take about a half of a step toward me. I closed my left eye and started to target Mark's head by getting it into my sights, preparing to take the head shot. Just as I was ready to squeeze off my shot I caught a flash of something blue within my peripheral vision, and just off to my right. It looked to be light blue-colored clothing. The same color of the Bellmawr police uniforms. Fearing someone may be possibly entering into my line of fire, I immediately went into a weapon retention position.

Basically, what this means is that I pulled my weapon down from the firing position, and into a downward-facing position, so that the barrel of my weapon was now aimed toward the floor.

After I had a moment to process what it was that I saw, I realized it was the Sergeant. My assumption was that when I fired at Mark, who was standing within two feet of the Sergeant when I pulled the trigger, the Sergeant must have bailed out of there and went running down the steps, in order to get out of the line of fire. Now, the Sergeant was moving back into his original position up against the wall. In my hypersensitive adrenaline-driven state what I thought I saw was a flash of blue moving directly into my line of fire. As I was processing this information, Mark began to succumb to his fatal wounds.

I took my gaze away from the Sergeant, and I looked back toward Mark. I watched him as he began to stagger backwards, and was heading toward the wall where I had been standing just moments before. He hit the wall with a hard thud, but remained upright and on his feet. Mark then bounced off of the wall, spun toward his left, and fell into the hallway. His body left a bright red blood streak on the white painted wall, as he did a complete 360-degree spin into the hallway. After Mark struck the partition in the hallway, which mercifully stopped his momentum, he slowly slid down and came to rest with the left side of his body pressed up against the bathroom door. Mark's final body position still haunts me in my thoughts. He was in a position where his one knee was on the floor, with his other knee propped up against the door, but slightly bent. His head hung down low with his chin on his chest, *and he was still gripping the knife*. He never let go of that knife. Even in death.

"Drop it–Drop it! Drop the fucking knife!" I was still screaming, like I was on autopilot.

I started to approach Mark with my weapon raised and my finger on the trigger, ready to fire again. I was fully expecting him to jump up and charge at me any second. After what I had just witnessed, with the horror of shooting him twice at point-blank range and seeing him covered in his own blood but still holding the knife—well, let's just say I didn't rule out any possibilities at this point. As I was making my approach, the Sergeant suddenly cut in front of me, and before I could get to Mark. He looked back toward me and put his finger up to his lips, like when you are telling someone to "Be quiet!" The Sergeant tip-toed over to Mark and smacked the knife out of his dead–clinched hand. The knife went flying across the room and landed somewhere in the dining room area.

I remember being absolutely terrified the moment the Sergeant approached Mark. First, the Sergeant didn't appear to have his weapon drawn, which I remember thinking was bizarre. Next, I thought for sure that just as the Sergeant approached Mark, that Mark would spring back to life, turn, and start to stab him. The Sergeant would have been directly in my line of fire at that point, so I wouldn't have had a shot. I still have that nightmare from time to time.

In my dream, I see the Sergeant just about to swat at the knife, when Mark suddenly turns toward him. He grabs the Sergeant by his collar, pulls him against him, and begins to stab the Sergeant repeatedly. In the dream

I am trying to get around the Sergeant so I can take a shot at Mark. But for some reason, there is no room to get around him. Mark is screaming as he stabs the Sergeant repeatedly. He is screaming and laughing like a completely sadistic madman! I can see the blood pouring out of the Sergeant as he is screaming, and begging me to help him.

My point of view in the dream is always from directly behind and over the Sergeant's shoulders.

I am screaming in the dream, "Stop Mark! Stop! Let him go! Just let him go!"

But Mark keeps stabbing away, while yelling, "Noooooo! Noooooo! Noooooo!"

Then the dream ends, and I wake up covered in sweat.

But Mark is dead. I've killed him.

After knocking away the knife, the Sergeant ran past me and down the stairs as he called out for the medics. I was once again alone in the apartment with Mark. And I let him have it!

"You stupid motherfucker!" I shouted. "Look at you! Really–this is what you wanted? You fucking idiot! Why, Mark, Why? Why couldn't you just put down the fucking knife? Why wouldn't you just listen? Why couldn't we just keep talking? No, instead you make me kill you!" Are you fucking happy now? You fucking piece of shit!"

I felt like I was losing my mind as I screamed at a dead man. It was rage! Pure, unadulterated rage. I was so angry. I felt this rage not only because he had forced me to kill him, and not just because he wouldn't listen to me. No–this was rage also directed at myself. I couldn't make Mark listen to me, and I didn't know how to handle it. This anger was because in that moment, I felt like I had failed. Suddenly, I heard someone coming up the stairs. Fearful that someone would think I was crazy because I was screaming at a dead man, I stopped yelling. I began pacing back and forth in the living room. My body was shaking and trembling all over from the adrenaline. The next thing that transpires has stuck with me for years. It still pisses me off so much, that even after all of these years I can barely write about it without wanting to smash something.

The first person to enter the apartment after I shot Mark was a female EMT. She came up the steps very slowly. She stepped up and onto the landing area at the top of the stairs, and stopped at the same spot near the wall where the Sergeant had been posted. Just like the Sergeant, she couldn't see into the rest of the apartment or down the hallway, unless she changed her position. She would need to either step further into the apartment to see where Mark was now positioned, or at the very least, she would need to lean forward and turn her head to her right. She did neither.

"Well, where is he?" She asked me, in an obviously annoyed tone of voice.

I gestured toward the far end of the hallway.

"He's right there!" I said, a bit annoyed with her annoyance.

The EMT took one step forward into the apartment and stopped. She looked to her right and down the length of the hallway where Mark was now lying–dead. She then let out an audible *gasp* as she turned toward me and said, "Jesus Christ! What the hell did you do to him?"

It struck me like a ton of bricks. I felt the rage just boil up inside of me.

*What did I do to him? You bitch–Look at what this asshole made me do to him!*

I didn't repeat any of these thoughts aloud, thank God. However, I thought it prudent at that moment for me to leave the apartment so I wouldn't commit *two homicides*! Without saying a word, I stormed past her and headed toward the stairs just as the Sergeant was coming up and back into the apartment. He must have heard what was said as he was coming up the staircase. Because after I pushed past her and started down the steps, the Sergeant turned and followed me down. He put both of his hands on the backs of my shoulders and whispered in my ear, "Chad, you did what you had to do. Don't fucking worry about her."

Nothing he said mattered. I was now on fire with rage. Between Mark forcing me to take his life, followed by one of the most callous and insensitive comments someone could make at that moment–well, I had just about had enough for today.

Once outside the apartment building, I began to look around. I tried to see what officers had arrived, since I assumed that once I fired the fatal shots the whole police world would show up. But there was hardly anyone here. I could see some of the other Bellmawr police officers standing just off in the distance, but no one approached me. The Sergeant had split off from me as soon as we had gotten outside. I overheard him get on the radio and request for dispatch to make notifications to his boss and the detective on duty, and to have them respond to the scene. I realized that I didn't hear the transmission come over my radio mic. As I had mentioned earlier, I had turned down my radio in order to concentrate on my negotiations with Mark, and I had failed to turn the volume back up. Even though the Sergeant's superior officers were now responding, and I was working under the "color of the law" in his town via the mutual aid agreement, I still needed to notify my superiors. I turned up my radio and took a deep breath. As calmly as I could, I advised dispatch to contact my bosses.

Once I had made the call, I attempted to reorient myself to my reality. *Think, Chad, think! What do you need to do now?* Then, an idea came to me. *Crime scene tape!* My Camden training had kicked in. *When in doubt, tape them out.* I recalled that little saying from one of our great street Sergeants in Camden. Whenever there is a crime scene, particularly in a place as densely populated as Camden, if you don't secure the area quickly your crime scene will get destroyed in a hurry. Whenever and wherever there is a crime scene, the police need to take up as much real estate as is practicable in order to protect it. The "When in doubt, tape them out" saying was a reminder to put up the tape.

Now, with a task to complete, I walked over to my police car and popped the trunk. I took out a roll of crime scene tape, and I started to put the tape around a pillar a few doors down from the apartment where the shooting had taken place. Just as I began to put some tape around the first pillar, two ranking officers, one a Sergeant from the Bellmawr Police Department and the other a Sergeant from neighboring Mt. Ephraim Police Department, began to walk past me on the walkway leading up to Mark's apartment. My back was facing them as they walked by me. As I was struggling to get the tape around the pillar, because my hands were still trembling so badly. The Sargent then asked me what was happening.

"Hey Chad, what's going on?" The Sergeant from Mt. Ephraim asked as he passed by. "Nothing. I just shot him." I replied very nonchalantly. But without my actually trying to be nonchalant about it at all.

They both stopped dead in their tracks. I heard them stop walking, so I turned to face them. The Sergeant from Mt. Ephraim had this incredulous look on his face. He took a step toward me and said, "What did you just say?"

"I shot him. I shot the guy." I replied.

I felt a bit perplexed at their lack of understanding. I mean, after all, hadn't they heard it on the radio? I couldn't understand how this information could be new to them. I had assumed everyone probably heard the call for "shots fired" go out over the radio once I pulled the trigger.

When a cop fires their gun it normally goes out over the radio almost instantaneously. So, I assumed someone must have made the call and I didn't hear it. Because my radio volume was turned down.

"Chad, what are you talking about? You shot who?" The Sergeant from Mt. Ephraim said, as he appeared even more confused.

"Jesus Christ, do I have to spell it out for you!" I replied. As I became rather annoyed.

"The guy in the apartment. I shot him! He's dead." It felt surreal for me to speak those words.

I was still holding the roll of crime scene tape when the Mt. Ephraim Sergeant took the roll of tape from my hand and said, "Come here, come with me. I don't understand what's going on."

As we walked together toward my police cruiser, I repeated those same words over again. Every time I said, "I shot him, he's dead" the more bizarre it felt to say. It seemed to be putting me further and further away from the reality of the situation. Once back at my car, with the both of us still as confused as when we started our conversation, the Sergeant and I parted ways. He walked back toward the crime scene to find out what was going on, and I stood by my car, alone, once again. At this moment, two things occurred to me.

The first thing I realized was that it was awfully quiet. When a *shots fired* broadcast happens, usually all other calls for service are held up from being dispatched, and the cops are responding with lights and sirens at warp speed from everywhere. It's basically like issuing a "May Day" call. The radio is kept clear until the cavalry arrives and gives dispatch a status on the situation. Yet, that is not what was happening. It was eerily quiet. As if no one knew anything had even happened. My mind started to run wild with bizarre thoughts. *Did the cops not give a damn? Why would no one come to a shots fired call to back me up?* Something didn't seem right, and it was playing with my head.

I would later learn that when the Sergeant ran outside to get the medics after I had shot Mark, he had also contacted dispatch over the radio. He told dispatch to have the tactical team and the negotiator "stand down," since they were no longer needed, now that Mark was dead. However, he never reported over the air that shots had been fired. So, everyone who heard the stand down call go out over the radio assumed it had been resolved peacefully, since there was no follow-up report of shots having been fired, or of anyone being down. This is why no one came in a hurry, and very few officers came at all. They simple thought it was resolved without incident. With my radio volume turned down I never heard the stand down order go out.

The next thing I recognized was, I began to feel as if I was losing my connection with everything around me. I started to feel "funny," as if I was in a dream-like state. Yet, I was still wide awake and functioning. It wasn't a feeling of being "high" that you would think one might experience from this type of incident due to the adrenaline. It was as if I was becoming a spectator to the world around me, and seeing things from a third person point-of-view. It is very difficult to explain. The best way I can describe it is that it felt like I was in a dream. Yet, I was conscious of the fact that I wasn't in a dream. Surreal is probably the better word to describe how I was feeling. As these bizarre notions were occupying my mind, another thought suddenly hit me like a slap to the face. *Oh my God, my wife! I have to call Suzanne–right away.*

I didn't want my wife to hear about the shooting on the news or from someone else calling her, since she would be terrified. I opened up the door to my police car, and I reached into my duty bag to retrieve my cell phone. I took a deep breath and pressed the speed dial button. Suzanne answered the phone in her usually silly and lighthearted playful voice.

"Hello, Mr. Holland." She said.

"Babe, I need you to listen to me."

I think she knew right away from the tone of my voice that this was not a normal call.

"What is it?" She asked.

"First, I'm okay." I began. "I just wanted to tell you I'm okay, and I don't want you to hear it on the news, or anything like that." I stumbled, while I was trying to find the right words.

"What happened, babe?" She asked gently, but a bit impatiently.

"I just shot and killed a guy who had a knife." I told her.

I realized during this brief conversation that I was laboring to get the words out, and I was struggling to put my thoughts together. While on the phone with my wife, something was happening to me. I didn't know what, but I was becoming very afraid. I felt like I was becoming increasingly detached from my reality. I had never felt like this before. It was almost like when you're on your way to passing out. You start to feel "different," and yet you can't describe how you are feeling. *Was I having a heart attack? Am I going to have a stroke? Or is this just what happens to you after you have killed someone?* I didn't like any of these possibilities, but I tried to stay cool, as I didn't want my wife to panic.

Suzanne asked me if I was okay. At that moment, I made up my mind that I was going to go to the hospital to get checked out. Still, I didn't want her to worry. She was in nursing school at the time, and she had enough stress going on in her life (As if her husband telling her that he just killed someone didn't add any more stress already!). The last thing I wanted to do was put anything else on her.

"I think I'm just going to go to Lourdes [Our Lady of Lourdes Hospital in Camden], just to get checked out. But I'm okay. Don't worry." I said, trying to reassure her.

Ironically, Our Lady of Lourdes Hospital was where my wife was currently attending nursing school.

"Do you want me to meet you there?" Suzanne asked.

"No, Jacob [our son] has school in the morning." I tried to play it off like it was no big deal. Even though I felt like I was about to pass out. "I'll be fine." I reassured her. "I have the guys with me. I'll call you as soon as I am done. It may be a while, anyway."

"Okay, I love you!" Suzanne said.

"I love you too, babe." As I tried to not to breakdown as I hung up the phone.

I tried to clear my head enough so I could think of my next move. No one had approached me since the Mt. Ephraim Sergeant had left me alone at my vehicle, and there were no other cops showing up. The whole thing was strange.

Just then, Officer Paul from the Gloucester City Police Department pulled up. Officer Paul and I had gone to high school together, and my nickname in high school was "The Duke," after the actor John Wayne (That's a story for another day). Officer Paul walked over to me and asked, "What's up, Duke! What's going on here?"

I damn near felt close to collapsing, so I just blurted out, "Can you take me to Lourdes Hospital?" I paused, as I gathered myself. "I just shot and killed that dude in there, and I am feeling a little weird."

The look on Officer Paul's face was one of disbelief. Yet, I think the Marine in him kicked in, and he knew what to do.

"Okay, let's go. Get in!" He said without hesitation, as we jumped into his car.

Officer Paul was driving about Mach 3 to the hospital with the lights and siren screaming, as if I had been the one who had been shot. At one point, because he was scaring the shit out of me with his driving, I said, "Hey, you can take your time. I'm not hurt or anything."

He just ignored me. I think he picked up on the fact that I wasn't well. Once at the hospital, Officer Paul grabbed hospital security and the nurse manager and told them why I was there, and I was immediately whisked away into a private room. Of course, of all the rooms, it had to be the room they kept available for the psych patients. Officer Paul remained in the room acting as my bodyguard while I awaited the doctor. He refused to leave my side, which felt comforting. Particularly, after my having spent so much time alone during, and right after, the shooting. Eventually, a nurse came and asked me why I had come to the hospital. I gave her a very brief explanation of what had occurred as she took down some info. The nurse then took my vitals—three times. With a very concerned look on her face, the nurse informed me that the doctor would be in shortly, and she quickly left the room.

In the meantime, I took off my duty belt, my uniform shirt, and my vest. I piled it on the far end of the bed that I was seated on while I awaited the doctor. At one point, my mind drifted off as I looked at the pile of gear. I had a vision of it being covered with blood—*my blood*. I pictured how the clothing would have looked had they needed to cut it off my body if I had been stabbed. Just as I was trying to push those images out of my head, the doctor arrived.

"Without getting into specifics Officer Holland. Can you tell me what happened to you tonight that brought you in here?"

I knew she didn't want to become a witness, so I just told her that I was forced to use deadly force on someone by firing my weapon, and that I was now feeling a bit strange. The doctor then took my vitals. I knew something was wrong when she took my vital signs not just once, not twice, but three times—just as the nurse before. The doctor took them again manually, and then once more, while using a different machine.

"Officer Holland, how are you feeling at this moment?" The doctor asked, calmly.

Ironically, as she was taking my vitals and listening to my breathing I was starting to feel a bit better. I was slowly starting to feel as though I was coming out of whatever *it* was.

"I feel okay. I'm feeling a bit better, actually." I said. "Why? Is there something wrong, doctor?"

The doctor turned the machine toward me which displayed my vital sign readings. My heart rate at that moment was clocking 198 beats per minute! This was about forty-five minutes, give or take, after my having pulled the trigger. I was sitting on the bed and talking to the doctor as calm as could be. In the meantime, my heart was running the New York City Marathon!

"I need to get you something to calm you heart down immediately." The doctor said, with a bit of measured concern in her voice.

It was pure adrenaline—the most amazing chemical there is. I couldn't even feel my heart beating that quickly, because I had become somewhat numb. At least that would be the only way to describe it. Still, the doctor needed to reverse the effects quickly. The longer my heart stayed jacked up that high, the more at risk I was of having a cardiac episode. This also accounted for my feeling "strange." While I was waiting the doctor's return, more and more officers began to show up and pile into the room. Even cops I hadn't seen in a very long time from other departments came to see me. Word got around fast. My youngest brother Michael, the Sheriff Officer, also arrived.

It made me feel better to have all these officers around me. Ironically, it made me feel safe. I never needed the presence of another cop or cops to make me feel safe before. However, as I looked around the room and saw all of these officers in uniform, all these amazing heroes I had come to know over the years, I had an overwhelming feeling of being safe and secure. It was an odd realization. Then my wife and youngest son arrived.

Suzanne, even though I had asked her not to, had come anyway. As soon as she saw me she lost it, holding onto me tightly while crying. She had brought our son Jacob with her, and while the three of us embraced, I could see the cops out of the corner of my eye starting to file out of the room. I'm sure in that moment, when the officers saw a cop's wife show up at the hospital with their child, and with the three of us hugging while my wife is crying, it must have struck a nerve with many of them. It likely made the officers think about the "*what ifs,*" and how their family would deal with it should something happen to them. This is something none of us in this line of work like to think about. Suzanne then held my face in both of her hands. With tear streaked eyes she looked directly into mine, and between sobs she said, "Babe. I don't care what you do. But I need you to do something else. I need you to do something else, because I can't lose you!"

That crushed me. To know that I caused her so much pain and anguish really hurt. This was the first time Suzanne had ever asked me to quit. I wasn't ready at that moment to even think about quitting. In my mind, I would be going back to work shortly, and everything would be okay with time.

The doctor returned and gave me some medication to settle my heart, and the rest of the night is pretty much a blur. I recall walking to the parking lot to get into my wife's car, then nothing after that. There is one event which took place at the hospital that I do recall vividly. It still makes me angry when I think about it.

While the officers were in and out of my room to see how I was doing, my Captain showed up. As police officers, we all know how important evidence is to a case. In the event of an officer involved shooting, it is most times necessary to collect the weapon(s) of the officer(s) involved in the incident, and in some cases even their uniforms. My Captain came to collect my weapon, which was fine, except for the way he went about doing it. The Captain walked into the room and without saying a word to anyone, he walked up behind me and whispered into my ear, "I'm taking your gun."

He then reached into my duty belt, which was still lying on the bed next to me, and in front of a room full of police officers, removed my weapon from the holster. He tucked it under his arm and left the room, again, without saying a word. Leaving me weaponless. At that moment, every set of eyes in the room looked toward me. Everyone had the same expression on their face. An expression of—*what the hell was that*? Talk about creating an atmosphere of suspicion! I was completely humiliated.

In that spirit, let me share a word of caution to all superior officers, detectives, or any others who investigate officer-involved shootings in your jurisdiction(s). As I mentioned, as cops we understand the value of evidence. It's universally understood that an officer's duty weapon is going to be taken from them for evidentiary purposes after a shooting. Still, it must be done in the least embarrassing way possible. First, do not remove an officer's weapon from him or her unless you have a replacement readily available. Additionally, do not remove an officer's weapon from them in front of anyone else, unless the officer gives you permission to do so. Even then, an officer is most likely just agreeing to let you do so because they fear if they say no they may be insubordinate, or suspected of hiding something. There is no need to have more than one other officer present as a witness while taking the officer's weapon into evidence—certainly not in front of a room full of cops. Remember to explain to them why you are taking their weapon at that particular moment, and have a replacement weapon available. If they do not accept a replacement weapon, make sure they are sent home with an armed escort.

Perception is an incredibly important thing to an officer during this emotional time. Please make the small, but important gestures to support the officer. Do not add any suspicion to the equation, or worse yet, humiliate them by making them feel like they've done something wrong. Even if the whole situation is sketchy, you have to give the officer the benefit of the doubt, and not form an impression for others. Okay, rant over.

# CHAPTER 19

---

# *MY FIRST BREAKDOWN*

The next day, Friday, April 27, 2012 was fairly uneventful. I remember waking up to a whole bunch of text messages of support, along with some voicemails. One text message I remember in particular is a perfect display of the sick sense of humor cops often use to bring levity to a tragic situation. It's just part of our coping mechanism—our *gallows* humor.

The message said, "Hey, Holland! I'm surprised you were able to hit him when you fired. Especially, since he was standing right in front of you!"

This particular text was in reference to my lack of proficiency at the shooting range. I will be the first to admit, when it came to standing in one place and shooting at paper targets my accuracy was a wild card. My scores ranged from the low 80s to the low 90s. I'd get so bored standing in place and shooting at the paper that I would lose focus. Whenever I was shooting and moving, like in a shoot house or on an obstacle course, I was a much better and more accurate shooter. I was also not a guy who took his time when firing his weapon. I got my weapon out quickly and got the rounds down range in a hurry.

Some officers like to draw their weapon slowly. They like to take their time getting their sight-picture, taking deep breaths, and then they *squeeeeeze* the trigger ever so slowly. These shooters consistently achieve scores of 100% accuracy. The only problem with that style of shooting is, it's not realistic! When you're in a gun fight, that gun needs to come out as quickly as possible, and you need to start firing rounds as fast as you can. That's how I shot my weapon at the range. I'd get the gun out of my holster as quickly as possible and—"bam-bam-bam-bam-bam!"—get the rounds out. So, my accuracy suffered a bit because of my rapid fire. Still, I thought losing some accuracy while practicing like it was the real thing was a fair trade-off. As opposed to shooting perfect scores. I'd still hit the target. Just not inside the lines where it counted for scoring. Anyway, my response to the text was, "I have only shot a 100 [100% accuracy] once. That was last night…when it counted the most. So go fuck yourself! ☺ "

I know you are reading this and probably thinking that I am some callous scumbag in order to make a comment like that. Specifically, after having taken a man's life less than 24 hours before. I'm not trying to defend it, but that's just cop humor. I'm not going to try to make you understand, nor am I going to apologize. I'm just telling you that's the way it is. Like it or not.

For the rest of the day I returned phone calls and text messages. I thanked everyone for checking in on me, and I had a couple of friends stop over the house to see me. Otherwise, I spent the day just trying to process my new reality. I was now a killer. I had taken another person's life. I committed a homicide. A legal and justified homicide, but a homicide nonetheless. I was trying to assess what changes (if any) were going on inside me.

Since this was my normally scheduled weekend off, I had planned to take Jacob to his ice hockey games on Saturday and Sunday. Attending Jacob's games has been a highlight of my life since he was five years-old. On Saturday, my father (with whom I was on good terms with at the time) and I, took Jacob to his game at a local rink. Just as the game was about to begin, I started to feel strange. I started to feel a bit unsteady on my feet, and my whole body was beginning to tremble. My father hadn't noticed because he was watching Jacob during the warm-up. I excused myself, and I headed for the bathroom. I barely made it. While walking to the men's room I felt like I was going to collapse to the ground. My body wasn't just trembling, it was literally jackhammering! *What was happening to me?* I was beginning to panic. I started to have trouble breathing, and my heart felt like it was about to burst out of my chest. As I made it into the bathroom, I was able to pull my cell phone out of my pocket and press the speed dial button. I called the only person I knew of at that moment who might understand what was happening to me. Particularly, since I didn't want to call 9-1-1, and alarm Jacob or my father.

"Jon, I can't stop trembling." I stammered into the phone. "I'm shaking all over. I can't stop. My body is jackhammering, and it won't stop!"

Jon is a paramedic and a flight paramedic, which means he flies on helicopters and treats extreme trauma victims. Jon once received the award of "International Flight Medic of the Year." Think about that for a moment. He was considered the best flight medic–internationally! What an amazing accomplishment. He was also a Lieutenant in the Gloucester City Fire Department as a full-time career firefighter at the time. Most importantly, besides being one of my closest friends, he was also a former police officer who had shot and killed a suicidal male while in the line of duty, and while he was working in Brooklawn. Just as I had now done.

Jon had called me right away when he found out about my shooting. His fatal shooting occurred almost ten years before mine, and I had been assigned to the team to help investigate his fatal encounter. Jon's shooting was what we call in the police world "a clean shoot." Meaning, that there were no factors that called for any further investigation beyond what was required, or anything that would be considered as questionable. Jon had followed all policies, procedures, rules, and regulations during his shooting. He was a true professional. Jon's fatal shooting is something of legend. He shot his subject from just over forty-six feet away in the pitch dark, while standing on top of a railroad crossing, and just as the subject drew and pointed a pistol (later found to be a plastic toy pistol) at Jon and another officer. He struck the subject in the upper right side of his chest, a fatal wound. Sadly, the subject had a long history of drug and alcohol abuse, and when he left the house that night he had told his family that "he was going to get a cop to kill him." Well, unfortunately he did.

Shortly after his fatal shooting, Jon left police work. Since he was only working as a police officer part-time. He continued his career with the Fire Department and the Medics, and at this moment he was the one person who understood what I was going through.

"Dude, relax." Jon said, as he tried to calm me down. "It's the adrenaline leaving your body. You're not having a stroke or heart attack. You're having a panic attack because of the adrenaline." He eased two of my biggest fears at that moment.

Jon continued. "The adrenaline has to get out of your system. Otherwise, it will wear your body down from keeping you so jacked up all the time."

I was in the midst of my first-ever panic attack. I couldn't recall ever having had a panic attack before, so this was uncharted territory for me. I stayed on the phone with Jon until everything subsided. He helped me with slowing my breathing and getting myself under control. Once I was calm, and I had hung up with Jon, I tried to clean myself up. I was completely soaked in sweat—absolutely drenched. I made it back to the stands just as the game had begun. My dad was focused on the game, so without him ever looking over at me he asked, "Are you okay?"

"Yeah, I'm good." I replied. "I just had to take a phone call." I lied.

During the game I continued to shake and shiver. Not because I was having another panic attack. It was because my clothes were so soaked with sweat and the ice rink was freezing!

* * *

I received a call later on that afternoon from my Chief. "You're coming back to work on Monday, right?" He asked.

Before I delve into the whole thing, let me just tell you up front that my Chief was a great guy. He was a good cop and a great guy to work for, because he didn't break your balls (except about your lack of tickets). He was never looking to jam anyone up, even when he could have very easily done so. As a matter of fact, there were times he *should have* handed out punishment to officers, myself included. But he was "old school" in the fact that he chose to just dig into your ass about whatever it was you screwed up, rather than "put you on paper," and charge you. These were all plusses to have in a boss. Especially in the deceitful world of policing. Where your friends can become your assassins rather quickly.

Still, the one thing I think the Chief lacked overall was proper personnel management skills. In this case, calling me up on a Saturday, and just two days after I had shot and killed someone to ask me if I was coming back to work on Monday—well, he might as well have been asking me if I was planning on taking a trip to the moon! The idea of being back in uniform and back in a police car seemed like such a foreign concept to me at that moment. As I said, my Chief was an old school cop. He believed the best way to get through this was to "get back on the horse," and get back to work. He wasn't necessarily wrong. Part of me wanted to do exactly that. I wanted to get back to work and get back to normal. I wanted to put this whole thing behind me. Yet, when the Chief hit me with the idea of coming to work just three days after my having killed someone I couldn't envision myself doing it. Not yet, anyway. I deflected, and I told the Chief that I wanted some time off to get my head together.

"Fine. But I'll call you on Monday." The Chief replied.

I spent the rest of the weekend wrestling with my thoughts. I was feeling different somehow. I was trying to chalk it up to the suddenness of everything. That I was still in a bit of shock, and simply feeling overwhelmed.

Still, there was something else. I was starting to feel like something deeper inside of me was now missing. Like I had lost something. It felt like a piece of me had disappeared, but I couldn't put my finger on what *it* was. Some of my cop buddies told me I should take some time off. Others were telling me to get right back at it.

"Chad. It was a good shoot." They'd say. "You should get right back to work."

Others would say, "Brother. Take some time off and come back when you're ready."

I was feeling conflicted to put it mildly. On Monday, my Chief called with some news that I didn't want to hear.

"Hey Chad. Before you can be cleared to come back they [the governing body and the municipal solicitor for the town] want you to go see someone for a fitness-for-duty exam. Also, I have to call the worker's compensation insurer (worker's comp) for the town and let them know you're out, and that you need to go for an exam. We have to start a claim, according to the solicitor."

This was not good news. When an officer is sent for a fitness-for-duty exam it's not as clear-cut as it may sound. You can literally be gambling with your career, depending upon whom the examiner is. Allow me to explain.

If an officer submits to a fitness-for-duty exam there are basically three possible outcomes. The first is, the officer can pass the test and is likely going right back to work. They will continue their career without any interruptions. The next, the examiner may feel the officer needs some counseling, and will hold them out of work for a while. The examiner has not found the officer "unfit for duty," and with some treatment that officer will likely be able to return to work as well. The final, and most stress-inducing outcome is if the officer fails the exam. This can lead to a variety of issues.

Initially, the officer will not be permitted to come back to work until they pass the exam. *If* they can pass the exam. Therefore, the officer will most likely need to seek a second opinion. Particularly, if the examiner who failed them does not think they can be rehabilitated enough to return to the job. By going for a second opinion, you are now asking one professional to go against the opinion of another professional regarding the fitness of the officer to perform their duties—and to carry a weapon. Both professionals probably interviewed the officer for a total of maybe an hour or so. Now, one professional is being asked to attest as to whether the officer is psychologically stable enough to carry a weapon. Versus the opinion of the other examiner, who has already said the officer is not. See the problem? The officer must hope their employer decides to go with the opinion of the second specialist—the one who cleared them, if that's the case. If not, they may be sent for a third opinion. If that practitioner sides with the one who failed them, then the officer will most likely need to fight the diagnoses, or be involuntarily retired. There is also a host of additional scenarios and issues that can arise. Such as, appeals and other variants too numerous to list. But you get the picture. Any way you slice it, a fitness-for-duty exam is a stressful activity.

"Chief, who does worker's comp want me to go see?" I asked, when the Chief called me back a few days later.

The name the Chief gave me did not put me at ease whatsoever. This psychologist had a reputation for finding officers unfit for duty. This happened to quite a few of the Camden officers I worked with who were sent to this particular specialist for examination. She always seemed to fail them.

"Chief, I don't want to see that doctor." I protested. "I want to see someone else."

This was the first time I ever had to be examined by someone regarding my fitness-for-duty, which I wasn't comfortable doing. Not many cops would be. This whole exercise forced me (too quickly) to come to terms with the fact that I wasn't ready to come back. By the township deciding they wanted a fitness-for-duty exam before clearing me to return to work, they were forcing me to make possible career-altering decisions that I wasn't prepared to make. If they were going to insist I see someone, then I wanted to pick the specialist. I wanted to be examined by a practitioner I heard had treated some of the Camden officers successfully. Furthermore, she had a reputation as being "pro-cop," and I didn't want to have to worry about the practitioner having any personal animosity toward cops, which could affect their conclusion.

It seems that some of these psychologists or psychiatrists, especially when contracted by the worker's comp insurers, tend to lean toward how the insurer wants things done. Additionally, it often appears these psychologists don't really fall into the camp of being *cop supporters*, and I didn't want the "who's paying the bill" bias (or any other bias) to come into influence.

"I want to go see Stephanie (Steph) Samuels of the Counseling and Critical Incident Debriefing Center." I told the Chief.

"Alright." He said. "I will tell the township and worker's comp that's who you're going to see."

I called Steph's office and made an appointment for the following Thursday. However, on Tuesday of that week I received a call from the worker's comp insurer for Brooklawn. I know this is going to sound harsh, but the woman I spoke with who gathered the information about my injury was, to put it simply, a cold-hearted bitch!

"Officer Holland. This is [so-and-so] from the Borough of Brooklawn's worker's compensation insurer. I would like to get some information about the injury you suffered on April twenty-sixth, two-thousand twelve."

"Sure, okay." I replied.

"Can you tell me briefly what happened?"

I went on to explain the nature of the call, and some of the other details. When I got to the part about it being a fatal encounter, that's where I became disgusted by her response.

"And after being warned several times to drop the knife and his refusing to do so, I was forced to fire my weapon twice, and the subject was killed." I said.

In what I can only describe as a bit of a "so what's your problem" tone, this was her response: "So, basically what you're telling me is, you had to shoot a guy in the line of duty, and he died, and you're upset now, and that's it. Is that correct?"

I was dumbfounded. Speechless, in fact. I am not ignorant to the fact that I was hypersensitive at the time to anyone's remarks, or even their tone of voice, when speaking to me or questioning me about the incident. Particularly, since it was all so new. You may be thinking I was simply taking her comments the wrong way, and that I was being overly sensitive, or overly dramatic. All I can do is ask you to trust me when I tell you she seemed like a typical heartless bureaucrat. She had a report to take, and the fact that I was "upset" because I had to "shoot a guy in the line of duty" and "he died" didn't seem of any consequence to her. As a matter of fact, she sounded almost skeptical that I was having any issues at all. It was as if she couldn't comprehend why a police officer would suffer an injury from such a thing. It would've been better if she just came right out and said, "Hey, you're a cop! Isn't shooting people part of your job?"

[Note: In case you were wondering why I am calling it an "injury," that's because whether or not an injury is physical or psychological in nature is of no significance to worker's comp. They are both classified as an injury by worker's comp.]

She continued. "And I understand you are requesting to see someone specific." The intake person said, but with an air of dismissiveness in her voice.

I couldn't take it anymore.

"Excuse me. But with all due respect," I began, "it seems to me you couldn't give a goddamn that I just had to kill someone." I was beginning to tremble.

"Officer Holland." She said in that still inflexible tone. "I am just trying to get your claim started. I just need to take down what you say happened." Her voice now in full and unfeeling pencil-pusher pitch. "I need to get you set up to see someone and tested for fitness-for-duty as soon as possible, so you can get back to work."

"But, do you think you could show some fucking empathy, for Christ's Sake!" I snapped.

"Officer Holland, do not curse at me again or I will end the call. And you will be marked as noncompliant." She stated, without a noticeable change in her tone of voice.

I could feel immense anger brewing inside of me. I was getting ready to blow!

"Let's just get this over with." I growled. And we finished the call.

One thing I learned during this call—whomever conducts your fitness-for-duty exam cannot treat you. It's a conflict. It's something that must be kept in mind when choosing a practitioner.

\* \* \*

"Worker's comp is a bunch of fucking heartless asshole bureaucrats!" I yelled at Roger my attorney during our first meeting, which occurred a few days after the shooting.

The PBA had sent me to an attorney within our legal defense protection plan. This was routine, and in order to prepare me for my forthcoming interview with the Camden County Prosecutor's Office investigator. Whenever an officer is involved in an incident, especially a deadly force incident, there are many legal factors are at play. Because of these legalities, the officer (or officers) involved need to be provided with legal protection. The responsibility of this protection usually falls onto one, or possibly two, entities. The municipality the officer works for is usually the first responsible party. The next would be the union that represents the officer (if they have a union). Unless the event appears to be a blatant act of criminality on the part of the officer, or some other obviously heinous act, the municipality will primarily bear the burden of providing and paying for the officer's legal counsel. Such as in my case.

The Camden County Prosecutor's Office is the lead law enforcement agency in Camden County, and acts under the directives of the State of New Jersey Office of the Attorneys General. They are charged with investigating all officer-involved shootings within the county, and would be directly responsible for investigating my fatal encounter, since Brooklawn and Bellmawr are located within Camden County. Because I was medicated right after the incident, I could not be interviewed by the investigator that evening. My statement would have been inadmissible due to my being under the influence of medication. I had gotten word while I was still in the hospital during the night of the shooting, that the preliminary investigation and initial witness statements were revealing that everything I did "to look completely clean and justified." I remember when one of the officers told me that. I was kind of surprised by that statement in the first place. In my mind, it was *obvious* that it was a clean shooting. Since I felt I had done everything humanly possible to *not* have to shoot Mark.

Nevertheless, the Prosecutor's Office investigator would be contacting my attorney to set up the interview in the coming days. This is what brought me to Roger's office, as we now had to prepare for the pending interview. Roger had asked me how I was doing as soon as I sat down. That is when I went off about the worker's comp bureaucrats being a bunch of heartless assholes. Roger saw I was really upset. After I got that off my chest and calmed down, he asked me to take him through the whole incident-start to finish. Before I even said a word, my heart began pounding so hard it felt like it was going to burst inside of my chest!

While I recounted the events of that evening, I was up and down in my chair and all over the room. I couldn't hold still. I would stand up and reenact different parts of the incident, and while doing so, I could feel myself getting to the edge of hysteria at times. As I relived the moment. I could see extreme concern in Roger's face as I was telling him the story. By the time I was done I was completely exhausted, and sweating profusely. Roger looked pretty worn out himself.

"Chad. I have got to tell you." He began. "I have had a lot of officers tell me a lot of stories about a lot of things over my thirty years of doing this. And I could see how it affected them right away. But *this!*"

He paused and took a long sip from a bottle of water. I saw that his hands were shaking.

"Jesus Christ, Chad." He continued. "I felt like I was in the goddamn room with you! I'm scared to death, my heart is pounding, I'm shaking like a leaf, and I wasn't even there!"

We set the interview with the Prosecutor's Office investigator for the following week. In order to give me a few days to prepare myself to recount the incident once again. The reciting of the event was already beginning to take a toll on me mentally. In the meantime, I had my first appointment with Steph.

Before I get into the details of our first session, I want to talk about Steph herself. You will never meet a bigger champion for the law enforcement and the military communities than Steph. I could literally spend chapters discussing all of her accomplishments and accolades she has rightfully earned. As well as, the many things she has fought for in the interest of law enforcement officers and our Veterans. One of Steph's passions has been the expansion of rights and resources for the treatment of mental health issues for law enforcement and the military. She has gotten legislation passed in New Jersey for this very topic. Which, if you are at all familiar with New Jersey politics, is not an easy task by any means. She has traveled all over the country, and to Capitol Hill in Washington, D.C. to give speeches and testimony advocating for mental health treatment for first responders and Vets.

Steph has personally been involved in the mental health treatment of those who responded to the fall of the Twin Towers during the 9/11 attacks, as well as the Boston Marathon Bombing. She has spent countless hours treating individuals *for free* in her practice, because they either couldn't afford to pay out of pocket, or their worker's comp (or personal insurance) wouldn't pay. I know this to be true, since I am one of those people. Steph is also the founder of COPLINE. A peer-to-peer crisis intervention hotline for law enforcement officers. COPLINE is staffed 24/7/365 by retired law enforcement officers who volunteer their time. She funds the maintenance and training of COPLINE out of her own pocket, along with any donations COPLINE receives. Above all, and first and foremost, Steph is a lifesaver! Through her personal practice and through COPLINE, this woman has saved more lives than you or I could ever count. And she continues to do so today. I am proud and honored to say I am a COPLINE volunteer. I have Steph to thank for that. She is by far one of the humblest human beings I have ever had the privilege to meet and befriend. And I am happy to say that she absolutely helped to save my life!

The first time I went to meet Steph in her office I was a nervous wreck. Worker's comp informed me that someone else was probably going to have to do my fitness-for-duty exam, but I decided that I wanted to go and speak with Steph anyway. I began to slowly come to the realization that I was not feeling like myself. Nor, was I bouncing back as quickly as I assumed I would. I thought it prudent to at least meet with someone before my fitness-for-duty exam. I was so anxious for my appointment with Steph that I asked a former Camden Police officer, and dear friend of mine (who had also treated with Stephanie before he retired), to take me to her office. I asked him to drive me so I wouldn't be able to change my mind, or be able to back out.

When I first met Steph, I knew within the first five minutes of speaking with her that she was the one I wanted my treatment to be with; if I was going to go for treatment at all. If I was going to start dealing with my fear and apprehension, which were already growing by the day, I would need to be comfortable with the practitioner. When I saw how Steph greeted my friend and her former patient, treating him like he was an old friend and not just a former client, I knew she was someone who truly cared about people.

I sat down on the couch in her office, with Steph facing me while she was seated in a large back chair. Her office is warm and comforting, decorated with law enforcement and military mementos, along with The Wizard of Oz characters. It is not the cold-sterile and stuffy type of office that you often encounter with practitioners in this field.

"Tell me what brings you to see me?" She began.

I proceeded through the whole incident, and at the end, I cried. For the first time since the whole thing had transpired, I cried my eyes out. This was the first time I felt as though I didn't have to hold back, and I let it all go. The emotions had been building up inside of me for days now. But, I couldn't cry in my Attorney's office when I told him. And I didn't want to cry in front of my wife when I recounted the event for her; albeit in very limited detail, for fear of upsetting her even more.

"That, my friend, was an extremely fucked up thing you just went through." Steph said, after I finished. Steph is known for her surly language, but in a good way.

"It's not normal, and it's not in our nature to spend that much time talking someone off the ledge like you did. Only for you to have to turn around and kill him to save your life and the life of your partner. It's painfully obvious you wanted to help him." She concluded.

"As a matter of fact, that's part of why you're hurting. You went to great lengths to try to not have it end the way it did. You even bonded with him when you made him laugh. And then you had to kill him. You killed him up close and personal, and in a very violent manner." Steph paused. "To have to shoot him like you did, and then to almost have to shoot him again after he stood up, and to watch him die." Steph's voice trailed off. "This was all by your hand, and this was not a normal event. The fact you are struggling and the fact you feel like you failed him is a perfectly normal reaction. You need to understand what you're feeling is normal, first and foremost. You would be a monster if this didn't bother you. I can see in your eyes that you're no monster."

I was relieved. She hit on every point as to how I was feeling. It was a huge relief to have someone who clearly understood what I was going through.

"So, what we have to do now." As she paused to think. "What we have to do now after watching you tell the story, and with all of the emotions you are feeling [I was all over her office while retelling the event, I couldn't hold still] is to make sure to not let this take over your mind. He (Mark) shattered your confidence in yourself when he forced you to kill him. Now, we have to rebuild that confidence, and that takes time."

That, my friends, is the power of Steph. When it comes to police officers and how we think, how we're wired, what we fear, and what our frustrations are, Steph understands us inside and out. She knows how to talk to cops. Steph knows when to be empathetic and compassionate, or when to give you a swift kick in the ass! She knows when to call you out on your "bullshit," and when to tell you to "stop being a little bitch." Which is definitely something I needed from time to time. Above all, she is genuine and she is honest.

"So, what do we do from here?" I asked.

"First, I want to ask you if you're sure you want to treat with me?" Steph said.

I found it to be an odd question. I had driven for over an hour to come see her specifically. So I thought the answer was obvious.

"Of course!" I said. "Why did you ask me that?"

"Because Chad, I want you to know up front that this won't be easy for you." Steph cautioned. "I will help you, but I won't baby you, and I can be tough on my patients. It's only because I want them to get better. I won't hold your hand. You have got to do the hard work. I'm just a tool. I also won't clear you just so you can go back to work." She warned. "If I don't think you're ready I'll tell you so, no matter how much you beg me!"

Steph paused.

"Now, your township wants you to have a fitness-for-duty exam soon, correct?"

"Correct." I replied.

"Well, I won't be able to do the testing because I am treating you, and that would be a conflict. However, what I will do is fight for you. This event is fairly new, and I believe your worst feelings are yet to come."

She sounded a bit ominous.

"I'm telling you right now, Chad. I don't think you have fully digested this yet. I don't think you're ready for a fitness-for-duty test, and you won't be any time soon."

In so many words, Steph was telling me I hadn't yet reached my rock bottom, and that was still to come. I wasn't aware of it at the time, but deciding to treat with Steph would be the best decision I would ever make. It would literally be a life-saving decision. From this point on Steph would be a part of my life, and she still is until this day. Not so long ago, I had a bit of a mental and emotional relapse. During one of our sessions, I told Steph I was waking up every day with a storm going on in my head. I just didn't know from one day to the next if the storm was going to be just a slight drizzle, or a full-blown category five hurricane! Steph has been my anchor during these storms. She's been my lighthouse guiding me safe passage, and she has never let me lose my way. For that I am eternally grateful, and love her dearly.

A couple of days after my meeting with Steph, I had my interview with the Prosecutor's Office investigator at my Attorney Roger's office. The investigator assigned to the case was a real gentleman. He was very respectful of the fact that I was already struggling with the whole ordeal, which was barely over two weeks old.

Fortunately for me, he had a reputation as being an honest broker, a straight shooter, and someone who would investigate the incident thoroughly and fairly. Even though I had always felt I had nothing to worry about, and that I had done my job properly, when it comes to a fatal shooting you can never be too sure of the outcome. Doubts begin to creep into your mind. I was already succumbing more and more to the notion that I somehow had failed Mark. My mind was torturing me with questions about what I could have, should have, and would have done differently. I wasn't sleeping. I was having constant nightmares. Panic attacks were becoming more and more frequent. I felt like I was very quickly falling apart.

I proceeded to take the investigator through the whole incident, start to finish. What I found during this particular recounting of the event was, that I was becoming acutely aware of when I was losing control of my emotions. Yet, there was nothing I could do about it. I couldn't stop myself, and I couldn't control my reactions. After my meeting with Steph, I started to believe that I would somehow make it out of this mental hellhole that I was slowly slipping into. But, and in a very short time, the guilt I was feeling over not having been able to convince Mark to put down the knife and spare his life was becoming overwhelming for me. I allowed him to shatter my confidence, which was already starting to pull me apart in my mind and in my soul.

As I was recounting that night for the investigator, I became aware of some new feelings I was beginning to have as well. It was a feeling and a belief that I almost had not acted fast enough when the time came for me to shoot Mark. The Sergeant had been only about two feet away from Mark when I finally pulled the trigger. The more I thought about it, the more I started to question why I didn't fire more quickly. On one hand, I felt guilty for having to kill Mark. On the other, I felt as though I almost didn't do it fast enough, and I had nearly gotten the Sergeant killed. Talk about being mixed up! These new doubts and emotions began to gain a foothold in my mind. This was permitting more self-torture to creep into my head.

"I don't know why the Sarge didn't fire!" I yelled while sobbing, as I told the investigator and Roger about that night. "I almost fired too late. He could have stabbed the Sarge to death, he was that close. I almost fired too late–I know it! But why didn't the Sarge fire? Why the hell didn't the Sarge fire?! Why did I have to be the one to kill him! Why did I have to be the one to do it?!"

I was getting to the edge of losing it completely. By the time I finished retelling the story I was completely spent emotionally, physically, and psychologically. I felt as if I had a complete breakdown. To make matters worse, Roger and the investigator looked at me as if they had just witnessed the total and complete devastation of someone. Looking back, this is exactly what they did see. I was acutely aware that I was slipping psychologically, but I didn't have the first clue as to how to stop it. Normally, once you talk about an incident a few times it gets easier to retell it. You start to rationalize the "how" and "why," and you begin to deal with it more logically. Yet, it seemed that the more I relived this incident, the worse I got. My mind was creating new and more effective ways to create doubt.

Once we finished, the investigator told me that my version of what had happened was exactly what the physical evidence had shown had occurred. It also fit the time line and the narrative of what the witness statements indicated. As well as the statements of the other officers at the scene. The investigator advised us there were *others* who had come forward with some additional information. Which further confirmed Mark's intentions of suicide. I was curious about who the "others" were who had come forward, and what information they had. Especially, since it was primarily just the Sergeant and myself in the apartment. The investigator told me that he couldn't reveal their identities or the information provided due to the investigation still being ongoing. He also said that although he couldn't officially "clear me" at the moment, he was very confident the investigation was proceeding in a fair and proper manner. And that everything appeared to be unfolding as was anticipated. Then, I was informed of a little tidbit of information that I was not aware of.

"So, when you conclude your investigation, I will get a call or a letter telling me I am cleared, correct?" I asked.

"Well Chad, here's the deal." The investigator began. "Per the AG's [AG-New Jersey Attorneys General] guidelines you are *never* truly cleared. What happens is, when the Camden County Prosecutor's office concludes their investigation we will send our findings up to the AG's office. We inform them [the AG's Office] of whether we believe there are grounds to pursue criminal charges, or if there's no further action to be taken based upon the evidence and conclusions from our investigation." He paused. "Now, they [the AG's office] can take our recommendation, which they usually do, and then they hold the case. *Holding the case* means *they will never actually close it*. Technically, what you did was commit a homicide. It was a justifiable homicide, but it was a homicide, nonetheless. Therefore, if they were to close the case and they received information later on that you actually killed him [Mark] for some other reason, which would then make it a murder, they could run into legal issues trying to reopen the case, or with charging you with the murder. To avoid that, they basically keep the case open, or on hold–*forever*.'"

I was dumbfounded. Talk about a bombshell!

"Let me get this straight." I began. "Are you telling me that I will basically have an open murder file for the rest of my life with the AG's office?"

"Unfortunately, yeah. That's pretty much it." The investigator replied.

"So, I'll never truly be cleared then?" I asked.

"Well, in one sense, no, I guess not." The investigator responded, somewhat embarrassed.

"Un-fucking believable!" I said. "So this never truly goes away." I said aloud, more to myself then to the investigator, or Roger my attorney. "This will never truly ever go away!" I repeated, as I tried to comprehend this stunning revelation.

"I'm sorry, Chad." As the Investigator tried to comfort me. "Look, I know you're a good dude and a good cop. You have a great reputation. But, try not to let it bother you too much. It's really just an administrative issue, when this is all said and done."

I appreciated him trying to downplay the fact I would have an open murder file on my head for the rest of my days on this Earth. Without saying such, I could tell he felt it was bullshit as well. Still, to know I would never get confirmation I was "all clear," and this would hang over me forever—well, at the moment it was the last thing I needed to hear. The investigator wished me the best, and told us to call with any questions. He assured us he would share whatever information he could when the time was right, and he left the office. Roger then sprung something on me I wasn't prepared for at that particular moment.

# CHAPTER 20

---

# *EVERYONE WANTS ME TO LEAVE*

"It's time we get your retirement papers rolling, Chad." Roger said out of
nowhere. And just after the interview with the Prosecutor's Office investigator had concluded.

"What?" I said, completely shocked! "What are you talking about?"
I asked, dumbfounded.

"Chad. I've watched you rehash this incident twice now." Roger
began. "You have to put this incident and this career behind you as much
as you can, and move onto something else. You just shouldn't do this job
anymore." He concluded.

His words hit me like a punch in the mouth. I had about four more
years to get my twenty, and I wanted to finish my career and leave on my
own terms. It had only been about two weeks and a few days since the
shooting. I still wanted to end my career by walking out the door, and not
be kicked out. I didn't want to feel the shame of quitting.

"Roger. I don't know if I'm ready to consider retirement just yet." I
said, trying to stall.

"I just started therapy, and I want to give that a chance to work. I know I may seem quite emotional now, but I think that with time I can get better. It's only been a couple of weeks for Christ's sake!" As I was trying to convince myself as much as I was trying to convince him.

"Alright." Roger responded, sounding somewhat disappointed. "But, I just want you to be aware that technically you only have a year at the most to make it back."

"A year. Why only a year?" I asked, surprised.

"Two reasons." Roger began.

"First, worker's comp will only cover you for a year. After that, you would either have to be back on the job, or have retired. Second, if you or someone else determines that you can't return to the job, like if you're declared unfit-for-duty, it takes roughly six to nine months for you to get a date with the pension board so you can retire. If worker's comp cuts you off before you retire, you could be waiting around for months without any money coming in, and until you have your pension hearing."

This was getting to be too much for me to handle at the moment. I didn't want to try and make such important decisions in my current state of mind. I had known plenty of officers who had gone out on psychological, as well as physical disability pensions, due to various injuries on the job. However, I never fully understood what the entire process entailed. I heard it was a pain in the ass. I was also aware there were different percentages that the pension board could award to the officer, based upon differing factors.

There is a 40% *ordinary disability* pension, which means that the officer would get 40% of their final salary as their pension figure. Which is fully taxable. Or, if the board found that the officer was *fully disabled*, they could award a disability pension equal to 66.66% of the officer's final salary. Which is an income tax-free pension.

In the first responder world, being awarded the latter type of pension was known to have gotten *The Golden Ticket*. It was looked upon as the officer hitting the jackpot. However, and depending upon the officer's reputation and the type of injury they suffered, some people considered it to be the equivalent of ripping off the system.

[Note: I am referring to the New Jersey Police and Fire Pension System [PFRS] whenever I refer to matters pension related in this writing.]

"Chad. If you do decide you want to retire, then there is a process we have to go through." Roger continued. "But first, I will need a two-thousand dollar retainer."

I was instantly turned off. At that moment, I suspected Roger didn't really want to help me deal with my problems, and that he just wanted to see me pension out. I began to get the feeling that Roger simply wished to secure some additional fees outside of what the PBA's Legal Defense Fund contract was paying him. I decided that I was going to get a new attorney, if I ever decided to retire.

I left Roger's office more confused and conflicted than ever. Trying to deal with taking someone's life just weeks ago, along with trying to handle worker's comp, the investigation, starting treatment, and the department's constant questions about my status, well, let's just say the stress was getting to me quickly. The following Monday, I received a phone call from my Chief.

"So, I heard you went to see Steph the psychologist, and that you gave your statement to the Prosecutor's Office the other day." My Chief said, in a cheery voice.

"Yeah, Chief, I did." I replied. Knowing something more was about to come of this conversation.

"Alright then. Once you pass your fitness-for-duty test you'll be ready to come back to work." The Chief replied, in a very matter-of-fact tone.

Looking to stall, I said, "Chief, I just started with Steph. Can you just give me some time to work through this stuff, please?" I was almost begging him.

"Chad." He began, with a new seriousness in his tone. "I want to ask you something."

I knew what was coming. Brooklawn is a small department. At the time of my shooting, we had only seven full-time officers. So, whenever even just one officer is out of the lineup for an extended period of time it plays hell with the scheduling for the entire department. I knew the Chief's "ask" was coming, and I braced for it.

"I just want to know if you even plan on coming back. Because if you don't, you know it takes at least a year to get a new officer on board. So, we need to get moving on it if you're leaving. Just tell me the truth!" The Chief said. While almost pleading for an answer.

Then he hit me with some additional upsetting news.

"By the way. The worker's comp insurer is already telling us that they're not going to pay for you to see Steph. You're going to have to see someone else that they approve of if you are going for treatment."

I was getting pissed!

"Chad, I have to ask." The Chief began again. "Wouldn't it just be easier for you to come back to work and deal with this stuff while you're back working?"

Now, I was getting really angry. The Chief was talking about this like I had a fucking shoulder injury, or something that just needed some physical therapy. He was absolutely not getting it! But, I tried to keep my cool.

"Chief." I began, as I tried to keep myself composed. "It's barely been over three weeks since I killed this guy." I was hoping the mentioning of my killing someone would snap him back into the weight of the situation. "And now you're asking me to determine my entire future. You're asking me to give you an answer on my entire career, after only a couple of weeks! Retirement isn't something that I have even seriously considered. At this point, I'm still trying to process all this shit. As far as worker's comp, I'm seeing Steph! I don't give a damn what they say. If you guys [Brooklawn] tell them that I want to see Steph, and you guys are permitting me to see Steph, well that should be enough. For Christ's sake, the body is barely fucking cold and I'm getting all of this shit thrown at me!" I was starting to lose my temper, despite my best efforts not too. "Can't everyone just back the fuck off for a while?"

"Look! I'm not trying to break your balls." The Chief said, a bit annoyed.

"It's just you know how hard it is working here with a cop missing. And if you're planning on leaving, the sooner we know, the better."

I don't want this to sound like I'm bashing my Chief, and believe it or not his heart was in the right place. Still, this conversation serves as a prime example of how we are all *just spokes in a wheel*. When one spoke gets broken they just want to replace it as soon as possible. So everyone else's life can get back to normal. It's like this in corporate America, and it's like this in the public safety sector as well.

We ended the conversation with my promising to think it over and to let the Chief know as soon as possible if I planned on retiring, or not. I felt like I was being pushed out the door. Then again, that was mostly my fault. If you recall in the earlier chapters, I had explained how I had become an arrogant prick, and how I was alienating some of the officers I worked with. The Chief and others had regrets about bringing me back by this point, and they saw this as a way of getting rid of me, without *them* actually getting rid of me. In many ways, I couldn't blame them. To this day, I look back on this period of my career with embarrassment. I had become the jerkoff cop that I never wanted to work with. The cocky, arrogant, burned-out-know-it-all. Even after the encounter with the woman I described earlier, the one who got me to "wake up" and caused me to start treating those around me better, the damage had already been done. They wanted me gone.

\* \* \*

During my next session with Steph, I told her how I was starting to feel pressured by the department to give them an answer about my future. Steph was furious!

"Let me get this straight." She began. "Your Chief is asking you already if you're going to retire?! What the fuck is wrong with these people!" She exclaimed. "The fucking body isn't even cold yet, but they want you to make a permanent decision about your career! Is there some fucking major emergency that they are having in Brooklawn that they can't give you some time to get your head clear, and get your shit together?!" Steph was pissed! "Just to let you know, I am going to be calling your Chief and having a heart to heart with him."

"Fine with me." I replied.

Not that I felt like I could have changed her mind anyway. Nor, did I really care too. If there had been any doubt about Steph's sincerity or her intentions to care for me (which there never were), it vanished right then and there. She was beside herself with anger. Steph and I then discussed the issues with worker's comp. They were starting to apply pressure on me with the constant phone calls, relentless requests for updates about my status and my treatment plan, and other mind-numbing inquiries. They made it clear they weren't going to pay for me to see Steph, and that I was going to need to start treating with their doctor. However, I was in limbo at the moment, because the Mayor was actually going to bat for me, and she was trying to get worker's comp to pay for me to treat with Steph.

"Chad, let me just tell you, worker's comp is not your friend." Steph began. "They are going to harass you and bust your balls until you either go back to work or pension out. Let me ask you something, and this is for me to better understand how to go about treating you." Steph paused, as she collected her thoughts. "I get two types of cops in here; those who want to get better and get back to work, and those who want to get better, but want to get the fuck out of the job. I'm not asking you for an answer right this minute. You've got enough shit on your plate right now. But, and at some point, you will need to tell me what you want to do. Because, if we decide together that you can't make it back after we've gone through your treatment for a while, then we'll need to move forward with getting you out in one piece—and without you losing any money in the process."

Her words really hit home. Did I really want to go back to the job? Did I want to get better and get back at it? Or, did I just want to get better so I could move on and leave police work behind–forever? I had been avoiding thinking about these questions, but each day seemed to bring more challenges, along with fewer answers.

\* \* \*

"Chad!" The call with the Chief began. "I spoke with your doctor Stephanie, yesterday."

"Yeah Chief. What did you guys talk about?" I asked, as though I didn't know what was coming.

"Let me tell you something." The Chief said, as his voice started to grow with anger. "She is a fucking bitch!" He hissed. "A disrespectful bitch!"

"Chief, why would you say that?"

"Because, she ripped into me for asking you when you're coming back to work! Chad, you know I care about you, but we're such a small department, and I just need to know if you plan on coming back or not so we can move forward." He paused, as he gathered himself.

"After all, this is my department. And I think I have a right to know if someone plans to quit!"

It had been just over three weeks since the incident and the conversations were already becoming more hostile and more difficult for me to deal with.

"Chief, that's part of the problem." As I tried to reason with him. "I'm trying to come back." I was trying to convince myself as much as I was trying to convince him.

"I want to come back. I want to get better. I think that is why she was so pissed when I told her what you said, and that is why she—" He cut me off.

"Why did you tell her what I said anyway?" The Chief questioned. "That's between us. She doesn't run this place!"

"Chief, Steph and I talk about everything. Part of my stress is trying to get well and get back to work. So, when people keep asking me when I'm coming back, or worse yet, when I'm retiring just a few weeks after this happening." I paused, "Well, Chief, it just weighs on me that much more. I don't know what else to do. I'm just trying to get myself well." I concluded.

"Chad, can I say something?" The Chief requested, in a lower tone of voice.

"I think you want to leave and you're just stalling. I know you haven't really been happy here since you got back, and I know some of the guys aren't happy with you either. If you want to leave that's fine. We'll help you any way we can. I just need an answer—and soon."

There was my answer. I felt that after this conversation, and no matter how much I progressed, I wasn't welcomed back anyway. However, I am a stubborn motherfucker at times. This conversation just ignited my fire to get back faster. Since I didn't want them to dictate when I could leave, or feel as though they successfully pushed me out.

The following months would be some of the most challenging of my life. The longer I was away from the job, the less confident I became that I could go back to doing it. My life became a constant battle of dealing with the worker's comp people, and going to see doctors that they insisted I visit. After about a month and a half of seeing Steph, the worker's comp insurer dropped a bombshell on me. They informed me they had come to a final decision, and that they would not be covering any of the costs of my treatments with Steph, at all. Period. End of story. Even the visits I had with Steph prior to their final decision, and while under appeal, would not be paid for.

Their decision was based on the fact that Steph was not on their *preferred provider list*. Additionally, they tried to say she wasn't qualified as well. Their position was since she didn't have a Doctorate or PhD she wasn't qualified to treat me, as per their guidelines. In other words, even though I had an established practitioner–patient relationship with Steph that was now almost two months old, they determined she would not be paid, and I could not see her. The Mayor of Brooklawn even wrote a letter to worker's comp appealing on my behalf, insisting they permit me to continue to treat with Steph. Worker's comp told the Mayor they would not cover her fee, and that was that. I had to hire a worker's comp attorney on my own to help me navigate all the red tape. I hired Scott Tashjy of the Tashjy Law Firm on the advice of Steph.

You will never meet a more compassionate individual then Scott. He doesn't treat you like a client, he treats you like a family member, and he fights for you just as hard. When I met with Scott in his office in Wall, NJ, he gave me the bad news. Scott informed me that essentially worker's comp controls the whole treatment process. They dictate what doctors you can see and when. If you fail to comply with their directions or directives, they can drop you and refuse to pay for your treatment, or refuse to reimburse the township for your salary and benefits while you are out of work. Even though they refused to pay for Steph, she refused to cut me loose. I told you this woman was amazing!

"Steph, you can't work for free!" I protested.

"Chad." She began, "You worry about getting well. I will worry about getting paid!"

Steph told me Scott would fight with worker's comp to get her paid. In the meantime, she would continue to treat me in conjunction with whatever doctors worker's comp insisted I see. So began my odyssey of treating with both Steph and the worker's comp doctors. This may sound like sour grapes, but the worker's comp doctors were complete quacks.

I was first sent to a psychologist who was constantly late for our appointments. He insisted I be penciled in as the first appointment of day, so he could get his worker's comp patients out of the way, and be able to treat his "money" patients later on. However, he could never make it to our early morning appointments on time. One day, he showed up almost a half an hour late. So I blasted him.

"So, Officer Holland. How are things going?" He said, as he began our session.

"Doc." I began calmly. "With all due respect, who the fuck do you think you are?!"

"What?" He asked, as he was completely taken off guard. "What did you just say to me?"

"You, sir, are one of the most inconsiderate and ignorant sono-fabitches I have ever met!" To say he was a bit taken aback would be an understatement.

"Excuse me?" He replied, quite startled. "I-I-I don't understand?"

"If I was half an hour late for this appointment, and late for all of our other appointments like you are, you would be on the phone telling worker's comp I was being 'noncompliant.' And you would be getting me cut off in a New York fucking minute!" I said through gritted teeth.

I won't lie. This guy was such an asshole that I was hoping he would fire me as a patient, and tell worker's comp to send me to someone else.

"Well, Officer Holland." He began, very contritely. "My apologies. I will admit, I do have some trouble getting here by 9 am sometimes. So, we'll just schedule you for later in the day. If that is agreeable with you?"

"Fine." I said. Disappointed that he didn't recommend I go elsewhere for treatment.

The worker's comp insurer decided after consulting with this psychologist, that I should see a psychiatrist in order to begin treatment with prescribed medication. At this point, I am about four months out from the date of the shooting, and I feel as though I am drifting further down the path of no return. Despite Steph's and my best efforts, I was getting worse. I wasn't sleeping. I was having panic attacks about three to four times per week. My flashbacks and nightmares were becoming more vivid and more bizarre. Cigarette smoke had become an easy mental trigger for me. The second I caught a whiff of cigarette smoke, I was instantly transported back into the apartment. I was struggling with rationalization of the whole incident. My mind and my thoughts were getting away from me, and my moods and emotions were all over the place. Heavy bouts of depression were setting in. I was starting to feel paranoid. When I was out in public, I swore people were looking at me differently, like they knew what I had done. I couldn't get past the feelings of failure. I felt like I had failed Mark, and I felt like I nearly failed the Sergeant, because I had convinced myself I had almost fired too late.

No matter how much we worked on my understanding that these emotions and feelings were irrational, and that Mark had forced my hand, and that the Sergeant was fine, I still couldn't stop my thoughts from torturing me. It was affecting my family and my home life, since it was wearing on my wife. She didn't know how to help me, or what to do. I could feel her pulling away from me. We were becoming distant, as she was trying to not get distracted from beginning her new career as a nurse. At the time of the shooting, I was taking courses at Drexel University and was maintaining a perfect 4.0 GPA, as I mentioned before. But, and after the shooting, my concentration went to hell and I had to drop out. Which broke my heart. It likely meant that my future as a PA was over before it even began. Everything in my life seemed to be falling apart all at once.

The worker's comp psychologist felt I needed medication to get me over the hump and hasten my healing. I was sent to a psychiatrist—to get me on psychotropic medications. Oh, what a fun ride this would become!

# CHAPTER 21

# *POPPING PILLS*

Dr. Lass seemed like a bit of an odd fellow. He dressed very eccentrically, and he appeared as someone who may have been sampling some of his prescriptions. If you get what I am saying.

"So, Officer Holland. Tell me why you're here." Dr. Lass began.

As I was explaining to him the events that led me to his office, I had a panic attack right in front of him. This one arrived without warning, which scared the hell out of me. Despite being a bit strange, Dr. Lass seemed compassionate. He helped me to get through the attack, and then prescribed me two different medications to get me started. I made an appointment to return in a week, and I left his office with the first of the many prescriptions he would write me over time.

In the interim, worker's comp had gone ahead and scheduled me for the fitness-for-duty exam. This was their way of expediting things. If I failed the fitness-for-duty exam they could have my agency push to force me into involuntary retirement. If my agency didn't wish to take that route, worker's comp could cut off their payments to the township, and force them to pay me out of pocket. That is their game. They get a doctor to say you're either okay or you're not. Either way, they can stop paying the township and bring the claim to a resolution. If you go back on the job to soon and wrongfully injure someone, or have some other type of meltdown, well, *the doctor* said you were okay, not us [worker's comp]. It wasn't our [worker's comp] fault. That is how they play the game. It's all about the money.

I was sent to a worker's comp doctor in Bala Cynwyd, Pennsylvania for the fitness-for-duty exam. I have to admit, the doctor was very compassionate. Not at all the persecutor I expected him to be.

The fitness-for-duty exam started off with a multiple choice test, which was conducted on a computer. While getting ready to sit with the doctor and review the results of the test, along with rehashing the events of the shooting, I had a panic attack—a major one—in the hallway right outside of his office. I was having trouble breathing, and I began to cry uncontrollably. I think with everything I had going on, and with the fact I was now on medication, the stress of the fitness-for-duty exam was just too much for me to handle. After several minutes, I was able to calm down. The doctor asked if we could review everything, if I was up to it. I acknowledged that we could.

The doctor began. "Officer Holland. I have read the reports, and quite frankly, you have been through a horrific event. I cannot even imagine what it was like for you to show someone the compassion that you showed this man, and then to have to turn around and take his life."

He paused, as he shook his head as if in disbelief. "It is obvious to me at this moment that you are struggling. You're clearly under duress, and there is no way you should be doing anything other than focusing on improving your mental health. At this point, it is clear to me that you are not fit-for-duty."

My heart sank. I was terrified of what would happen next. How would I take care of my family? How would I pay my bills? What the hell would I do with my life? What would I do for a living? These questions started to flood my mind all at once. However, and before I could begin to object to his findings or express my concerns, the doctor put my mind at ease.

"Officer Holland. I'm not going to inform worker's comp that you cannot continue as an officer at this time. If I were to do so, they will force you to make a decision you're not prepared to make. I can see by the doctor's reports that you are truly trying to get better, and I think you should be given the proper amount of time to let the therapy and the medications begin to work."

He took a moment before continuing.

"You have given sixteen years of your life to this profession. I think they [worker's comp] can at least give you some time to try and get yourself together, and before you make a final decision about your career. Would you agree with that, Officer Holland?"

"Yes doctor." I said softly. "I agree." As I began to weep. He was throwing me a lifeline, and just when I needed it the most.

"So." The doctor began. "I'm going to recommend to worker's comp that you be permitted to continue with your treatment, and that we reevaluate you in a few months. This will do two things for you." He paused. "First, it will permit you the time you need to start to recover properly. Next, and if things are not progressing accordingly, it will permit you the additional time you may need to put in for your retirement without getting cut off financially by either worker's comp or your employer. Does that make sense to you, Officer Holland?"

I couldn't believe it! Here was a doctor willing to help me get around worker's comp's bullshit, and give me time to get my act together. I tearfully thanked the doctor for his help, and I left the office. I would later learn that when Steph had found out what doctor I was being sent to for the fitness-for-duty exam, she had made a call. Steph and the doctor had a professional relationship, as well as a mutual understanding. This understanding was the result of a prior situation in which the doctor had severely screwed up in the diagnosis of a mutual patient he and Steph shared.

This doctor had gone against Steph's diagnoses. The mutual patient was a police officer, who this doctor found was fit-for-duty, and who he had sent back to work before the officer had fully recovered. The officer was soon back on the street. Shortly after the officer returned to duty, he was involved in another fatal shooting that never should have occurred. This was due to the officer still being hypervigilant to danger, or *perceived danger*. The officer inadvertently fired his weapon during an encounter, killing an innocent person. This doctor swore to never again go against any diagnosis Steph ever made. Especially, after he was forced to eat a huge piece of *humble pie* in the ensuing wrongful death lawsuit that was filed by the victim's family. Steph had called him to make sure the doctor didn't forget his promise.

Worker's comp continued to send me to both the psychologist and to Dr. Lass the psychiatrist, and I was still treating with Steph on the side. I visited with the worker's comp psychologist once or twice a week, Dr. Lass once a week, and Steph two to three times a week. I was literally going to one practitioner or another on an almost daily basis. This was now my life. Around my fifth month of treatment, Steph broached the retirement subject with me again.

"Chad, here's what I want you to do." She began. "Let's put your papers in [retirement paperwork], just in case you decide to pull the plug. That way, we're not behind the eight ball trying to get you out if you decide to retire, and you're not sitting at home without any money or benefits coming in."

No matter how screwed up I was feeling—and now that I was on medication I was feeling more screwed up than ever—I didn't want to concede that my career was ending. I had been a cop since I was twenty-three years-old. I was now thirty-nine. I had no other skills. Being a cop was all I knew! What would I do? What kind of work does a mentally screwed-up thirty-nine year-old retired cop with no other job skills do in life? Officers would always joke about going to work for Home Depot when they retired.

I felt like I couldn't even do that! I had little to no knowledge of plumbing, construction, or any other home improvement aptitudes.

My plan on becoming a PA seemed like a distant memory, and from a lifetime ago. How would I ever be able to pass the rigorous courses, let alone the testing, when I couldn't even read two pages in a book without losing my focus? Besides, would they even let someone who left police work on a psych pension treat patients? How did my mind and my life go off the rails so quickly? I couldn't understand why I couldn't just *get over it* and move on. Why couldn't I just rationalize the whole thing and chalk it up to what it was—a troubled and suicidal individual who wanted someone else to end his life and his pain—and that someone ended up being me! Why was this destroying my mind? I had no answers. So, I stalled.

"Steph, can we just keep working?" I asked meekly.

"Chad." She began sympathetically, "We can do whatever you want to do. But, I just want us to cover our bases. Why don't you think about it over the weekend and let me know on Monday."

I agreed to give her my answer on Monday. On my hour-long drive home from Steph's office I replayed her words over and over in my head. Steph doesn't recommend something unless she already knows the answer. I came to the conclusion that she probably realized I was already too far gone to make it back, and she was just helping me plan my next move without my realizing it. I was staring down the barrel of no longer being a cop; the only thing I had been for almost my whole adult life. The prospect of no longer being a police officer didn't seem as appealing when it was being forced upon me, versus when I had planned to leave in a few years, and of my own accord.

"Alright Steph. What do we have to do?" I asked, as I gave Steph my answer the following Monday.

"Listen." Steph began. "I want you to understand something. If you do progress enough over the next few months to where we feel you will be okay to go back, then we can always try and pull your papers [meaning withdrawal the retirement papers]. My concern is we are already five almost six months into your treatment, and let's be frank, things haven't gone well. You are really hurting, and things are not moving in the right direction as of yet. They will—but they just haven't gone that way as of yet." She continued, "And my fear is that we'll run out of time. It takes at least six months to get a hearing before the pension board if we file your papers now. So, we can hopefully get you in under the wire, and before worker's comp cuts you off. I'm concerned that if we wait any longer to begin the process, you'll have to wait God knows how long before you have money coming in."

Stephanie paused. I could see she was deep in thought.

"I'm going to say something that you may not like, but I want to be straight with you."

I braced myself.

"I believe you're not going to be able to make it back onto the job in the short time we have left to get you well. I believe that you took a psychological blow so hard and so devastating, and it has set you back severely. You're struggling with guilt and doubt. You're struggling with negative thoughts and emotions. Your confidence is shot. And the physical manifestations of these things you aren't remotely capable of handling right now. The thought of you going back out onto the streets in a department where you have to work on the street alone, which is fucking insane to begin with—and I don't give a damn how close your back up is, you're still working alone! That fact in and of itself, makes me want to not see you go back. I think you should focus on getting out of this job and getting well. I'm sorry. I know that's not what you wanted to hear."

Steph and I sat silently, as I digested what she had just told me.

"Steph, I know you're right." As I acknowledged the obvious. "I think I've been trying to hang onto a piece of me that I lost that night. A piece that is no longer there." I paused, as I began to cry. "I've been searching for an innocence that I lost, and that I'll never get back. I lost the confidence

I had, a confidence that's now shattered. I've lost the ability to believe in myself and maintain the bulletproof mindset I need to do this job."

I paused once again, as I became really emotional. "The last thing I ever want to do, and something I couldn't live with, is if someone got hurt because of my inability to react." I stopped talking, as I was now in a full blown cry. "You're right Steph, I'm done. I just can't do this anymore. I know that now, and it hurts. As much as I hated the job sometimes, bitching about shift work, the bosses, whatever--it's killing me now to know it's over. But, it's over. It's just over. I understand that now." Tears streamed down my face.

They say the hardest part of overcoming a problem is first acknowledging you have one. The hardest part for me was acknowledging that I was not the same person anymore that entered the apartment that night. My swagger was gone. My confidence was shot. I felt shaken. I was frail and weak. I felt like a part of me had died. If you would have said to me before the incident that I would suffer like this for taking the life of someone who came at me and another officer with a knife—someone who left me no choice but to end his life—I would have told you that you were crazy! After all, I did everything I felt I could have done at the time to save him. Still, my inability to reconcile the facts with my feelings would haunt me for years to come.

The thoughts and emotions from the shooting, along with my inability to resolve them, were the basis of what was ruining me. Along with my inability to accept that I wasn't going to make it back to police work. It was time to let it all go. It was time to move on. I needed to focus on getting better. The start of my recovery would have to begin with my admitting that I was no longer the same man I was before. Nor, would I ever be that same man again. I could no longer do the things I once did. I could no longer be the officer and the protector that I once was. Once I faced this truth, and I stopped chasing the fantasy of going back to police work and recapturing my former self, only then could I truly begin my healing.

Steph walked me through the pensioning out process step-by-step. First, the pension board would cobble together all my medical records. They would compare the evaluations and the different treatments I had gone through among all the doctors I had been seeing, in order to gain some insight into my ability, or my inability, to continue to do the job. Next, I would be sent to see a doctor who worked for the state for a final evaluation. Finally, I would be scheduled for a pension hearing, where I would appear before the board and who would determine the amount of pension money I would receive every month. If I wasn't awarded the full 66% I could file an appeal. However, that is a whole other process that can take months or even years to resolve.

Steph knew a person who specialized in this entire process, and who was a former member of the board. This person knew what the board was looking for in order to make the best case for me to get the maximum amount of pension allotment. This former board member would gather all of my medical records and put together the paperwork. I felt beaten. This was the end of my career. In the meantime, I would have to continue to follow the plan of care with worker's comp.

The pressure on me to give the police department a definitive answer on my plans was growing by the day as well. It was now about six months after the date of the shooting. My fear was if I told them I was retiring, they would make a move to have it happen as quickly as possible, which could further complicate my situation. Additionally, the township had an obligation to tell worker's comp of my plans if I told them I was retiring. This could result in worker's comp dropping me completely, and before I had my pension hearing. That would leave me without any money or benefits to live. I felt like I was letting everybody down. I felt like I was disappointing everyone, because I knew how tough it was on the other cops to work with even just one cop out of the lineup. So, I felt guilty on top of everything else. Furthermore, it was getting old answering the same questions of "When are you coming back?" or "Are you coming back?" These questions came up again when I spoke with my Chief on the phone a couple of days later.

"Chief, with all due respect, I am trying to get well. I'm going for my treatments. I'm taking my medication, and I'm still going through hell. I'll be back when I'm back, and that's it."

I felt terrible that I couldn't confide in him my true feelings. But, I was also getting annoyed with the constant grilling.

"Chad, I have to ask you." The Chief began. "And I don't mean to sound like a dick. But, why are you having such a hard time? Especially, since you didn't do anything wrong. I've spoken to the Prosecutor's Office, and they said everything was cut and dry."

He continued. "What you said happened matched what the Sergeant said happened, almost identically. I just want to understand why you're having such a hard time with this. You did what you had to do, what you're trained to do. You did your job, and you're alive. He [Mark] is dead! I just don't get what you're having trouble with."

The Chief seemed unable to comprehend what I was going through. I softened a bit, since I felt that the Chief truly didn't understand what was happening to me. Hell, neither did I. But, for the first time, it seemed as though he was really trying to understand my issues.

"Chief, the truth of the matter is I don't understand it myself. I tell myself every day that I did what I had to do, and that I should be happy the Sergeant and I are okay. I try to convince myself of that all the time. But, I just don't know. I just can't get it straight in my head."

"Chad, I really think Camden fucked you up more than you thought. And this is just what pushed you over the edge." The Chief surmised.

"Well Chief, I can't say that you're wrong. I think that may have made me somewhat predisposed to how I'm feeling now. I just don't know. All I know is, that no matter how much I try to control my thoughts and emotions, I can't. I feel like I'm on an emotional roller coaster ride at all times. I feel like I have no control over myself."

SCARS OF BLUE

At this point, I was feeling mentally and physically exhausted. I had recently been put on another medication by Dr. Lass. This medication seemed to be making it more difficult for me to think clearly. It was literally physically exhausting for me to have a conversation.

"Well." The Chief concluded. "Just keep working on yourself and keep me in the loop, please."

"Sure, Chief. No problem." I said, and we hung up.

# CHAPTER 22

# BACK FROM THE DEAD

My visits with the worker's comp doctors continued without much progress. The particular psychologist I was assigned would occasionally come up with some new theory about why I was struggling, but at no time did I feel we connected on any level. I'm sure much of it was because I was putting up a bit of a mental wall whenever I was in his office. At the end of the day, I wanted to treat with Steph and Steph only. This was an exercise in futility in my opinion. To force someone to go to a practitioner whom they didn't connect with, or even respect, was a waste of everyone's time. Worker's comp was getting fed up with my lack of progress under Dr. Lass as well. So, they sent me to a different psychiatrist to be re-evaluated.

Having been a police officer for sixteen years, I had come across my fair share of drug addicts. I had heard the term "pill factories" more than once during my encounters with many of these addicts. These are places where many of these addicts began their habit, but I had never actually witnessed one in action. For someone who is addicted to legally prescribed medications, doctors who operate pill factories are like finding a gold mine. These doctors don't give a damn about healing folks. They just want to write as many prescriptions as possible, in order to get their bonuses and other goodies from the drug companies who provide the medications. That is exactly where worker's comp sent me, to a pill factory.

I sat in the waiting room and watched as addict after addict walked in and out of the office. These people were freaking zombies. They were the walking dead! This was the type of place where the opioid epidemic began, and it felt like I was sitting at ground zero. After about an hour or so, I looked up to see this skinny dark-haired woman walking in through the front door. Right behind her was a man whom she was leading by the hand. The man could have been Mark's twin brother! He was an exact replica of Mark, the man whom I had shot and killed just months before. It was as if he were back from the dead. This gentleman was just a few inches shorter and not quite as broad in the shoulders. But his face, the bushy hair, the straggly beard, and the piercing eyes, it was like I was looking at Mark reincarnated.

Needless to say, I damn near pissed myself! I started to tremble all over as my heart rate jacked up and my breathing went shallow. I couldn't sit still in my chair. Especially, since I was sitting almost directly across from the both of them. I was afraid to look up. Because every time I did I thought for sure I was going to be attacked. I had gotten up to go to the bathroom about four or five times, just so I could catch my breath and throw cold water on my face in order to keep from having a full-blown panic attack. Whenever I would cast my gaze toward him, I would see him staring right back at me. At one point, I was acting as if I was thumbing through a magazine. Every time I would look just over the top of the magazine, I could see he was staring directly at me. He had the same thousand-yard stare Mark had in his eyes just before I shot and killed him. I began to not only question my sanity, but whether this was God's way of punishing me somehow. This was way too creepy to be a coincidence.

Finally, after almost two hours of sitting in the waiting room, I was called to the back waiting area. Which was just outside of the doctor's office. As fate would have it, the skinny dark-haired girl joined me in the back waiting area. Just after I had sat down. However, Mark's look alike remained seated in the front waiting room. I could clearly see this girl was an addict. She couldn't hold still in her seat, not even for a second. She kept fidgeting with her hands, her hair, her purse, and her clothes. The woman kept licking her lips, because her mouth was so dry from all of the drugs she was taking. She would slump over in her seat like a heroin addict on "the nods." But then she'd suddenly jump up and onto her feet. The woman would sigh deeply and loudly, as she carried on a conversation with herself, aloud.

Then, she spoke to me.

"Hey, excuse me!" She said to me, in her slurred speech.

"Yeah, what's up?" I replied.

"Can I go before you please?" She pleaded. "I need to get out of here. Pleeeease!" she slurred, and as she held the word for emphasis.

I had already been here for over two hours. I was getting worried that I was going to be late picking up Jacob from the bus stop. The last thing I wanted was to wait any longer.

Very gently, I tried to break the bad news to her.

"I'm sorry. But I have to pick up my son from school. If I had nothing to do I would let you go first. But I have to get out of here too. I'm sorry."

"What-the-fuck-ever, asshole!" She snapped. And as her demeanor did a 180.

*This cannot be happening.* Not only does her man look like the guy I killed, but now his girlfriend is giving me a hard time. To make matters worse, she had yelled at me so loudly, that I thought for sure the Mark look alike was going to come charging into the waiting area and attack me. To my great relief, I was called into the doctor's office about thirty seconds later.

The doctor directed me to sit down in a chair that was about ten feet away from the front of his desk. I assumed he put the chair so far away from his desk for a couple of reasons. First of which, he probably didn't want the addicts breathing on him. Additionally, he had probably been attacked on an occasion or two from the junkies he dealt with. After not prescribing them all of the drugs they had wanted. In a very thick and heavy Middle Eastern accent, he gave me a thirty-second run down of his credentials. He attended university in Bombay, India, and he did his doctoral studies and fellowship here in the states, etc., etc.

"So, I understand you are here because you had to kill someone in the line of duty. Isn't that correct, Mr. Holland?" He said.

"Yes. Yes that's correct." I replied.

"And I understand that you have been prescribed several medications, but without any positive results. Is that correct?"

"Correct."

"Okay then. I am going to prescribe you three new medications. I want you to take these for thirty days. After thirty days, we will reevaluate. Understood?"

"Wait a second, doctor." I began. "You have spoken to me for what, two minutes. Yet, you've already determined that these are the meds I need? Three medications! How is that possible?"

"Mr. Holland." He replied. And without any noticeable change in his demeanor. "I have reviewed your medical history and the medications you are currently on. I feel as though this is the best course of treatment for you."

"Ok, whatever!" I said. I didn't want to argue. I just wanted to get the hell out of there. The whole place gave me the freaking creeps.

The doctor handed me the three prescriptions, and he told me to make a follow-up appointment with the front desk on my way out. I stopped at the reception desk, made the appointment, and started to walk out the front door. And there he was, waiting for me.

Standing next to the wall smoking a cigarette (of course he had to be smoking a cigarette, as if there weren't enough triggers already) was Mark's doppelganger. I didn't notice him at first. As I stepped out the front door I was looking down while reading my new prescriptions. So, I didn't see him. But, as I stepped outside I suddenly *felt* someone standing there, looking at me. That's when I looked up and encountered my new nemesis.

"Hey, asshole!" He began. "What the fuck did you say to my girl?"

Even his voice sounded like Mark's. He had that same cigarette-induced raspy voice.

To say I was dumbstruck would be the understatement of the decade. I wasn't immediately putting the whole situation together either. Because my mind was too busy comparing the "old Mark" to this "new" version.

"What girl? What are you talking about?" I asked confused, as I had gone blank.

I began having a flashback, and I felt like I was right back in the apartment.

"My girl." He yelled. "Don't play fucking dumb with me!" He roared. "You disrespected my girl. She asked you if she could go first, and you called her a bitch!"

*That lying little bitch*! I thought. As I snapped back into the present.

"Listen. That is not what happened." As I was trying to reason with him. "She asked me if she could go first. I told her that I had to pick up my son from school, and that I couldn't switch. That's it, dude. I didn't call her any names. I even told her I was sorry!"

I hoped my rationalizing with him would calm him down, unlike it did with Mark.

"Are you calling my girl a liar–you asshole!" He screamed at me. As he threw down his cigarette, and started to curl his fist.

Then something started to happen to me. At first, I had felt frail and weak. But after he called me an "asshole," and when he threw down his cigarette while clenching his fists––well, that was my breaking point. I had-had enough of feeling like a weak little bitch! I dropped my folder full of papers and prescriptions on the ground, as I felt the rage begin rising up inside of me.

"Listen to me, motherfucker!" I literally hissed at him. "I didn't call your girlfriend a bitch! I'm dealing with some shit right now that I don't want to deal with."

"I don't give a fuck what you're dealing with!" He yelled, and as he cut me off.

"Listen to me." I tried again. "I'm a cop. And I am dealing with some major shit right now. So, I don't have time for you or your girl's fucking bullshit!"

"I don't give a fuck that you're a cop!" He shot back.

"I'm not telling you I'm a cop for you to give a fuck that I'm a cop." I said in a low and evil voice. One that I barley recognized coming out of my mouth. I could feel my body getting ready to pounce. "I'm telling you I'm a cop because I killed a guy recently, and that's why I'm here."

This seemed to get his attention, as his face and body language changed slightly.

I continued. "It just so happens the guy I killed looked, sounded, and acted *just like you!*" A look of puzzlement was now on his face.

"So, I am telling you right fucking now. You either back the fuck off, or I swear to God, I am going to kill you too!" I then got into a fighting stance, with my hands up and my fists clenched, ready to go.

I could tell he didn't know what to make of me. At first, I was this meek and mild guy who appeared to be very scared. However, and within a matter of just a few moments, I was now in a fighting stance, my face contorted, and I was threatening to kill him. I started to take a couple of steps toward him. He had been leaning on the wall while we were speaking.

Now, he had stepped away from the wall and took about a half a step or so backwards.

"Alright-alright!" He began in a much lower and calmer tone. "I'm going to let this slide." He said, as he tried to make it appear he was still in control. "But, it's not because you're a cop. Because I don't give a fuck that you're a cop!"

"It doesn't matter that I'm a cop!" I barked. "But, you either back the fuck off, or I am going to end your life, right here, and right now, you motherfucker! Do you understand what I am telling you? Back off, or you are going to die!"

I couldn't believe what I was saying. What scared me the most was that I had zero reservations about literally beating him to death! If we had gotten physical, I think I would have killed him. I was now that far gone. He looked at me like I was some crazy person. Then, the Mark look alike turned and walked toward the parking lot.

"I'm giving you a pass this time. But next time–Not so much!" He said, as he walked away, and as he tried to save face.

I gathered up my loose papers as my hands were trembling almost uncontrollably. Then, I slowly walked to my car while I continued to watch him. Once I was inside my car I almost threw up. I began to have such a violent panic attack that I thought I was having a heart attack. The panic attack became so bad that I almost called 9-1-1. I could barely breathe. However, after some time, the attack passed. As I was sitting in my car recovering, I looked across the parking lot and there was the dark-haired little bitch who had created this nightmare for me. She was walking out with her new prescriptions in her hand, practically skipping with joy, and I became angry all over again. I am going to confess something I've never confessed to anyone before. It was at this moment that I understood why perfectly *normal* people sometimes commit murder.

I started my car and put it into drive. At this moment, I had all intentions of plowing my car into her just as she got to the door of her boyfriend's car. I envisioned the whole thing happening. After running her over, and when her boyfriend got out of the car to see the carnage of his dead girl-friend, I was going to back my car up and run him over as well. Still, one thought stopped me from following through on this course of action–I thought of my wife and kids. The thought of my family snapped me out of this morbid vision and back into reality. *You're going to be late picking up Jacob!* I suddenly realized. I immediately pushed the thoughts of revenge out of my head, and I called someone to talk too as I drove away—someone who had been though his own deadly force encounter years before.

"Jim, its Chad Holland." Jim could tell right away from my voice that something was wrong.

"Brother, you alright! What's going on?"

Jim Michaels had been a police officer in Woodbury, NJ. Which is a couple of towns away from Brooklawn. Jim had been involved in a deadly force encounter when someone he stopped on foot for investigative pur-poses, pulled a gun on him and stuck it in his stomach. He shot the suspect from a weapon retention position, and before the suspect could get a shot off. How Jim and I first met has much irony to it.

Jim's wife Jen is also a police officer. They have several children, so a night out for the family was usually going to Weber's Drive-In, the restau-rant my wife and her family owned. They would come to the restaurant to get some burgers, fries, hot dogs, shakes, and some ice cream for the kids. Somehow, my wife found out they were police officers, and she had told them I was a police officer as well. From that day on they became very friendly with my wife. After my shooting, my wife saw them at the restau-rant and told them what had occurred. Up until that time, I had heard all about Jim and Jen from my wife, but I had yet to meet them.

As fate would have it, Jim and I also had another connection. After Jim's deadly force encounter, he too was treated by Steph. My wife told them I was also treating with Steph, so Jim and I began to talk.

"Jim, I'm just leaving a doctor's office that worker's comp sent me to." I was saying between heavy breaths. "And the guy, the guy—" I stumbled.

"Chad. Slow down bud. What guy? What guy are you talking about?" He asked.

"The guy I killed." I was having a hard time catching my breath still. "The guy I killed was there at the doctor's office!" I couldn't slow my thoughts or my speech down enough to make sense. The fact that I was driving about 90 miles-per-hour to get home to meet Jacob at the bus stop on time wasn't making things any easier for me.

"Chad, I don't understand what you're saying, brother. Just slow down. What do you mean the guy you killed was at the doctor's office?" Jim said, as he tried to make sense of me.

I paused and took a deep breath. "Alright." I began, as I tried to keep it together. "There was a guy at the doctor's office that looked just like the guy I killed. I swear to you, it was his fucking twin. It was his fucking identical twin! And I almost got into a fight with him." I was becoming completely exasperated.

"Bud, where are you now?" Jim asked, as he was starting to grasp what I was saying. "I'll come to you right now! Where are you?"

"I already left. I just need someone to talk me down. Just help me calm down, please." I begged him.

On the ride to the bus stop I recounted the whole incident for him. Everything about the girlfriend, the guy, the doctor, how the place was a pill factory, everything. Jim had also had his battles with worker's comp, so he was familiar with their bullshit. He said I should call them and blast them. Jim told me to contact Scott, my attorney, and have him tell worker's comp I refuse to go there again for my safety.

"Brother." Jim began. "Have your attorney call them up and tell them if they try to send you there again you are filing a fucking lawsuit!"

"I got one better. I am going to call the AG's office [Attorneys General] and get that motherfucker shut down!" I replied.

"That's a great idea!" Jim affirmed.

I never did call the AG's office, but I called worker's comp and blasted them. Afterwards, I called Scott my worker's comp attorney and told him what had happened. He assured me I would not have to go back to that doctor. Steph called me to check on me, after Jim had called her and told her what had occurred. While all this drama was going on, I still had to keep a smile on my face and act like everything was okay when I picked up Jacob from the bus stop. I was dying inside when I saw Jacob's beautiful and sweet innocent face through the window of the big yellow school bus. But, I refused to let my kids see me crumble.

"Hi, Daddy. How was your day?" Jacob beamed, as he ran off the bus and into my arms.

I almost burst into tears right then holding him. There is nothing like the love and the innocence of a child to make you realize how lucky you are to have them, and appreciate how much you love them. I had damn near carried out the act of killing two people because of a confrontation that didn't even turn physical. It was only by the grace of God, and the thoughts of my wife and children, that kept me from doing something I would have forever regretted. Still, I was that unstable, and that was truly frightening to me. I never would have ever thought of doing something like that before. I had to get off these meds and get my head straight before it killed me. Or, before I killed someone else.

# CHAPTER 23

## *ONE LAST LIFE TO SAVE*

As the months went by, and I awaited my date with the pension board, I knew I was completely broken. There was no way I could ever return to a job that required me to maintain such a mental edge. My older son Chad told me not that long ago (when we were discussing my career as a police officer), that he once watched me as I was putting on my uniform as I was getting ready to go to work. He watched me getting dressed from behind my bedroom door. Chad told me that he saw my facial expressions change as I was putting on my uniform piece-by-piece. And he could tell by the look on my face that my mind had clearly gone elsewhere. He was exactly right. I used the ritual of putting on my uniform, and the various stages of my getting dressed, as a way of getting my mind right and ready to go to work. I was setting my *mental edge.*

My preparation went like this: First, as I put on my pants I would pray. Next, as I put on my boots I would run various scenarios of what I would do, and how I would react, if I had to chase someone on foot. Then, as I put on my vest I would think about how I would handle being shot. I would picture the scenario playing out—how I wouldn't let the bullet that struck me knock me down, or kill me. How I would stay in the fight. As I was putting on my uniform shirt, I would think about all types of various situations. I would let the different notions come into my mind, and I'd sort my way through them. They could be as diverse as car chases, gun battles, hand-to-hand fighting, fighting with edge weapons, or even running into a burning building. I would just let the ideas come and I would mentally drill through all of these fictitious events, while picturing what my response would be. Finally, as I put on my duty belt, I would double and triple check all my equipment.

*Are both sets of my handcuffs where I want them?* (One set on the front of my belt, the other on my left side just behind my left hip.)

*Is my pepper spray still full?* (I would shake it to check the volume.)

*Do I have rubber gloves in my pocket?* (Left-front pants pocket.)

*Where is my handcuff key?* (Fastened behind my handcuff case on the front of my belt.)

*Is my portable radio fully charged and in a good spot?* (Radio on my left hip, mic clipped at the center of my chest.)

*Do I have my leather gloves?* (Right-rear pocket.)

*Is my gun secured in my holster?* (Right-hand side of my belt.)

*Is the path to my holster clear of anything that would block me from drawing quickly?*

*Is my weapon "hot" and ready to go?* (Check.)

*Is the fifteen-round mag full, with one in the chamber?* (Check.)

*Are my extra magazines fully loaded?* (Ammo pouch on the front left side of my belt, two magazines fully loaded to their fifteen-round capacity.)

*Where is my knife?* (On the opposite side of my body from my gun.)

There were a couple of other items (notepad, pens, etc.) that I would make sure I had as well. Once I was fully dressed, I would let myself "come down" from having my game face on until I actually hit the street. When I tried to picture myself preparing like this now, I couldn't. That person–Chad the Cop, seemed like someone from long ago, and he had largely faded from my mind. However, I still needed to know for sure.

In the beginning of December 2012, about eight months after the shooting, and just after my 40<sup>th</sup> birthday, I tried putting on my uniform and going through this ritual once again. I needed to make sure that I was *truly* done. I turned on my radio to listen to the calls going out as I was getting dressed, and as I tried to get into my work mindset once again. Suzanne and Jacob were at Suzanne's parent's house visiting, and Chad was at his mom's house. So, I decided I would get dressed in full uniform (minus my duty weapon, but carrying my off-duty gun), and drive to the Brooklawn police station. Once there, I would sit in the police station parking lot in one of our patrol cars and just listen to the radio. There would, of course, only be one officer on duty at the time. So, my plan was that as soon as the officer on duty got a call, one that I knew would keep him busy for a bit, I planned to go into the station and grab a set of keys to one of the patrol cars. I would then get into the car–fire it up, and at that point I would see how I felt.

I went through the ritual of getting dressed, but was still unable to answer the nagging question as I stood in my bedroom–*could I possibly do this job again*? Only one way to find out! I got into my personal vehicle and drove to the police department. It was already dark due to the short winter day when I arrived at the department parking lot. After about twenty minutes or so, the officer on duty received a call for a two-car crash. *That will keep him tied up for a while.* I watched him pull off and waited until he signed out at the location of the crash before I made my move.

Walking into the police station in full uniform felt both normal and completely strange at the same time. I found myself doing the normal things I would do to get ready for a shift, almost automatically. I went straight to my locker and grabbed a couple of items I would normally take on the road with me. My duty bag would have come with me under normal circumstances, but I didn't want to take up too much time. I certainly didn't want to get caught by the officer on duty gearing up. For him to see me in full uniform and getting ready to hit the road, well that would have been a pretty tough one to explain. I quickly grabbed the keys to one of the cruisers and headed out to the parking lot. I climbed into the police car, fired the engine, and turned on the radio. Then I just sat back to take it all in.

My heart was pounding, and my senses were already in overdrive as I was shaking like a leaf. Yet, all I had done up to this point was start the car and turn on the radio. Still, I was determined to hang in for as long as I could. As fate would have it, and just as I was starting to relax, a call came over the radio for the neighboring Gloucester City Police Department.

"District fourteen." The dispatcher began. Which meant she was giving the call to any and all available units in Gloucester City. "Be advised, a ten fifty-six [ambulance] responding to––for a report of a male threatening ten seventy-four [suicide] by unknown means."

*This can't be fucking happening! The same call. The same fucking call!*

This was the exact nature of the call I responded to the night of my shooting. I nearly picked up the radio and screamed into it for them not to go, as I was instantly gripped by fear.

Two or three of the Gloucester City units reported that they were responding. I sat in the patrol car completely spellbound. As I was listening to the radio as they arrived on scene, I fully expected one of them to call out with "shots fired," or the dreaded "officer down" at any second. I actually considered responding to the call myself. My thinking was that I could just show up, and if everything was okay I could just drive away, and maybe that would help me get over my fears. But what if it went badly? Could I shoot someone again? Would I shoot someone again? Or, would I freeze? Sitting in the cold patrol car, while watching my breath fog the windshield as I panted heavily from the anxiety, I realized I couldn't answer any of those questions with any degree of certainty.

I had been diagnosed by four different practitioners with PTSD by this point, and I had been on countless medications. Yet, I was still fighting.

I still wanted to get the old me back. However, as the Gloucester City officers radioed to dispatch that everything was 10-6 (under control) I felt no relief. I was happy no one was hurt, of course. But, I realized at that moment that it was over for me. I felt like a part of me had just died, *again*. A part of me was now gone forever. All that was left for me to do was to bury that lost part of my soul. I began to cry.

Fearing the ramifications of the Brooklawn officer on duty pulling up any second and catching me crying my eyes out while sitting in a patrol car, I quickly shut off the engine and ran into the police station. I hung up the keys for one final time, and I left.

The next topic is very hard for me to discuss and to confess to. Because for years, I have lied about it to almost everyone who has ever brought up this subject. Whenever I've been asked if I ever thought of killing myself, I have answered with a resounding *no*! I once told Steph that I had thought about what my death would be like, but I never actually thought of committing suicide, no plan, nothing. That was a stone cold lie!

Driving home that night from Brooklawn with tears in my eyes, I pulled off of route 295 with a plan to end my life. I drove to a park which is located in the town of Haddon Heights. This particular park had been dedicated years before to a Haddon Heights Police Officer, John Norcross, who was killed in the line of duty, along with Investigator John McLaughlin, a member of the Camden County Prosecutor's Office. They were killed by Leslie Nelson, a transgender person who had killed Officer Norcross and Inv. McLaughlin with a high-powered rifle.

Once at the park, I parked in a dark space toward the back of the lot. I pulled my gun out of the holster, and I sat there with the gun on my lap, staring down at it.

*Is this how you want to go out? You just want to blow your brains out and let them find you in your car. Why can't you just snap the fuck out of it!*

I began shouting at myself in my own head. *Just get the fuck over it already and stop being such a sensitive little bitch! Fuck him! You shot him, he's dead. Fuck him! It's his fault! He wanted it, and he used you he so could die.*

"Fuck him-Fuck him-Fuck him!" I screamed out. As I was trying to push the thoughts of taking my life out of my head. Then suddenly, and out of nowhere, I began to laugh hysterically. The thought had suddenly entered my mind of how crazy it would look if someone found a cop in full uniform, sitting in his POV (personally owned vehicle), while screaming aloud at himself, and holding a gun. I laughed for a few moments, and then I cried more heavily than I think I have ever cried in my life. I completely broke down. I was conscious of the fact that I was completely losing my mind. At least, it felt like I was losing my mind. I was thinking about ending my pain by ending it all, because I just didn't know what else to do. I looked down again at the gun on my lap.

*You can't do this to Suzanne and the kids. This isn't their fault. They were just along for the ride. They never asked for this and you have no right to leave them like this.*

As I tried to talk myself out of pulling the trigger, I turned the gun toward my face and stared down the barrel. I slid my finger onto the trigger, and depressed the safety to release it.

*They deserve better. You're no good for them anymore.*

The demons in my mind were telling me to leave Suzanne and the kids behind.

"No!" I yelled out. *You can't let him win.* (Meaning Mark) *You can't let him win. You can't let him kill you!*

I slowly put the gun back into my holster, wiped my tears, and drove home. I had come that close to ending it all. My career was over, and I almost let my life end with it. Yet, there was a part of me that was still fighting. A part of me that was determined to not let this whole thing defeat me. After the realization completely sank in that I wasn't going to make it back to the job, I fell into such a deep and dark depression that I thought I was literally going to just fade away. Like someone who is slowly dying from cancer, I just wanted to fade away into nothingness.

At home, and while I was alone during the day, I would re-enact the whole night of the shooting in my living room, trying to change the outcome and to have it end peacefully. It was around this time that I was served with the initial notice of the wrongful death lawsuit by the deceased's family. They were planning on suing me personally. As well as, the department, the township, and everyone involved. I was being sued for a violation of Mark's civil rights due to use of excessive force. In other words, because I shot and killed him, they were saying I violated his civil rights. One piece of information which was now confirmed for me by being served with the lawsuit was that Mark had two daughters. I remembered us talking about his kids the night of the shooting. But for some reason, I completely forgot if he had said whether he had sons or daughters.

Over the years I often had the same recurring nightmares about the incident. I had the one I mentioned earlier, where Mark is stabbing the Sergeant. Another nightmare I had was of Mark standing in front of me while he was bleeding. He would look at me and say, "Why? You were supposed to help me!" That dream would morph into me watching helplessly as he stabbed the Sergeant over and over. I had dreams about not being able to pull the trigger because it was too heavy, and Mark would begin stabbing me. Another, where I pulled the trigger and the gun would not fire. Crazy dreams and nightmares! However, once I knew for certain Mark had two daughters I started having recurring nightmares about the girls.

I pictured both of them being about six or eight years-old, although I didn't know their ages. The girls would look at me and ask, "Why did you kill daddy? You were supposed to help daddy, not kill him! You're a policeman, and policeman are supposed to help people."

The worst one I can remember is one in which the girls were standing by his dead body. They were covered in blood, and one of the girls looked at me and said, "You killed daddy and you killed us too. You just kill people. That's all you do is kill people!"

It was horrible. I was afraid to go to sleep because I didn't want to face them anymore.

After my incident with the Mark look alike at the pill factory (doctor's office), worker's comp decided to send me back to Dr. Lass. Dr. Lass continued to prescribe me new medication after new medication when the last two or three he had prescribed didn't work. We were heading toward the end of December, just around Christmas time, when I realized these meds were doing me more harm than good. None of the meds seemed to help me in any way, whatsoever. They just made me tired and they killed my sex drive, which certainly didn't help matters at home any. I couldn't think clearly, and it was during this time that I was trying to seriously contemplate what to do with the rest of my life after retirement. All while I was battling PTSD and a deep depression.

I knew I had to get off these meds ASAP when one day, and shortly after my attempted suicide in the park, I was napping on the couch when I suddenly awoke from a dead sleep. I sat straight up on the sofa and the first thought that entered my head was of killing myself. This wasn't just a thought, it nearly became a task. The intrinsic pull I felt to walk upstairs and get my gun out of my safe in order to finally end my life by blowing my brains out was so strong and so overwhelming, that I had to force myself out of the house just to keep from doing it. I had to walk around the block three or four times in the cold December air in nothing but a tee shirt and sweats just to get the thought out of my head.

"Jesus Christ." I said to myself aloud. "What the hell is happening to me?"

It was the psychotropic medications. After doing some research, I found out that the one particular medication I was on had a high rate of users having suicidal ideations. Dr. Lass changed my medication to something else after I told him about the couch incident. This new medication seemed to have no effect on me whatsoever. Which was just fine with me. I told him that I felt better from taking it, just so he wouldn't put me on something else. He credited himself with finding "the breakthrough" medication we needed to finally get me feeling well again. I didn't care. I just didn't want to take anything else. Specifically, anything that was going to make me want to kill myself.

In the beginning of February, 2013, I received my date to go before the pension board. The date was set for the first week of March. It had been ten months since the shooting, and the relief I felt about getting the date was palpable. Since I had no way of knowing if I would get the 66% or 40% pension award. I was also faced with a new problem—my health benefits. More specifically, the lack thereof.

There is false narrative that in New Jersey all police officers automatically receive health benefits for life when they retire. This is simply not true. Not all police officers will get benefits upon retirement, and they are certainly not free. Health benefits are contractual, meaning that each individual police department must have the benefits spelled out in their contract. There is no unilateral provision for automatic health benefits upon retirement for police officers working in the State of New Jersey. This, was about to be the crux of my problem.

In Brooklawn, there were only three police officers who worked their entire careers and retired from the Brooklawn Police Department. All three were already age sixty-five when they retired, and were automatically eligible for Medicare. Since age sixty-five is the maximum age you can work as a municipal police officer in the State of New Jersey. Therefore, no one who had previously retired from the Brooklawn Police Department required medical benefits from the municipality. Once I informed Brooklawn of my intention to retire, which was after I received my date to appear before the pension board, it was assumed I would receive my benefits from the State Health Benefits Plan. Only there was a hitch. When Brooklawn sent in my paperwork to have me enrolled into the State Health Benefits Plan, my application was rejected.

It turns out that in 1998, the State sent word to all of the townships in New Jersey that if they did not currently offer health benefits upon retirement for their officers, they would have to pass an ordinance declaring they would not offer health benefits upon retirement now, or in the future. By passing this ordinance, the townships would be making their retiring officers eligible to enter into the State Health Benefits Program. Brooklawn had failed to pass this ordinance within the allotted time frame. As a matter of fact, the original paperwork was found buried in the drawer of a desk kept in storage. This was a major issue for me. If I couldn't somehow get into the State Health Benefits Program, my family and I would be left without any medical coverage. This was additional stress I did not need.

Fortunately, the CFO (Chief Financial Officer) of Brooklawn came up with a plan. He wrote a letter to the commission who oversaw the State Health Benefits Program explaining the whole situation. He requested a hearing before the board to further plead my case. Just days before I was scheduled for my hearing before the State Pension Board, he went before the State Health Benefits Commission. They ruled in our favor, and I was permitted to enter into the State Health Benefits Program upon retirement. The board later revealed in a conversation with the CFO, that the only reason they permitted Brooklawn entry into the program was because of my current situation. They told the CFO they didn't want to see me punished for the sins of those in the past. Now that my health benefits issue was resolved, I had to prepare to face the pension board.

\* \* \*

I was both relieved and afraid that it was all coming to an end. I was looking forward to putting all this behind me and moving on with my life, if that was possible. I still had no answer for what my future held, or any plans for how I would take care of my family long-term. First, I had to hope and pray that the pension board would take mercy and award me the full disability pension, just so we could survive. My wife was still finishing up her nursing program, and we had no other income at the moment to fall back on. My police salary was it. The last stop before my hearing with the Board would be my visit with the state's doctor. He was the one who would be conducting the final exam to determine if I fit the definition of "Fully and Permanently Disabled."

As to how this definition pertains to police work, it basically states that for whatever the reason(s), you can no longer perform the functions of a police officer to any degree. In my case, I didn't suffer from any type of physical injury that would prevent me from performing these functions. Although, I later realized I had suffered some hearing loss from firing my weapon in such close quarters; but I never pursued that issue. In my particular situation, because I suffered a psychological injury, we felt I could no longer function as a cop. My injury was my inability to be able to use my firearm again with any degree of certainty. This is what the doctor would have to determine for certain.

The ability of an officer to use their firearm when necessary is a subjective topic to begin with. When the chips were down, I have witnessed cops not fire their weapon—even though they would have been fully justified in doing so. As violent as many people think police officers are, or feel we can be, I will let you in on a little secret: There are some officers who are not only pacifists, but they are also deathly afraid of firing their own weapon. There are some cops who would just as soon throw it at someone, and use it like a brick, before they would fire it. The assumption that the law enforcement community operates under is, that once an officer has been trained in how to use their weapon and trained as to when they are justified in doing so, the officer will use their weapon whenever it is so required. However, everyone has a different fight-flight-freeze response. So, the notion that a well-trained officer will fire their weapon when it is required is an estimated probability, not an absolute.

When you are declared fully and permanently disabled due to a psychological injury, it is understood that you no longer can be counted on to fire your weapon (or perform other police functions) when, or if, required. Therefore, you are now a liability on the street and are not fit to carry a weapon. Rendering you irrelevant. This is what I needed the doctor to recognize as my disability–my inability to be counted on to pull the trigger when or if necessary. Otherwise, I had no idea what would come next.

# CHAPTER 24

# *THE HOME STRETCH*

When the day came for me to go for the exam with the state's doctor I had a panic attack. Still, I was determined to get through this exam. I *had* to get through this test. Ironically, the office where the assessment would be conducted is literally a three-minute drive from my house. I got there fifteen minutes early, checked in, and waited. Listening to my *thought voice* narrating everything that had occurred over the past year, I ran through the whole incident through my mind as I waited to be called.

*Just tell him everything that has happened and he will understand. Just remain calm. Otherwise, he will probably think you're just faking it, and he won't believe you.*

I tried to coach myself up to remain calm. The thought that concerned me the most was I didn't want to lose control of my emotions in front of the doctor, and have him think I was just playing it up to get the full pension. Let's face it, there are some officers who get a full disability pension who don't really deserve it. If someone has ruined their shoulder or destroyed their knee on the job, the doctor who examines their case can see the physical evidence and determine the actual damage. However, whenever you're dealing with a psychological injury there is bound to be some skepticism, since no one can see inside your mind. No one can read your thoughts. That is why there's a combination of evaluations required to "prove" you are incapable of performing your duties any longer. The state's doctor was my last checkpoint in this journey before my appearance before the board. If he had any suspicions whatsoever that I wasn't 100% disabled, he would reflect that in his report. Then, I would be in a world of trouble.

"Officer Holland, please come in." The doctor greeted me.

The room was nondescript. The doctor and I sat down across from each other at a small round table.

"Officer Holland, as you know you have been referred to me by the State. My job today is to discuss with you a great many things. First, I'm going to ask you some basic questions about yourself, your employer, your education, how long you have been a police officer, those sorts of things. Then, we are going to get into the particulars of the night of the incident. I also want you to tell me about the treatment you have received, and by whom. Is that okay so far?"

"Sure Doctor, no problem." I replied.

"Is there anything you don't understand or have questions about so far?" He asked.

"No, sir. Everything seems clear. Thank you."

The doctor seemed kind enough so far. I wasn't detecting any hints of him being biased. Nor, did I sense he had already made up his mind about me. Over the next hour or so, we went through my pedigree information, my personal history, and my work history. We covered the specifics of where I worked, what I did, why I left, and so on. Then we got to the night of the shooting. It had been quite a while since I had recounted from start to finish the events of that evening. Having to relive it during such a pressure-packed moment, along with how the past year had worn me down both mentally and physically, and despite my best efforts, I broke down right in front of the doctor.

I was telling the doctor as calmly as I could about how I spoke with Mark about his life, his kids, and so on when suddenly, I had a complete meltdown. It was such a sudden shift in my demeanor and change in my emotions that it took me completely by surprise, and it obviously shocked the hell out of the doctor! I had simply lost control, and I was sobbing profoundly. I was sobbing so severely while trying to continue to speak, that the doctor finally put his hand on my shoulder and said, "Officer Holland, please stop talking. You need to just breathe.

Breathe–Breathe. You need to calm down, or you're going to have a panic attack."

Still, I couldn't stop crying. Each time I tried to speak this sudden rush of emotions would overtake me, and it would literally take my breath away. I would then breakdown all over again. I couldn't slow my breathing, and I began to have an actual panic attack. My fear was that he was going to think I was faking it, and that this was all an act just to get the full pension. After the doctor helped me get through the attack, he got me a glass of water. After drinking the water, he requested I go to the rest room and put cold water on my face. I returned to the table and sat down across from the doctor once again. Several minutes had passed since my breakdown had ended, when the doctor asked if we could just talk a little bit more. I started quietly sobbing again as we began speaking. I was trying to suppress my crying as much as I could while we spoke. He clearly noticed. I felt humiliated, and I began to apologize to him for my loss of control. The doctor cut me off.

"Officer Holland." He began. "You have nothing to apologize for. Look. I'm going to be quite frank with you. I have read your file, and I have read the report of the incident. And, I have seen the numerous medications you have been on. Quite frankly sir, you have been through hell. For you to have spoken with someone you were trying to help, and then for you to have to turn around and shoot and kill that person is a horrific thing to have to go through. Plus, the ridiculous amount of medications your doctor has had you on…." His voice trailed off, and he just shook his head side to side.

After a brief pause, he continued. "My point is, it's obvious to me you can't function in the type of environment that's required for a competent officer to function within. I can't tell you what the board's decision will be, but I am obviously of the impression that you are struggling with the events of that evening. You are unfortunately going to continue to struggle with these issues for a long–long time."

*He gets it. Thank God! He understands.* I was relieved. The doctor knew I was truly suffering, and that I wasn't just trying to get The Golden Ticket. He was telling me, without him actually telling me, that he was going to find me fully and permanently disabled. But, he left the door open to the fact that it was ultimately the pension board's final decision as to whether or not to accept his findings. As we spoke some more, the doctor asked me some general questions about what I planned to do with my life. I really had no idea, and I told him so. He made sure I was okay to drive and wished me luck. To this day, I am so grateful for his compassion and care. So many times you come across someone who is there just to do a job, and is cold and uncaring. This doctor clearly put the person before the task, and that helped a lot.

\* \* \*

On the day of my pension hearing I drove to Trenton, NJ, where the hearing was to take place. My wife had a class at nursing school, and I felt like this was something I wanted and needed to do alone. I sat in the waiting area as they called officer after officer into the adjoining room where their fate would be determined. You could tell after an officer had appeared before the board how things had gone for them. I remember one guy coming out and mumbling under his breath "motherfuckers," which was not reassuring. While I waited for my number to be called, I saw a long-time PBA attorney who was a friend of mine. He came into the waiting area with one of his clients.

Sam Altman had been the attorney for many years for PBA Local 30, the Union Local for both Brooklawn and Somerdale, and I knew him well. The night of the shooting, he had responded to the hospital to see me and the Sergeant. Sam gave me some quick advice while in the waiting area about what to do should things not go my way, or what to say if I was asked any questions that I wasn't prepared to answer while in front of the board. He told me that if they did not find in my favor, he would be happy to handle the appeal for me. I was grateful for his advice and guidance. [Note: I failed to mention this previously, but the Sergeant had chosen not to retire. He was up for Lieutenant and apparently wasn't having any issues after the shooting. So he chose to stay on the job.]

When you appear before the pension board they don't call you by name for privacy reasons. You are given a number. They called my number, and I entered the room. I was strangely calm. No butterflies, no nerves, nothing. I simply felt emotionally flat. I recall the room being large. It was comprised of a group of four large tables, which were joined together and formed one large square table in the middle of the room which was surrounded by chairs. I was directed to sit at the far end of the table, and in front of a microphone. Several board members were present, with the Chair of the Board sitting directly in my line of sight across from me. Behind the board members and spread throughout the room were numerous assistants, note takers, stenographers, and other staff members. There were probably twenty to thirty people in the room—the place where my career was about to officially end.

"Officer Holland." The Chairman began. "You are appearing before this board for an incident that took place on April 26, 2012, during which you were forced to use deadly force in order to protect your life and the life of others. Is that correct?"

"Yes, sir." I replied.

"Excuse me!" One of the board members suddenly interrupted.

The Chairman recognized the board member, who then requested permission to ask me a question.

"Go ahead." The Chairman said to the member.

The member looked at me and asked, "Pardon my ignorance, but where the heck is Brooklawn?"

I explained the logistics and location of Brooklawn in relation to where we were presently, which was Trenton, New Jersey.

"Brooklawn is located about four or five miles south of Camden." I explained. "You can stand on the shoreline of the west side of Brooklawn by the Delaware River and look directly across the river at Citizens Bank Park [home of the Philadelphia Phillies], and Lincoln Financial Field" [home of the Philadelphia Eagles].

"Oh!" The board member exclaimed. "I thought you were from *Brooklyn* (NY), not Brooklawn. I was hoping you were New York's problem!" He said sarcastically, and as he began to laugh.

He and the Chairman then bantered back and forth for a moment joking some more, and thinking somehow this whole thing was funny. Me. I was seething inside!

*My fucking career is ending and you jerkoffs are making shitty jokes. Ha-ha! What a fucking riot!*

I wanted to scream at them. Instead, I sat there stone faced. I could see the other board members looking at me and squirming in their seats. They knew it was distasteful as hell, and finally one of them spoke up.

"Excuse me, Mr. Chairman. We are here to decide the fate of Officer Holland's career, as well as the careers of numerous other individuals. I think we should show Officer Holland the respect of us taking this decision seriously." She said respectfully, but obviously annoyed.

I looked over at her and our eyes met. She mouthed to me, "I'm sorry."

I mouthed back to her, "Thank you!" Truly appreciative of her stepping in.

"Yes, of course." The Chairman said awkwardly, and as he picked up on the vibe in the room. He was obviously embarrassed.

"Officer Holland. This board has reviewed the findings of numerous evaluators of your inability to continue to function as a police officer going forward. It is of unanimous opinion of this board that you are found to be *fully and permanently disabled*, and you will receive a pension allowance that reflects the same. Thank you sir for your service."

That was it. It was over. I felt lightheaded. I was afraid I would have trouble standing. I sat there for what felt like a long time, but was really only a few seconds. After I processed what had just happened, I whispered softly, "Thank you."

I could feel myself begin to well up with tears as I made my way toward the door, but I didn't want them to see me cry. Especially, that asshole who made the poorly timed joke. I opened the door and stepped out into the rest of my life. For the first time in seventeen years and two months I was no longer a police officer. And I would never be a police officer again.

\* \* \*

All was not over the day the pension board made their decision and my career ended. I still had the pending wrongful death lawsuit to deal with. In addition, I had the lawsuit that had been filed for the Violation of Civil Rights and Wrongful Termination under the Whistleblower Act against Camden and the Camden Police Administration. Which I had mentioned previously. It never sat well with me the way I was pushed out of Camden. The suit was based upon my being "constructively terminated." Which basically meant they had forced me to leave or be fired, even though I had transferred willingly. I felt it was purely retaliation toward me (and others) for bringing our concerns to the administration about possibly violating the rights of citizens, along with all the grievances I had filed. I had voiced my concerns and paid the price.

# SCARS OF BLUE

As fate would have it, I had to go to the depositions for both the wrongful death lawsuit and the wrongful termination/civil rights lawsuit during the same time period. Sometimes, I could barely keep one thing straight from the other. As far as the Camden lawsuit, it would take ten years for it to finally go to a trial. Camden won. When all was said and done, I got what I had always wanted. Which was the Chief being forced to admit during the deposition(s), and while on the stand at trial, that my concerns should have been acknowledged and treated legitimately. And I should not have been disciplined or threatened to be fired. That acknowledgement would have to be good enough for me.

# CHAPTER 25

# *A WRONGFUL DEATH*

Mark's family had filed the lawsuit for Wrongful Death and a violation of Mark's civil rights by use of excessive force (as previously mentioned). However, the wrongful death lawsuit never made it to trial. The case was settled out of court. We conducted only one deposition that I was a part of. During the deposition, the attorney for Mark's family requested I go through the shooting step-by-step. While walking him through the incident, we wound up in a back-and-forth argument about specific details, and it got ugly. [Note: I do not have access to the transcript of this deposition. The questions, answers, and other statements are from my memory only and to the best of my recollection.]

"How many times did you say you fired, Officer Holland?" Their attorney began.

"I fired two shots, sir." I replied.

"Two shots, you said. Is that correct?"

"Yes, sir. Two shots."

"Are you sure about that, Officer Holland?" He asked. With the tone of when someone is trying to get you to question yourself, as well as change your answer.

"I am sure, sir." I replied.

"How can you be sure, Officer Holland? I mean, after all, you said the whole thing was pure chaos! How can you be so sure you only fired twice? Are you sure it wasn't three times, four times, maybe?"

"Sir, I fired twice. I am sure of it." I replied.

"But you're not answering my question." The attorney persisted. "How can you be *sure* you only fired twice?"

It was clearly a question meant to throw me off my game. How did I know for sure I only shot my weapon twice? Well, there was the crime scene evidence. I was told during my interview with the Prosecutor's Office (and after I had told them I had fired twice), that they had recovered two .40-caliber shell casings at the scene which matched my weapon. Furthermore, both of my shots had struck Mark, with both being fatal shots according to the autopsy report. The first shot, the one I didn't see hit him, entered somewhere at the top of his chest and just around his heart. The second shot, the one I did see strike him, entered into his midsection around his liver area. Exactly where I saw the blood pouring from almost immediately.

"I know I only fired twice, sir." I responded.

"So, let me get this straight. You know you fired two shots, and yet you only saw one of those shots hit the victim. Is that correct?"

I was starting to get where he was going with this. It was all about getting me to doubt myself, and "admit" to something different than from what the evidence showed. It was all smoke and mirrors.

"Correct." I replied.

"So, Officer Holland. If you only saw one round hit the victim, then how do you know you fired two rounds for certain? You keep insisting you only fired twice. And yet you say you only saw one shot hit the victim. And that the scene was pure chaos. I just don't think it makes sense what you are saying." He concluded.

"Training! Years of training." I responded. "Training to the point that I could have fired my weapon with my eyes closed and my ears covered, but I still would have known I only fired two shots because of muscle memory. That sir, is how I know I fired two shots. From years of training and muscle memory. Now, are with done with this bullshit, and can we please move on?" I asked, as I was getting aggravated.

"Fine, I'll move on." He replied.

"So, Officer Holland. We will assume you knew you fired two shots. And we'll assume you are being truthful when you say you didn't see the first shot hit, but you did see the second shot hit, as you said. Is that correct?"

"Correct." I was becoming exasperated. As I was recounting the shooting in such vivid detail, I was transported back into the apartment. I could literally smell the cigarette smoke while I was sitting at the table in the attorney's conference room, and no one was smoking. This whole line of questioning was wearing on me. And no matter how many times I told myself that he is just playing his game, and that it's his job, I couldn't suppress the feelings of anger rising up inside of me.

"So, Officer Holland. Let me ask you something." Counsel began, and with a hint of cockiness in his voice. "You shoot this victim, and you see the bullet hit his body, and now you see blood." He paused. "Let me ask you—*was there a lot of blood*?"

*Snap!* I felt the button go off in my head.

"What kind of a fucking question is that?" I shouted. "Was there a lot of blood?! Goddamn right there was a lot of fucking blood! You fucking asshole!"

"That's it! How dare you." My attorney chastised the opposing counsel. "Chad, get the hell out of here." He yelled to me.

I stormed out of the room. After several minutes, my attorney emerged from the conference room.

"Are you okay?" He asked, as he put a hand on my shoulder.

"I'm sorry." I began to apologize, but he cut me off.

"Fuck that Chad! You have nothing to be sorry for. That asshole was way out of line, and I told him so."

After a few moments of silence between us he asked, "Do you think you can you come back in and finish up? He (the opposing council) promised to move on and not get out of line again. If he does, we're done."

"Fine, sure." I said reluctantly, as we returned to the conference room.

We finished up the deposition with no further issues, but I feared that the damage had already been done. My outburst gave the opposing attorney everything he needed. Part of his job was to prove that I was unstable, or at the least, to learn how he could press my buttons and set me off during the trial. He succeeded on both counts. I felt terrible. I left there feeling defeated. But not nearly as bad as I was about to feel after the Sergeant gave his deposition.

# CHAPTER 26

# *THERE'S ONLY ONE TRUTH*

"Chad. The Sergeant changed many of the details from the statement he gave to the Prosecutor's Office. He altered his story about what happened that night." My attorney shockingly explained to me during a meeting in his office.

"What the hell are you talking about?" I asked in complete shock. "What is there to change? Everything happened the way we said it did. What other possible way is there to tell what happened?"

I was completely stunned and thoroughly confused. My attorney proceeded to lay out the Sergeant's *new version* of actions as they occurred that evening. Which he told during his deposition. First, it should be noted that the Sergeant and I had *never spoken* about the events of that night. Not once did we discuss what had occurred, and I certainly never thought there was a need too. As far as I was concerned, there was never a reason to "get our stories straight." The Prosecutor's Office had told me during my interview, that other than some minor variances, our (Sergeant's and my) stories were almost identical. The only inconsistencies were things that were considered to be *point-of-view* alterations. Such as, the angle from which I saw Mark approaching, and how I was discerning certain movements. As opposed to how the Sergeant was seeing things as they were happening (i.e. the angle Mark was holding the knife, and some differences in perceptions of distance).

One of the more apparent differences was that the Sergeant never realized Mark was as close to him as he actually was. The Sergeant thought Mark was still further away when I fired. Yet, I had fired for exactly that reason. Because I could see that Mark was damn near on top of him. Originally, the only discrepancy that could be considered a "major" difference in our stories was what occurred just after I shot Mark.

Right after I opened fire, I watched Mark spin about 180-degrees and go down onto one knee, and place one hand on the ground to hold himself upright. He then stood with the knife still in hand, and attempted to walk forward again, unsuccessfully. The Sergeant couldn't recall seeing any of that. What bothered me about the Sergeant saying that he couldn't recall seeing Mark spin and go to the ground and stand back up after I shot him was, that the Sergeant already knew why he didn't see that occur. It was because as soon as I fired, he ran down the stairs and out of the room. Who could blame him! With that .40-caliber handgun going off right near his head that was the smart thing to do—get out of the line of fire. Fair enough. But, of course he wouldn't see Mark spin and fall to the ground and then get back up and onto his feet—because he wasn't in the room. So why not just say that? Just say that is why you didn't see him fall. Because you weren't there! Don't go and contradict my version of what occurred and create doubt.

Now, there were *new details* in his version of what occurred, and which he failed to disclose during his original statement. These new proclamations conflicted with the prior testimony the Sergeant made to the Prosecutor's Office back when the incident first took place. The depositions for the wrongful death lawsuit are taking place around 2014. About two years after the original date of the shooting. My attorney informed me that the Sergeant was now describing Mark as not being all that upset during the encounter. Nor, was the scene chaotic, like I had described it. Amazing! This was just simply amazing. In his deposition, the Sergeant was now saying that Mark's demeanor was calm, and that he didn't recall him crying, or even really yelling. I felt like I was living in the twilight zone.

"You have got to be fucking kidding me!" I said to my attorney. "Okay, let's just think about this logically for a moment. How does that even remotely make any sense? If Mark isn't upset, then why the hell are we even there in the first place? If he's not upset, then why were we responding to a report of male threatening suicide? If he's not upset, then why is the Sergeant calling for the tactical team and the negotiator? If Mark is not upset, then why isn't he surrendering, rather than coming at us with a knife?"

What the Sergeant was saying just didn't make any sense.

"If Mark isn't upset, then why did the Sergeant bring Mark's brother back into the apartment to try and talk Mark down?" I countered.

Now angry, I blurted out, "That's what gave Mark the chance to say goodbye in the fucking first place! And that's why I had to kill Mark. Because he got the chance to say goodbye! Whose fucking fault was that? Huh! Whose fault was it that he got to say goodbye? Not mine. That's for damn sure!"

I was livid. To say that a suicidal man whom I wound up having to kill, to even remotely suggest that he wasn't upset had to be the most bizarre statement I had ever heard. But, there was more. We had found out during the investigation that Mark had called his ex-girlfriend just prior to our arrival. Mark had told her that "he was going to get a cop to kill him." How's that for not being upset! Why would he plan *suicide-by-cop* if he wasn't upset? My attorney continued with even more bazaar and terrible news.

"The Sergeant also said he couldn't recall Mark ever holding the knife up high and in a threatening manner, like you said he did, and prior to you shooting him. As a matter of fact, he said he never raised the knife up high at all. He only carried it low by his waist at his side, and he never turned toward him (the Sergeant) to stab him."

I wanted to throw up! I felt lightheaded and sick. *This cannot be happening. This has to be a mistake.*

"Ike." I said to my attorney. "Let's for just a minute take my statement, and the Sergeant's statement, and take them both completely out of the equation. The physical evidence alone, as well as the statement from his brother, clearly demonstrates my version of the events to be accurate–correct? Hell, even the dispatcher that night reported how on Mark's voice mail he said he was now dead."

"No doubt you're correct, Chad." Ike replied. "But, you know their attorney only has to create reasonable doubt, and the Sergeant just did that for them.

But why? I had my own suspicions as to why. None of which were good.

"Ike, am I going to lose everything?" I asked, desperately.

I was still being sued personally by the family. Now, with these new revelations I was worried about the New Jersey Attorneys General Office reopening and reinvestigating the case. I wasn't concerned out of guilt. I knew I hadn't done anything wrong. It was just the fact that this thing would drag on even longer. I felt like I had very little left in me to give. If I were to be put through the whole process once again, well, I wasn't sure I could handle it. And I wasn't sure if I wanted to live through it.

*What the hell kind of jam did the Sarge just get us into?*

"Ike, his new statement doesn't make any sense." I continued, as I was still trying to wrap my mind around this turn of events. "Essentially, and if you go by his version, I shot and killed a guy who wasn't upset and who was just walking toward us with a huge knife down at his side. Never threatening to stab anyone, but just refusing to put it down. Am I understanding this correctly?"

"Yeah Chad." Ike replied. "That would be the gist of it. It makes zero sense. He makes it sound like you killed a guy who was very calm, and who was never a danger to anyone. And other than the fact that he had a knife in his hand, he was of no real threat. Despite everything pointing to the contrary. It's very bizarre."

"Ike. The first time he even saw Mark wasn't until he came out of the bedroom and started walking toward us with the knife in his hand. I know he never saw him while he was sitting on the floor in the bedroom, when he was upset and crying. He never saw him twisting the knife into his thigh like I did. He never saw the transformation I saw after Mark said goodbye to his brother. The Sarge never saw any of that! But, he sure as hell had to hear him screaming and yelling." I was still desperately trying to make sense of this whole thing.

The Sergeant knew Mark was uncooperative. That is why he got his brother to come back inside. In order to try and talk him down. So, how the hell could he say he wasn't upset? Why would he say he wasn't upset? Unless he just didn't agree with me killing him? That is what I was starting to suspect. I think at the end of the day, the Sergeant felt I didn't need to end Mark's life. He never said that to me, but what other explanation could there be? Mark was two feet and some odd inches away from the Sergeant and looming over him with a knife when I fired. For him to turn the whole story around and make it sound like it really wasn't as dangerous as it was, and to undercut me in the process by creating doubt as to why I fired-- well, it was just insane!

I was never comfortable when people would say to me that I saved the Sergeant's life. I may have saved his life, but I also saved mine. I was never looking for thanks. His going on and living his life was thanks enough. Still, I wasn't anticipating that he would undermine me and change his story of what happened that night. There was only one truth of what occurred that evening. A truth that only he and I knew.

"Well, Chad. Unfortunately, what you're saying doesn't help us." Ike began.

"He changed his story, and right or wrong it doesn't matter. It hurts us because he changed his version of the events—period. Now, we have got to figure out what to do about it."

Ike and I sat in silence for a moment. "I know one thing." Ike continued. "He just lost us any chance of winning this case. At the least, he may have cost both towns [Brooklawn and Bellmawr] a lot of money."

I left Ike's office feeling lower than at any point in my life. If it hit the newspapers that the story changed, I would be portrayed as though I was lying about what happened that night. Or at the least, it would be implied that I had made up my version of events. I felt like this was the end for me. I felt angry and I felt betrayed, but I also felt lost. I had been struggling this entire time with the guilt of having to kill Mark in the first place. Along with the doubt that I had almost fired too late to save the Sergeant's life. Now, here was the Sergeant basically saying that I didn't need to kill Mark. That the circumstances didn't warrant my use of deadly force. He and I are the only two people who knew exactly what happened in that apartment that night. The only other person was dead. For the Sergeant to turn around years later and change his story was simply incredible. To run the risk of putting both of our families through further hell with a brand new investigation--well, I had no words.

That night, I fell into such deep despair that I contemplated suicide again. Just to spare my family the torture and humiliation of what I thought was sure to come. Over time, I was able to push the thoughts of suicide out of my mind. I decided that I would suffer whatever fate awaited me, and do my best to protect my family. The papers did run new stories about the "discrepancies" in our statements. Along with the fact that the judge overseeing the case ruled that it could go to trial based upon my "possibly" having violated Mark's civil rights with the excessive use of force. However, the backlash that I thought would occur never really materialized.

Although it may not appear so, I harbor no ill will or negative feelings toward the Sergeant. I'm happy that he was able to continue his career. Unfortunately, and in this particular instance, I feel he failed us both. I'm certain when he (and others) read this book, they will misinterpret it as me taking a cheap shot at him. That is not my intent. Still, I wasn't going to hold back on telling the truth for the sake of sparing hurt feelings.

Five years after the wrongful death lawsuit was filed, and years after the depositions and court motions were completed, I received a call from my attorney.

"Chad. I just wanted you to know that we agreed to a settlement with the family. It's over."

"What happened, Ike?" I asked. As I was completely stunned. "What changed?"

I felt relieved, and yet I was afraid to learn the answer.

"His daughters." Ike said softly. "When we took their depositions they were very impressive girls. Great kids! We felt that if they were called to the stand during a trial they would make very good witnesses for their side, and the jury would most likely be very sympathetic. At that point, the damages could be astronomical." Ike paused for moment. "I want you to know that the settlement included that we did not admit to any wrongdoing or anything that would damage your reputation. I want that to be clear, Chad. We all know *you did nothing wrong*. Despite the Sergeant having changed his story, this was strictly an economic decision. After five years we just thought it was the right thing to do."

It was over. I was now free from living under the specter of being sued into oblivion and worrying if I was going to lose everything.

"Ike. The girls." I started to choke up with tears. "Are they—," He cut me off.

"Chad, the girls are doing very well. I mean, it's not an ideal situation they live in. They live with extended family, I believe. But they are doing okay. One is still in high school, the other goes to community college."

I had tears flowing down my face. I had always assumed Mark's daughters were just little girls. In my nightmares, I had always pictured them as between six or eight years old. For some reason, with my now learning they were older, it actually made me feel somewhat better. I guess it was the fact that since they were older than I originally thought, I somehow assumed they would be better equipped to handle the loss of their father. I imagine it was more of my trying to lessen the burden on myself than anything else. I don't know why I thought it would be less painful for them. But, in my mind it seemed like they stood a better chance of surviving the loss of their father since they were older.

"Ike, are they angry with me?" I asked. "I mean, do they understand that I didn't want to kill their father, but that he gave me no choice?"

Ike paused for a moment before answering.

"The younger daughter is very angry. She wanted to see you go to jail. But the older daughter knew he had tried to kill himself in the past. So, she kind of expected this to happen at some point. Still, she was angry that a cop killed her father. However, I think she understood the circumstances better than her younger sister."

[Note: I found out over the years that followed the shooting that Mark had previously attempted suicide.]

"Ike, do you think I could write them a letter?" I asked.

He sat quietly on the other end of the line for what seemed like several moments, but was actually about twenty or thirty seconds.

"Chad, I'm going to say no. My suggestion is to let them move on. The truth is, it doesn't sound like he was very much a part of their day-to-day lives to begin with. Hopefully, and with time, their life will return to how it was before. Unfortunately, it seems as though they are used to him not being around. It has been five years since his death. I would just leave it alone."

"Okay Ike. Thanks for everything." I said somberly, as we hung up.

I was now free of the burden of the lawsuit. But I would never be free of the burden of taking away the father of those two girls—no matter how dysfunctional their relationship was.

# CHAPTER 27

# PTSD-DEPRESSION & SUICIDE

I feel it's only appropriate to end this book by discussing mental health as it relates to law enforcement. However, I do not proclaim to be, nor, do I hold myself to be an authority on the subject.

When I left police work in April, 2013, I felt ashamed. What affected my self-esteem and my self-worth the most was that I was made aware there were peers who assumed I had faked having PTSD and depression, in order to get The Golden Ticket (the tax-free disability pension).

I was cognizant there were people I worked with who assumed I was using this opportunity to bail out of the job early. Especially, since it was well known that my plan was to work twenty years and leave the job, taking the partial pension. There was another issue that officers in my department were aware of. One I suspected thoroughly convinced them I was faking my PTSD.

In my notepad that I carried on duty, I had written some things in it which could have been interpreted as my voicing my desire to leave the job. I made these notes several months prior to the shooting, and while I was attending my psychology courses at Drexel University. One of our assignments for class was to focus on depressive thoughts you may have during the day. We were to write these thoughts down as we were in the midst of those feelings, so we wouldn't forget them. We were to later use these notes for class discussion purposes. One night, during my overnight shift when I was sitting in the police car and feeling very alone and down, I wrote down some thoughts in my notepad that just came into my mind, as per the assignment. Thoughts, such as, "Help!" "I hate my job." "I can't do this anymore." and things to that effect.

As fate would have it, I dropped my notepad in the police station parking lot, and one of the officers found it. I guess I don't really have to explain what happened next. Or, maybe I do. Nothing! Nothing happened. Nothing initially, at least.

The officer who found the notepad returned it to me a few days later. He asked if I was okay. I assumed he had read the notes, so I explained to him that I was simply doing stuff for my classes, and he seemed like he was fine with that answer. I would later find out that copies had been made of my notes and were passed around the department. I'm sure these went into someone's "little black book" for safekeeping. Since everyone in the department had access to these notes, I was certain they thought it was predetermined that I wanted out of the job after my shooting. Based upon what I had written in my notebook, and not from my actually suffering from PTSD. The thought of my peers thinking I faked having PTSD pushed me further and further down a mental rabbit hole.

I began to cut off most of the people in the outside world, because I assumed they all thought the same things about me. I became more and more alone, as I began to suspect there were those who believed I should not have killed Mark, once the new version of the Sergeant's story came out in the papers. This created a suspicion in my mind that my co-workers may have thought I took the life of an innocent man. This was a very painful period in my life. My mind often drifted to thoughts of suicide during this time, because I didn't think I would ever be able to get back to normal. I have only begun to feel like my old self again, over the past year and a half, or so. It has been a monumental struggle. What helped me personally get back on track were several things.

First, the love of my family and the help of Steph kept me alive. That is how I began my path toward healing. Without the love of my wife, my kids, and the support of Steph I would have likely been gone long ago. I can say that without a shadow of a doubt, there would have come a time where I would have cashed in my chips and called it a day. It got to the point where I no longer feared death, and I was welcoming it. Without these people in my life I just don't think I would have made it. Next, I recently have reconnected with my cousin Kristen. As kids, we were like brother and sister. After fifteen years of little to no contact, I am happy to say that we visited with each other in early 2020 (before Covid-19), and we now talk on the phone almost every night. Reconnecting with her has been huge in my recovery. But by far, the most important element in my recovery was learning to forgive myself.

We are our own worst critics. I am certainly no different. A lot of that self-criticism manifests itself into negative thoughts and feelings when we are unable to forgive ourselves for actions we either took, or failed to take. Once I chose to forgive myself for my lack of knowledge on how to diffuse Mark from his suicidal intentions. And once I chose to forgive myself for not knowing how to handle the situation. And once I chose to forgive myself for having to take Mark's life–only then was I truly able to begin healing. Forgiveness. That was the key to my beginning to getting better.

Another aspect that has helped in my recovery is my introduction to religion. Before you roll your eyes and think that I am now some religious zealot, and that I am going to start preaching the Gospel to you, trust me, that is not the case. I believe in each to their own when it comes to religion and politics. I was raised in a home without religion. Although, I was always curious about it, I was too intimidated to pursue religion because I had no understanding of it. I have always wanted religion to be a part of my life, because I always felt I was lacking spiritually. Still, I didn't know how to go about it. Kristen, and her husband Tory, have helped to guide me down my spiritual path. Kristen has truly been an angel that arrived in my life when I needed her the most.

I mentioned earlier in the book that I had a bit of a "relapse" not long ago. It was during this relapse that I told Steph one of my issues was that I didn't feel of value anymore. I felt I had all this knowledge and experience from having been a police officer and from my suffering, but I didn't have any positive place to direct it. I felt that pull to help people once again, but I didn't know how. That is when Steph recommended I become a call-taker with COPLINE. Traveling to Texas in early 2020 to not only reconnect with my cousin Kristen, but to also take part in the week-long training course for COPLINE was like having a born-again experience for me. It is literally what got me over the top of the mountain I have been climbing emotionally, mentally, and spiritually since my career ended. I now feel as though I have value, that I am of service, and that I have purpose–again. The feeling of purpose is immensely important to police officers, or former police officers, especially.

Fellow police officers, superiors, family members, friends, and others oftentimes don't understand why an officer can't just "get over it" when something traumatic has occurred. When someone says they are struggling with an injury that cannot be seen by the naked eye, such as a psychological or emotional injury, the level of suspicion rises. So, and oftentimes, officers suffer in silence. Police officers tend to be suspicious and cynical by nature. Cops sometimes think that a colleague just wants to *pension out* and take an early retirement, or they just want to get off the street when they claim to be suffering from mental issues. This type of thinking not only hurts the individual who's struggling, but the profession overall. Many officers struggle with various mental health ailments. Conditions such as, burnout, depression, substance abuse, and anxiety to name a few. How many of us know cops that drink too much? So, when our peers create an environment of "don't ask, don't tell," or an atmosphere of just "suck it up," or worse yet, "that officer is full of shit and just wants out of the job" it hurts everyone.

The thoughts of our peers (or loved ones) doubting us when we express we are in pain, or someone we value thinking that we are just faking our injury to get out of the job or off of the street, can be devastating. Couple these suspicious with the loss of self-esteem and self-worth, and an officer can easily fall into a deep depression. This deep depression is too often ending in police suicide. Officers just don't wake up one day and decide they are going to stick their gun in their mouth and pull the trigger. It has to start somewhere. Rarely, is suicide the result of just one incident. It is usually the cumulating of events that lead to this ending. We in the police profession, have got to learn not to dismiss anyone who is exhibiting signs of struggling. There is too much at stake if we are wrong in our assumptions.

When a cop is battling PTSD, anxiety, or depression the feelings of being an outcast are exasperated by the illness. The officer is already in a weakened state of mind. When they start feeling as they are no longer part of the team, they feel rejected. When they feel rejected, they begin to feel lost, they feel worthless, and they feel useless. Furthermore, they feel like they have now lost their identity and their sense of value and purpose in the world. So, the mental spiral begins, with suicide too often being the end result. Since 2016 (and as of this writing), there have been 827 verified police suicides. In 2016 alone there were 143. In 2017, 172. 2018, 174. 2019, 228. As of August 2020 there have been 110 police suicides. (www.bluehelp.org).

Most police suicides occur when an officer has suffered some type of an injury, is under investigation, experiencing financial pressures, coping with a divorce, dealing with an affair, or experiencing child custody issues. Suicides sometimes occur at or near retirement, because that officer is about to lose their only identity—or so they believe. We are now seeing an increase in suicides post-retirement. Part of the problem is that loss of purpose. Police officers are in a profession where they are responsible for solving important problems, and even making life and death decisions. Nothing they will do post-retirement will likely reach that level of importance, or fill that void. This can lead to feelings of loss of self-worth, and a state-of-mind in which they feel they now lack value in the world, as I previously mentioned. These factors, along with many others, are what causes officers to end their lives. These are some of the same thoughts and feelings that caused me to almost end my life. So, we have to do better. But how?

First, we must no longer place a stigma upon each other when we need help. Mental health checkups should become as commonplace as a yearly physical, or qualifying with your weapon. They need to be embraced. Each and every officer, no matter where you work, sees and experiences things that ninety percent of the population will never deal with. We only have so much room in our soul for the horror we experience. We must, from time-to-time, unpack that treasure trove of hell that is living rent-free in our head by speaking with a professional who can help us sort through the muck. In other words, you have got to empty the mental bucket before it overflows. Mental health must no longer be looked upon in our profession as a sign of weakness. Our leaders must stop being afraid of introducing mandatory mental health checkups for fear they will open "Pandora's Box," and have their officers start leaving the job in droves. I am fairly confident that only those who are truly suffering will even consider taking that path. And that would only be after meeting with numerous practitioners to begin with.

In simpler terms, we need to encourage, embrace, and employ mental health treatment regularly in our profession. We need to speak up when we see or suspect an officer is hurting, and not be afraid of doing so. There cannot be any repercussions for the officer reporting it, as well as for the officer who needs treatment. An officer should never lose an assignment, a chance for promotion, their job, or suffer any damage to their reputation because they are suffering from a mental health crisis. Too many innocent police officers are taking their lives because they don't know how to deal with the pain.

And it has to end…

# SPECIAL THANKS

A special thanks to my editor, Jamie Clayton. The hours we spent on this project are forever engraved in my memory. The passion you showed for this assignment will always remain in my heart. Thank you!

Thank you to Carol B, Joe G, Michelle T, and Nick R for acting as my brain trust for this writing. I would still be revising chapters and making corrections if it wasn't for your love, support, guidance, and feedback. I am forever in your debt. I love you all!

To my "hockey family." You guys have no idea how much you kept me going when the days were dark and the future looked bleak. Thank you!

I am certain there are those I am overlooking. You know who you are. Thank you!